Fragile Governance and Local Economic Development

Much of our understanding of local economic development is based on large urban agglomerations as nodes of innovation and competitive advantage, connecting territories to global value chains. However, this framework cannot so easily be applied to peripheral regions and secondary cities in either the Global South or the North.

This book proposes an alternative way of looking at local economic development based on the idea of fragile governance and three variables: associations and networks; learning processes; and leadership and conflict management in six Latin American peripheral regions. The case studies illustrate the challenges of governance in small and intermediate cities in Latin America, and showcase strategies that are being used to achieve a more resilient and territorial vision of local economic development.

This book will be of interest to students and researchers of local economic development, urban and regional studies, and political economy in Latin America as well as to policy-makers and practitioners interested in local and regional economic development policy.

Sergio Montero, Ph.D., is Assistant Professor of Urban and Regional Development at CIDER (Centro Interdisciplinario de Estudios sobre Desarrollo), Universidad de los Andes, Colombia.

Karen Chapple, Ph.D., is a Professor of City and Regional Planning at the University of California, Berkeley, USA.

Regional Studies Association
THE GLOBAL FORUM FOR CITY AND REGIONAL RESEARCH, DEVELOPMENT AND POLICY

Routledge
Taylor & Francis Group

Regions and Cities

In today's globalised, knowledge-driven and networked world, regions and cities have assumed heightened significance as the interconnected nodes of economic, social and cultural production, and as sites of new modes of economic and territorial governance and policy experimentation. This book series brings together incisive and critically engaged international and interdisciplinary research on this resurgence of regions and cities, and should be of interest to geographers, economists, sociologists, political scientists and cultural scholars, as well as to policy makers involved in regional and urban development.

For more information on the Regional Studies Association visit www.regionalstudies.org

126 Smart Transitions in City Regionalism
Territory, Politics and the Quest for Competitiveness and Sustainability
Tassilo Herrschel and Yonn Dierwechter

127 Territorial Designs and International Politics
Inside-out and Outside-in
Edited by Boaz Atzili and Burak Kadercan

128 Universities and Regional Economic Development
Engaging with the Periphery
Edited by Paul Benneworth

129 Fragile Governance and Local Economic Development
Theory and Evidence from Peripheral Regions in Latin America
Edited by Sergio Montero and Karen Chapple

Fragile Governance and Local Economic Development

Theory and Evidence from Peripheral Regions in Latin America

Edited by Sergio Montero and Karen Chapple

Routledge
Taylor & Francis Group
LONDON AND NEW YORK

First published 2019
by Routledge
2 Park Square, Milton Park, Abingdon, Oxon OX14 4RN

and by Routledge
52 Vanderbilt Avenue, New York, NY 10017

First issued in paperback 2020

Routledge is an imprint of the Taylor & Francis Group, an informa business

British Library Cataloguing-in-Publication Data
A catalogue record for this book is available from the British Library

Library of Congress Cataloging-in-Publication Data
Names: Montero, Sergio, editor. | Chapple, Karen, editor.
Title: Fragile governance and local economic development : theory and evidence from peripheral regions in Latin America / edited by Sergio Montero and Karen Chapple.
Description: New York, NY : Routledge, 2019. | Series: Regions and cities ; 129
Identifiers: LCCN 2018015255 | ISBN 9781138106529 (hardback) | ISBN 9781351589444 (pdf) | ISBN 9781351589437 (epub) | ISBN 9781351589420 (mobi)
Subjects: LCSH: Regional planning—Latin America. | Rural development—Latin America. | Economic development—Latin America. | Latin America—Politics and government.
Classification: LCC HT395.L3 F73 2018 | DDC 338.98—dc23
LC record available at https://lccn.loc.gov/2018015255

ISBN 13: 978-0-367-66582-1 (pbk)
ISBN 13: 978-1-138-10652-9 (hbk)

Typeset in Bembo
by Swales & Willis Ltd, Exeter, Devon, UK

To our city planning and regional development students, at the University of California, Berkeley and the Universidad de los Andes, who always push us to ask more questions

Contents

Contributors

Nathalia Calderón (Researcher, Universidad de los Andes, Colombia): Nathalia is a research associate with CIDER, Universidad de los Andes. She is an expert in local economic development policy.

Karen Chapple (Professor, University of California, Berkeley, USA): Karen Chapple, Ph.D., is a Professor of City and Regional Planning at the University of California, Berkeley. Chapple, who holds the Carmel P. Friesen Chair in Urban Studies, studies the governance, planning, and development of regions in the US and Latin America, with a focus on housing and economic development.

Miren Estensoro (Researcher, Universidad de Deusto, Spain): Miren Estensoro is an expert in local development, in particular providing public–private collaboration processes in local development agencies. She holds a Ph.D. in Economics from the University of the Basque Country and her current research focusses mainly on the facilitation of action research processes for regional development.

Susana Franco (Researcher, Universidad de Deusto, Spain): Susana Franco is a professor at Universidad del País Vasco and researcher in topics linked to economics, cluster, innovation and regional competitiviness.

Andrés Matta (Professor, Universidad Nacional de Córdoba, Argentina): Andrés Matta is an expert in Local Economic Development – University of Córdoba. He has a Ph.D. in Economics, National University of Córdoba (UNC). He is a researcher in topics related to economic sociology, territorial development, and employment policies based on the strengthening of productive practices.

Sergio Montero (Assistant Professor, Universidad de los Andes, Colombia): Sergio Montero, Ph.D., is an Assistant Professor of Urban and Regional Development at the Universidad de Los Andes in Bogotá, Colombia. He is based at CIDER, an interdisciplinary research center for development studies. His interests are in urban politics and governance, comparative global urbanism, and local and regional economic development, with an emphasis on Latin America.

Pedro Peterson (Planner, San Francisco City Planning Department, USA): Pedro Peterson has a Ph.D. from UC Berkeley's Department of City and Regional Planning. His research focuses on public–private governance and local economic development policies in Brazil.

Acknowledgments

This book grew out of a visit of a group of Inter-American Development Bank (IADB) officials, led by Claudio Cortellese and Bob Daughters, to the verdant campus of the University of California at Berkeley. As a leader of the Bank's Multilateral Investment Fund (MIF), Cortellese had started to fund many local economic development projects in Latin American countries, and he and his staff were observing what they believed was remarkable innovation in territorial governance. Yet, he and his team were frustrated that many of these outcomes were not being captured by the IADB's traditional evaluation metrics, led by its *randomistas*. Might a team of Berkeley researchers, working with Orkestra-Universidad de Deusto in the Basque Country, be interested in conducting qualitative research on these projects to see if there were lessons for the theory and practice of local economic development?

Thus started an adventure, with chapter authors conducting fieldwork over a period of almost three years in Peru, Brazil, Chile, Argentina, and Guatemala (based on fieldwork by a group of Berkeley graduate students). Two years later, we organized a summer course on governance and local economic development at Universidad de los Andes in Colombia and decided to add one additional case study – Mompox – with the research assistance of a group of graduate students of the Interdisciplinary Center of Development Studies (CIDER) of this university. In the meantime, back at the IADB, chapter authors and a MIF team worked to distill lessons from our cases studies for local economic development practitioners and eventually published a manual, *Una Guía para la Práctica: Mecanismos de Gestión Publico-Privada para el Desarrollo Económico Territorial.*

Thus, this book is truly the product of a village, and we have many people to thank. At the IADB, we benefited tremendously from lengthy discussions with MIF staff, including Claudio Cortellese, Bob Daughters, Monica Romis, Natalia Laguyas, Alejandro Pardo, Anabella Palacios, Hector Castello, Ernesto Stein, Claudio Maggi, and Betsy Murray, among others. We extend special thanks to Monica and Natalia, who served as editors and project managers as well.

Case study research would not have been possible without the people that took the time to answer our questions and the assistance of local leaders who supported our work, even arranging interviews in some cases. In Lurín, Juan Sánchez Barba and Jaime Giesecke, Elizabeth Minaya and Teodoro Rojas; in Arauco, Heidi Inestroza and the team of Cidere Bio Bio; in Córdoba Felix Mitnik and Andrés Matta; in Xela, Alejandro Arango and Roberto Gutiérrez; in Mompox, Alberto Escovar from the Colombian Ministry of Culture.

We also had a great many research assistants assisting us along the way, each with extraordinary contributions. Virginia Rodríguez Nuño de la Rosa, Miriam Chion, and Sonia Cordova Lagrevere helped us in Lurín (Perú); Victoria Liberatore in Córdoba (Argentina); Rucker Alex, Kelan Stoy, Shannon Rieger, Tiffany Eng, Lilija Rudis, and Natalie Camarena Lopez were a very committed research team of UC Berkeley graduate students in Xela (Guatemala) while Nathalia Calderón, Michelle Calderón, Daniela Corzo, Mary Luz Escobar, Daniella Hernández, Natalia Herrera, Ana Maria Navia, Luisa Payán, Octavio Rengifo, Carlos Sandoval, and Carlos H. Suárez, grad students from CIDER-Universidad de los Andes, provided us not only with interview data but with exciting discussions about governance and local economic development in Colombia during our fieldwork in Mompox.

We also want to thank the editors at Routledge *Regions and Cities* series, particularly Susan Christopherson, who supported our work enthusiastically from the beginning. We are deeply sad not to have a chance to interact with her at the end of the project, due to her passing.

Finally, as we concluded the manuscript, we held a conference to discuss it, funded by the UC-Berkeley Institute of International Studies. We are deeply grateful to the participants for extremely thoughtful comments that helped shaped the final of this book: Alison Post, Markku Sotarauta, AnnaLee Saxenian, Charisma Acey, Miriam Chion, Anna Cash, Matt Wade, Oscar Sosa, and Adrián Hernández García. In the final stages, Yuko Aoyama pushed us to clarify our contribution and Beth Chapple served as an able editor.

Sergio Montero and Karen Chapple
Bogotá-Berkeley, October 11, 2017

1 Peripheral regions, fragile governance

Local economic development from Latin America

Sergio Montero and Karen Chapple

In 2015, the Brookings Institution published a report that identified and listed the three hundred largest metropolitan economies of the world. The front page was a world map with three hundred bubbles that showed how economic wealth concentrated not only in certain countries but specifically in particular metropolitan regions within those countries. With only 20 percent of the population and less than 2 percent of the planet surface, these bubbles accounted for nearly half of the world's gross domestic product (Brookings Institution 2015).

Uneven development across regions, particularly the higher rates of economic growth in large urban regions compared with smaller cities and rural regions, has for a long time caught the attention of researchers and policy makers interested in local and regional development (Friedmann 1986; Hirschman 1958; Saxenian 1996; Storper and Walker 1989). Interestingly, the last few decades of globalization have heightened this dynamic. Since the 1990s, economists, geographers, and planners have repeatedly shown that despite the technological and transportation advances of the last decades that have significantly decreased the costs of moving information and goods around the world, firms still tend to cluster in large urban regions seeking the benefits of agglomeration economies (Krugman 1991; Porter 1998), dense labor networks (Saxenian 1996) and favorable local and regional institutional contexts (Amin 1999). However, this rediscovery of cities and regions as important sources of competitive advantage in the context of globalization draws mostly from studies of successful and highly dynamic large urban agglomerations (Amin 1999) or what Scott and Storper (2003) have called *global city-regions*.

In contrast to the burgeoning literature on large cities and global city-regions, the economic potential of cities and regions outside large metropolitan regions has caught the attention of fewer urban and regional researchers in the Anglophone world, apart from a plethora of cluster studies (Bell and Jayne 2009; Clancey 2004; Ketels 2013). While the literature on the Third Italy sparked interesting debates during the 1980s and 1990s on the economic development possibilities of smaller cities through small enterprise spatial systems (Bagnasco and Messori 1975; Bagnasco 1977), studies of innovation hubs, and how other cities can – or cannot – become the next Silicon Valley, have dominated recent local and regional economic development debates as well as the aspirations of urban policy makers (Bresnahan, Gambardella, and Saxenian 2001; Florida 2002; Parthasarathy 2004; Piscione 2013). In this context, ideas such as public–private collaboration, brain circulation, information spillovers, and global value chains have captured the imagination of many academics and policy makers of cities of both the global North and South, in the hopes of achieving global city-region status (Keating 2001; Stren 2001; Montero 2009; Saxenian 2007; Storper 2013).

We see this not only as a worrying gap in the literature but also as a problem for practitioners in small and intermediate cities. Theories and strategies that seek to support the ascent of global city-regions, such as export zones, high-tech clusters, and business and talent attraction, do not transfer well to the economic development reality of smaller cities and peripheral regions, where local officials are learning new administrative responsibilities and experimenting with policy models to promote economic development. As they strive to diversify their economic base in the face of youth migration to large urban centers, to improve public–private synergies in the context of low levels of trust and a weak private sector, or to manage the environmental consequences of extractive industries, these regional planners find little of relevance in the dominant theoretical and policy approaches to promote local economic development. Instead, stakeholders must develop new ways of organizing themselves, expanding networks and learning processes, and achieving more sustainable and endogenous development (Camagni 1991; Davoudi et al. 2008; Morgan 1997; Teitz 1993). While recent theoretical frameworks to study local econonomic development have tended to overrepresent the urban and regional dynamics of large cities of the global North (Robinson 2002; Roy 2009), it is imperative to better conceptualize the challenges of smaller cities in either the North or the South, which are following different development trajectories and modes of insertion to the global economy while still subject to all the forces of globalization, financialization, and planetary urbanization that affect large urban agglomerations (Soja and Kanai 2007; Brenner and Schmid 2013). Similarly, the vast empirical experience on the failure of "one-size-fits-all" regional development policies (Pike, Rodríguez-Pose, and Tomaney 2006), or what Chien (2008) has called "isomorphic approach to development," require a renewed place-based approach to local economic development theory and practice that emphasize institutional diversity as well as a detailed attention to the "soft" or informal institutional aspects that make places different from each other (Barca, McCann, and Rodríguez-Pose 2012; CAF 2010). This book seeks to address this gap in theory and practice by analyzing how six peripheral cities and regions in Latin America – Arauco, Chile; Córdoba, Argentina; Mompox, Colombia; Espíritu Santo, Brazil; Lurín, Peru; and Quetzaltenango, Guatemala (see Figure 1.1) – are experimenting with different governance mechanisms to promote local economic development.

Developing new theories and policy strategies that fit better with the challenges of small and intermediate cities in Latin America is important at the

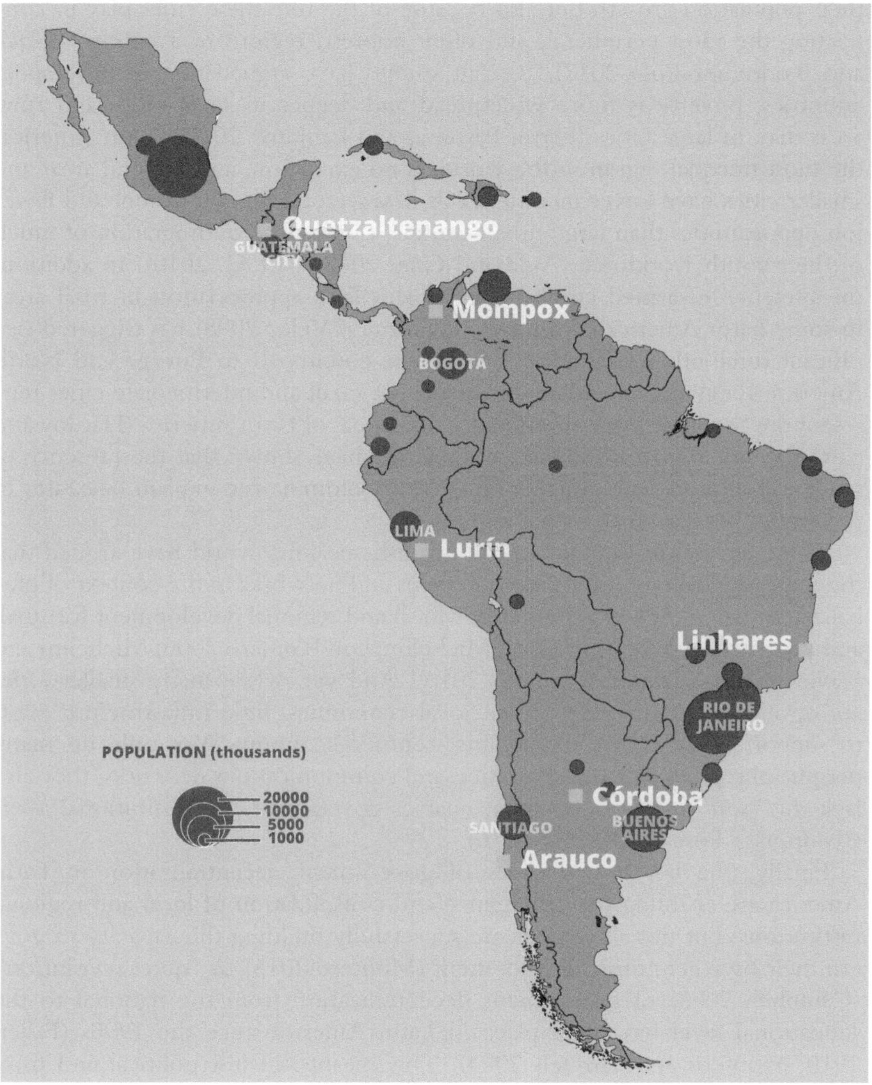

Figure 1.1 Location of case studies

moment for several reasons. First, intermediate cities in Latin America are projected to grow rapidly in the coming decades (Dobbs et al. 2012). Recent Latin American studies show that the population growth of the largest cities in the region is stabilizing (Dureau et al. 2015), while intermediate cities continue to grow (Roberts 2015; Sassone 2000), thus diminishing the urban primacy of capital cities that has characterized the region during most of the twentieth century (Cuervo González 2010).

Second, small and intermediate cities are important not only because of their population growth but also because of the role these cities play in connecting the most peripheral, and often poorest, regions of a country (Frick and Rodríguez-Pose 2017). Recent studies have argued that in developing countries, poverty is more widespread and deeper in small cities and rural areas than in large cities (Ferré, Ferreira, and Lanjouw 2012). Latin America, the most unequal region in the world, is no exception, and its rural areas and smaller cities have lower income levels, less sectoral diversification, and fewer job opportunities than large urban centers, causing the outmigration of much of their youth workforce (Aide and Grau 2004; CEPAL 2010). In addition, the presence of armed conflict and violent land appropriation in rural areas in some Latin American countries (Ibáñez and Vélez 2008) has triggered significant rural–urban migrations within the country or to Europe and North America. Reviving an earlier argument that small and intermediate cities represent the "economic heart" of many rural areas of Latin America (Hardoy and Satterthwaite 1986), Berdegué et al. (2015) have shown that the presence of small and intermediate cities in Chile and Colombia can explain decreases in poverty in peripheral and rural regions.

Third, several researchers in the Spanish-speaking world have argued that the increasing role of informal institutions and networks in the context of globalization brings new possibilities for local and regional development for small and intermediate cities (Méndez, Michelini, and Romero 2006; Michelini and Davies 2009; Vázquez Barquero 2010). And yet, while many smaller cities are developing their own vibrant local economies, little infrastructure exists to support entry in the twenty-first-century economy. Not only do many peripheral regions lack transportation and communications networks, they also lack the "soft" infrastructure that enables governance and institutional assets (Rodríguez-Pose 2013; CAF 2010).

Finally, the last few decades of government decentralization in Latin America are enabling the emergence and consolidation of local and regional institutions, but not all regions are successfully building the capacity to govern their own economic development (Montero 2015). A "quiet revolution" (Campbell 2003) of government decentralization from the national to the subnational level has taken place in Latin America since the 1990s (Falleti 2010; Montero and Samuels 2004). This meant not just political and fiscal decentralization, but also administrative decentralization, which has forced localities to develop capacities for policy making, even when new local and regional institutions were still quite fragile (Wilson et al. 2008). In this context, public officials, sometimes working with nongovernmental organizations (NGOs) and the private sector, have experimented with a variety of practices to help localities develop new capacities to participate in markets (Post 2014). The new role for the subnational scales of governance in the formulation and implementation of public policies and planning has empowered smaller cities in Latin America even if their institutional capacities and governance structures were often fragile compared with capital cities and large urban centers

(Chapple and Montero 2016; Grindle 2007). While flirting with the dominant menu of policies – providing direct assistance to businesses, supporting clusters, connecting to global value chains – localities, and particularly small and intermediate cities, have become aware of the critical need to strengthen territorial governance so that local and regional development policies can be effective (Daughters 2012; Barca et al. 2012).

Peripheral regions, fragile governance

There are two important categories of analysis that we introduce in this book to examine local economic development processes: peripheral regions and fragile governance. Many authors interested in studying smaller cities, in Latin America (Jordan and Simioni 1998) and elsewhere (Lang et al. 2015), have argued that giving a universal definition of what constitutes a small or an intermediate city is not possible. We use the concept of *peripheral region* rather than small or intermediate city to emphasize that the possibilities of development in these urban and regional spaces are not defined merely by their population size or location but also by broader and parallel social, economic, and cultural processes such as isolation, dependency, or migration pull factors in relation to larger cities. Latin American dependency theorists and Marxist geographers have long understood the core-periphery dynamic as shaped by processes of capital accumulation, which draw from the differential economic environments of core and periphery in a perpetual search for higher rates of return (Harvey 1975; Prebisch 1976; Wallerstein 1979). In recent years, several authors have returned to the idea of periphery as a useful term to analyze political economy and cultural changes in cities in the context of globalization (Lang et al. 2015; Caldeira 2017). In these new interpretations, however, peripheries are considered dynamic and socially constructed processes rather than geographical or structural characteristics of particular spaces. For instance, Lang et al. (2015) have used the idea of *peripheralization* as a wider and multidimensional process that can produce different kinds of inequalities, not only economic ones and not only at the global nation-state level but also within countries and regions. In this book, we concur with these recent conceptualizations of peripheries. One key characteristic that all the cities and regions in this book share is that many of their young residents are moving to larger cities, either within their country or in other countries, in search not only of better job opportunities and livelihoods but also of the urban amenities, diversity, and consumption patterns of our increasingly urban-centered representations of culture. This out-migration of young people for economic, social, or cultural imperatives is, for us, a key marker of whether a city or region is peripheral in local economic development (LED) terms, more so than its size.

Our notion of peripheral region seeks also to bridge two debates that have often remained separate despite the increasing connections between cities and rural areas: local and regional economic development studies and rural development studies. In a world in which the boundaries between the rural and the urban are increasingly blurring (Woods 2009; Brenner and Schmid 2013), recent advances in rural development that emphasize the importance of creating new viable livelihoods (Bebbington 1999) and how existing social networks can facilitate new processes of innovation and learning in rural areas (Murdoch 2000) have much to offer to researchers and practitioners of LED. Decentralization processes are empowering local actors and creating new interdependencies and joint action between local and national institutions, and thus also may strengthen the rural periphery (Ward, Wilson, and Spink 2010). Our preference for conceptualizing our case studies as peripheral regions rather than small or intermediate cities follows logically. The concept of *region* allows us to emphasize the complex connections between urban and rural dynamics that take place in these territories against the urban bias that involves calling them small, intermediate, or second-tier "cities." Bringing together these debates through the notion of *peripheral region* opens up new ways of thinking about LED and brings to the stage a different and more diverse set of concepts, actors, and city models beyond the agglomeration economies, dense networks, and venture capitalists of Silicon Valley and other global city-regions. This then allows us to better understand the development bottlenecks and opportunities of smaller cities and regions, which are simultaneously affected by rural, urban, and global forces.

We argue that peripheral regions in Latin America are often characterized by *fragile governance* dynamics. By governance we mean the "process of co-ordinating actors, social groups and institutions in order to reach objectives which have been collectively discussed and defined in fragmented, even nebulous environments" (Bagnasco and Le Galès 2000, 26). As much as the region has been rediscovered in recent years, so have institutional approaches to explaining regional disparities and local and regional development outcomes (Rodríguez-Pose 2013). In this context, urban and regional scholars, in Latin America and elsewhere, have realized that institutional aspects such as the rule of law, government capacities, social capital, or trust levels are key to explaining why certain cities and regions do better than other over time. For instance, in their study of urban management and planning capacities in six intermediate cities in Latin America, Jordan and Simioni (1998) found a common incapacity to translate elements listed in plans, programs, and projects into reality due to several reasons, including the preponderance of higher-level government priorities, poor distribution of updated information, lack of availability of implementation planning mechanisms, and dispersion of planning responsibilities among different agencies. In addition, the pervasive preference of local political powers to focus on short-term projects that are perceived as urgent made long-term planning and implementation even more difficult. On the positive side, the authors found increasing participation of civil society in processes of urban change and planning in these cities, as well as some positive pilot experiences with public–private collaborations that have translated into positive LED outcomes. Yet, as Ward et al. (2010) note, despite decentralization efforts in recent decades, civil society participation in Latin American countries remains weak. We encountered this double-sided aspect of local governance in all of the empirical cases in this book: while long-documented institutional weaknesses in these territories persist to this day, new logics of local and regional governance are emerging in the context of the decentralization and democratization of the traditionally centralized Latin American state (Grindle 2007). We also found that the literature on small and intermediate cities in Latin America is often divided between studies that see great economic development potential for smaller cities as endogenous and local assets have become more important in the context of globalization (Méndez et al. 2006; Michelini and Davies 2009; Vázquez Barquero 2010) and those that highlight the deficiencies and weak institutional capacities of Latin American small cities and rural areas (Jordan and Simioni 1998; Bolay and Rabinovich 2004; Machado 2000).

Rather than focusing on identifying the institutional weaknesses of peripheral regions or celebrating their potential, we chose to focus this book on identifying key areas of transformation where new yet also fragile possibilities of coordination and collaboration for LED are emerging. Thus, by *fragile governance* we refer to emergent processes of coordination and collaboration of local actors to promote common endogenous development goals in the context of weak institutional capacity. Fragile governance also calls attention to the possibility that these emergent processes of collaboration can be easily broken or stopped by certain lock-in situations or bottlenecks. Yet, in using the term *fragile* as opposed to *weak*, we seek to emphasize the temporal and evolutionary possibilities of governance and institutional transformation. In other words, we look at fragile governance in peripheral regions as a dynamic process: while institutionalist development economists have often analyzed developing countries as "weak" (formal) institutional environments (Aron 2000; Kaufmann, Kraay, and Zoido-Lobatón 2000), the increasing importance of place, social networks and informal institutions in the context of globalization open up new, albeit fragile, possibilities for economic development. Fragile governance is therefore about emergent processes rather than a static (weak) governance structure. In doing so, we stress the evolutionary possibilities of governance and local economic development in these peripheral economies while acknowledging the possibilities of bottlenecks in the process.

On methods: analyzing fragile governance qualitatively through social networks, learning processes, and shared leadership

Fragile governance often occurs through informal institutional processes and therefore is invisible to the quantitative methodologies through which development economists, particularly those at the World Bank, have attempted to measure the relationship between institutions and economic development (Aron 2000; Kaufmann et al. 2000) under the "good governance" paradigm (Santiso 2001). As Amin (1999), and more recently Rodríguez-Pose (2013), have argued, most of the literature on institutions and economic development has focused on using quantitative indicators, econometric models, and game theory to analyze the role of formal institutions such as the rule of law and property rights, as well as corruption. When informal institutions have entered the equation, it has often been through quantitative attempts to measure social capital and trust. Less, however, is known about other types of informal processes such as, for instance, the role of leadership (Sotarauta, Horlings, and Liddle 2012), despite its importance for local and regional innovation (Uyarra et al. 2017). Therefore, to better conceptualize the "soft" (or informal) governance mechanisms at work in peripheral regions we need not only conceptual innovation but also more qualitative approaches and ways to systematize findings resulting from case study research. In the following paragraphs, we give more details about the origins of this book and our chosen qualitative methodology to conceptualize and analyze the relationship between fragile governance and local economic development from the experience of peripheral regions in Latin America.

This book emerged in the context of a research project at the University of California, Berkeley, commissioned by the Inter-American Development Bank (IDB) to better understand the relationship between governance and local economic development in small and intermediate cities in Latin America. All cases, with the exception of Mompox (Chapter 8), are based on research conducted for the IDB project "Public–private mechanisms for local economic development," led by Dr. Karen Chapple and a team of researchers from UC Berkeley and Universidad de Deusto-Orkestra. The Mompox case is part of a research project led by Dr. Sergio Montero and conducted during the summer of 2016 with a team of researchers from Universidad de los Andes, using a similar theoretical and methodological approach. Initially, the project sought to explore the relationship between governance processes and local economic development in six Latin American regions: three sparsely populated rural regions (Arauco, Chile; Lurín, Peru; and Mompox, Colombia) and three intermediate cities (Córdoba, Argentina; Linhares, Brazil; and Quetzaltenango, Guatemala). Arauco, Lurín, Mompox, and Quetzaltenango are stories of bottom-up governance networks that strive in different ways to connect to higher levels of government and with peasants, artisans, and associations of small businesses struggling to reach national and international markets. With political obstacles impeding relations between the regional and national government, Córdoba and Linhares turn instead to bolstering local association structures to gain competitive advantage.

Each of these cases contributes in a different way to our understanding of fragile governance. Rather than focusing on the impact of economic development initiatives, we are interested in understanding the institutional factors and governance dynamics of local actors that facilitate the emergence and consolidation of LED processes. Because we consider these processes to occur in a context of fragility, we focus not only on success stories but also on "governance failures" (Jessop 1998), which are situations in which the collaboration of actors failed in achieving economic development or ended up in lock-in situations. Like Ostrom et al. (1999), we believe there are valuable lessons in analyzing the reasons behind governance failure as much as in explaining success.

Based on two hundred interviews in these six Latin American regions over a four-year period (2012–16), thorough feedback from practitioners affiliated with the Inter-American Development Bank and several discussions of our conceptual frameworks and results in courses and academic conferences celebrated at UC Berkeley and Universidad de los Andes, we identified three key areas where the six peripheral regions we studied are transforming their fragile governance to trigger new LED initiatives:

1 Creating networks and associations that can connect the horizontal and vertical dimensions of governance needed to promote local economic development;
2 Acknowledging the existence of diverse forms of learning and the potential of learning processes to generate new forms of collaboration and economic development;
3 Nurturing individual leadership, facilitating the transition to shared and inclusive leadership processes, and managing conflicts in emerging collaborative schemes.

Our case studies help us illustrate and analyze how transformation takes place in one or more of these three key areas. By including cases from six different countries, we seek to analyze fragile governance processes in the context of different decentralization processes and governance structures. Decentralization varies across countries, driven by factors such as democratization, electoral imperatives, neoliberal reforms, industrialization, and urbanization, among others (Montero and Samuels 2004). But what Latin American countries share is an increasing attention to the local level as a scale for local economic development and a strengthening of social fabric, with a new emphasis on the third sector (Wilson et al. 2008). In countries with a history of decentralization, like Argentina and Brazil, established secondary cities develop associativity to compete with global city-regions for national markets. Where decentralization processes are incipient, as in Peru and Guatemala, small cities build on thick existing networks and institutions to establish their own identity in the shadow of capital cities. Peripheral regions in Chile and Colombia, where the national government remains dominant and local resources are scarce, negotiate their course directly with outside actors, whether NGOs or higher levels of government.

Introducing the cases

The southernmost of three river basins in the metropolitan region of Lima, the Lurín River Basin extends from the Andes to the coast, with a population of over 165,000, half of whom are impoverished. Locals have traditionally relied principally on agriculture and cattle for their livelihoods, but more recently tourism and food processing have emerged as well. The region has a complex relationship with Lima. While youth are departing for the city and abandoning agricultural land, some areas are seeing new real estate development, summer homes for Limeños. The fortunes of local farmers depend heavily on demand from the city, creating an ongoing need to upgrade product quality and access supermarket chains to keep a share of the competitive market. Multiple actors engage in economic development activities: regional and provincial governments, the provincial municipality, seven district municipalities and the Mancomunidad that they form, 20 *comunidades campesinas*, associations of local producers, and two NGOs headquartered in Lima. In Chapter 3, "From learning to fragile governance in Lurín: rural economic development in rural Peru," Karen Chapple and Sergio Montero analyze the potential of learning processes to promote governance and economic development in rural areas. The chapter examines how three types of learning in the Lurín River Basin – technical expertise, storytelling, and experiential knowledge – combine to empower rural communities to act collectively. Based on an analysis of three community-led economic development processes – irrigation improvements, tourism, and food processing – we show that learning can result in new, albeit fragile, forms of governance and social capital. Fragile governance can turn into regional economic development when learning results in the development of a regional narrative and coordination occurs across both vertical and horizontal network dimensions.

At 225,000 residents, Quetzaltenango (also known by its Mayan name Xelajú, or Xela) is the second-largest city in Guatemala. While agricultural production has dominated the economy, ranging from produce to coffee and cocoa, recently the region has seen growth in manufacturing and services, particularly health care, education, and tourism (specializing in Spanish language schools). However, infrastructure is minimally developed and the business climate is challenging, leading many young people to emigrate to Guatemala City, Mexico, or the United States. With decentralization occurring at a slow place, local associations of private sector and civil society actors (Grupos Gestores) have emerged to tackle some of the country's most urgent economic development challenges. In Chapter 4, "Learning via communities of practice: the experience of Grupos Gestores in Guatemala," Karen Chapple, Sergio Montero, and Pedro Peterson chronicle the emergence, spread and current challenges of Grupos Gestores in Guatemala, a model of associations of private sector and civil society actors that seek to collaborate to promote processes of local economic development in smaller cities and peripheral regions of the country, illustrating a process of governance and learning embedded in territory. Ironically, replication is occurring due more to the mobilization of strong tie networks by policy entrepreneurs and communities of practice rather than by any proven effectiveness of the model. Through a comparative case study on the role of Grupos Gestores in promoting tourism in Quetzaltenango and Totonicapán, the chapter illustrates the challenges of promoting public–private collaborations through the Grupos Gestores model. Ultimately, the chapter shows the ways in which a governance model for local economic development can spread in the context of small cities and peripheral regions while, at the same time, it shows the limits of models and "best practices" to promote local economic development and public–private collaboration.

Argentina's second-largest city Córdoba lies at the intersection of two rivers on a plain east of the Sierras Cordobesas foothills. In recent years, the information and communications technology (ICT) industry in Córdoba has grown from 1,600 workers in 2001 to more than 10,000 in 2016 (MTEySS 2017; CTC 2017). ICT industries moved from representing only 2.4 percent of industrtial employment in the 1990s to 8.6 percent in 2016. In Chapter 5, "Córdoba, the Argentinian Silicon Valley? Common narratives, institutional experiments, and mutual adjustments to develop a regional innovation system outside Buenos Aires," Andrés Matta and Sergio Montero analyze the opportunities and difficulties in articulating public and private actors in a new and emerging set of economic activities in Córdoba, Argentina. In Córdoba, this public–private articulation was not achieved through a single or paradigmatic organization. Instead, public–private collaboration in Córdoba's ICT (Information, Communication, and Technology) sector has taken place through considerable institutional experimentation and circulation of people between public and private organizations. But if there has been a constant variable in this frenetic process of institutional experimentation, then it is the strength and continuity of two associations of local small and medium enterprises established in the early 2000s. The process followed by Córdoba's ICT industry illustrates also the transition from an economic development strategy based on the idea of "industrial complex" or "growth pole" to another approach more aligned with the more endogenous idea of LED. The case of Córdoba is also interesting because it is a Latin American city trying to reinvent itself to become a regional economy based on technology and innovation-related economic activities. Despite the fact that Córdoba has 1.3 million inhabitants, we consider it a peripheral city given the primacy that Buenos Aires has traditionally had in the distribution of economic activity and highly skilled workers. A businessman in the sector we interviewed echoed this idea with a phrase well known in the country: "God is everywhere, but he attends in Buenos Aires."

Historically one of the poorest states in Brazil, Espírito Santo was for many decades an agricultural region specializing in growing coffee. Increasingly focused on extraction and manufacturing, the region is now a leading exporter of iron ore, steel, paper, and granite. This chapter explores a territorial approach to LED policy in a city in that peripheral region, Linhares. Linhares is located hundreds of kilometers from Brazil's main urban centers, yet since the 1990s it has emerged as one of Brazil's most successful furniture producers and has built an industrial infrastructure that has attracted plants from a range of other sectors. The development of the furniture sector in Linhares has generated broader developmental spillovers, such as an improved workforce, a higher capacity for innovation, infrastructure that can be used and appropriated by other economic sectors, and improvements to living standards and reductions in poverty and inequality. In Chapter 6, "Against the grain: networked governance and local economic development in Linhares, Brazil," Pedro Peterson argues that the success of these LED efforts owes to intricate forms of networked governance at multiple scales and across the public/private divide, from horizontal and vertical production arrangements between furniture firms, to a thickening of the local production chain, to the mobilization of state resources to improve productive conditions in the region.

A coastal province in the Chilean region of Bío Bío, Arauco, includes seven municipalities with a population of almost 170,000. A high poverty area dependent on social assistance, Arauco's economy specializes in agriculture, fishing, tourism, forestry, and commerce. Though located about two hours' travel from Chile's second-largest conurbation, Gran Concepción, the economy is not well connected. Engaged in economic development is an array of local, provincial, regional, and national actors, with active participation from the private sector in joint governance. In Chapter 7, "From individual to shared leadership in Arauco, Chile: elements of an emergent process," Miren Estensoro and Susana Franco analyze the elements of an emerging process of shared leadership in the province. The case focuses on the Public Private Board (PPB) created to articulate the implementation of a project of territorial economic development. Despite the lack of collaboration culture in the area and the centralist policies in the country, the actions of several catalytic agents were crucial to spark a process of dialogue to generate a shared vision for local development. This emerging process enabled their collaboration to respond to complex situations, such as the low level of human capital in the area, by setting *ad hoc* initiatives for training different collectives. For shared leadership processes to advance, Estensoro and Franco argue, it is important to develop a sense of belonging facilitated by nurturing institutional, networking, and socialization capabilities. In the case of Arauco, the replacement of the charismatic president of the PPB and the changes in its governance structure are evidence of how these capabilities were put in practice.

Mompox, with 44,000 residents, is a Colombian municipality in the department of Bolívar that draws on a rich cultural heritage dating from the sixteenth century. Its economy revolves around jewelry, fishing, agriculture, and increasingly, tourism. In 1995, after UNESCO declared it a World Heritage site, tourism took off rapidly. Mompox, Colombia, is known worldwide for its artisanal filigree jewelry. Yet only a few artisans are reaping the benefits of this recognition, while most local artisans are disconnected from national and international markets. In this context, different local and national government agencies, international development organizations, and NGOs have attempted to organize filigree local artisans in cooperatives and associations to improve their production processes, decrease their costs and increase their sales. In Chapter 8, "Intergenerational leadership and local economic development: towards a new kind of artisan association in Mompox, Colombia," Sergio Montero and Nathalia Calderón analyze the dynamics of local associations of artisans in Mompox and discuss the current disenchantment with traditional associations, in which a small number of leaders – often older *maestros* – often become the representatives of local artisans. Some of these leaderships, however, reinforce existing hierarchies among artisans and do not allow younger generations to be represented or feel that they have a voice. This results in little product innovation, youth migration to larger cities, and fragile association structures that often disappear after some years. In this context, they analyze a new kind of association of young artisans that provides an interesting example of a new wave that breaks with the older model of associations built around traditional community leaders and gives a renewed force to collective action among the younger generation.

Towards the governance of local economic development in peripheral regions

Large or global city-regions are not the only locomotives of national economic development. Smaller cities and rural regions in Latin America, or what we have called *peripheral regions* in this book, play a vital role in decreasing poverty and enhancing the economic development possibilities of the poorest regions of a country (Berdegué et al. 2015; Frick and Rodríguez-Pose 2017). In this introductory chapter, we argued that peripheral regions in Latin America are often characterized by *fragile governance*. By this we mean emergent – and often informal – processes of governance taking place in contexts with weak institutional capacities and low levels of social capital. Together, our cases illustrate not only the challenges and fragility of governance in peripheral regions in Latin America but also the variety of governance processes and solutions these cities and regions are innovating and implementing to achieve a more territorial and inclusive vision of LED. The cases illustrate how these regions are actively transforming their fragile governance in practice by fostering new kinds of local associations, how multiple forms of learning combine via these networks to catalyze change, and how leadership and conflict management are important mechanisms to avoid governance failure. Fragile governance often grows out of regions' deep experience in managing the commons and relying on local and informal assets: "it is essential to draw on cultural endowments and their knowledge of local resources to find innovative institutions that fit local conditions" (Ostrom 2002, 16). By following a unified research design with a common theoretical framework and three associated categories of analysis, combined with systematic qualitative research based on in-depth interviews, we have built a series of case studies with a strong internal coherence that illustrate the role that networks, learning, and leadership can play in processes of LED in Latin American peripheral regions. Together, these cases illustrate not only the challenges of governance in small and intermediate cities in Latin America but also the variety of governance approaches these cities and regions are innovating and implementing to achieve a territorial vision of LED.

The book is structured as follows. After this introductory chapter, the next chapter (Chapter 2) situates our notions of fragile governance and peripheral regions within recent theoretical debates on local economic development and governance in the rich literature in geography, development, and planning that exists in both the Anglophone and Spanish-speaking worlds. In that chapter, we also develop in more detail the three categories – networks, learning, and leadership – that we use to analyze our case studies. Although each case has elements of the three themes, some themes will be more prominent than others. Thus, we organize the cases by pairs to explore each theme in turn. To illustrate learning, the case of Lurín (Chapter 3) shows how in rural areas learning should be conceptualized as a combination of technical expertise, experiential learning, and storytelling. Given that learning is a social and interactive process, the case of Quetzaltenango (Chapter 4) shows how new "communities of practice" can construct meaning and transmit knowledge in rural areas. Learning occurs through social networks and it is this theme that the Córdoba (Chapter 5) and Linhares (Chapter 6) cases help to develop in detail. Finally, understanding the dynamics of leadership is also an important contribution of this book. Arauco (Chapter 7) and Mompox (Chapter 8) are distinctive cases that reveal the difficulties of moving from individual towards shared and inclusive leadership. Based on the experience of the cities and regions analyzed in the book, the concluding chapter (Chapter 9) summarizes insights and discusses lessons for LED policy and institution-building efforts in fragile governance contexts. In doing so, we seek an audience not only among local economic development academics but also in the world of practitioners who seek concepts and tools that can be applied to the practice of local and regional economic development planning in small cities and peripheral regions, in Latin America and beyond.

References

Amin, A. 1999. "An Institutionalist Perspective on Regional Economic Development." *International Journal of Urban and Regional Research* 23(2): 365–78.

Aron, J. 2000. "Growth and Institutions: A Review of the Evidence." *The World Bank Research Observer* 15(1): 99–135.

Bagnasco, A. 1977. *Tre Italie: La problematica territoriale dello sviluppo*. Bologna, Italy: Il Mulino.

Bagnasco, A., and M. Messori. 1975. *Tendenze dell'economia periferica*. Torino, Italy: Valentino.

Bagnasco, A., and P. Le Galès, eds. 2000. *Cities in Contemporary Europe*. Cambridge, UK: Cambridge University Press.

Barca, F., P. McCann, and A. Rodríguez-Pose. 2012. "The Case for Regional Development Intervention: Place-based Versus Place-neutral Approaches." *Journal of Regional Science* 52(1): 134–52.

Bebbington, A. 1999. "Capitals and Capabilities: A Framework for Analyzing Peasant Viability, Rural Livelihoods and Poverty." *World Development* 27(12): 2021–44.

Bell, D., and M. Jayne. 2009. "Small Cities? Towards a Research Agenda." *International Journal of Urban and Regional Research* 33(3): 683–99.

Berdegué, J. A., F. Carriazo, B. Jara, F. Modrego, and I. Soloaga. 2015. "Cities, Territories, and Inclusive Growth: Unraveling Urban–Rural Linkages in Chile, Colombia, and Mexico." *World Development* 73: 56–71.

Bolay, J. C., and A. Rabinovich. 2004. "Intermediate Cities in Latin America: Risk and Opportunities of Coherent Urban Development." *Cities* 21(5): 407–21.

Brenner, N., and C. Schmid. 2013. "The 'Urban Age' in Question." *International Journal of Urban and Regional Research* 38: 731–55.

Bresnahan, T., A. Gambardella, and A. Saxenian. 2001. "'Old Economy' Inputs for 'New Economy' Outcomes: Cluster Formation in the New Silicon Valleys." *Industrial and Corporate Change* 10(4): 835–60.

Brookings Institution. 2015. *Global Metro Monitor 2014: An Uncertain Recovery*. Washington DC: Brookings Institution. Available at: www.brookings.edu/research/reports2/2015/01/22-global-metro-monitor (accessed March 1, 2016).

CAF. 2010. *Desarrollo Local: Hacia un Nuevo Protagonismo de las Ciudades y Regiones*. Caracas: Corporación Andina de Fomento (CAF).

Caldeira, T. P. 2017. "Peripheral Urbanization: Autoconstruction, Transversal Logics, and Politics in Cities of the Global South." *Environment and Planning D: Society and Space* 35(1): 3–20.

Camagni, R. 1991. *Innovation Networks: Spatial Networks*. New York: Wiley & Sons.

Campbell, T. 2003. *The Quiet Revolution: Decentralization and the Rise of Political Participation in Latin American Cities*. Pittsburgh, PA: University of Pittsburgh Press.

CEPAL. 2010. "La hora de la igualdad: Brechas por cerrar, caminos por abrir." 33rd conference of CEPAL, Brasilia, Brazil. May 30–June 1, 2010. Available at: repositorio.cepal.org/bitstream/11362/13309/1/S2010986_es.pdf (accessed March 20, 2016).

Chapple, K., and S. Montero. 2016. "From Learning to Fragile Governance: Regional Economic Development in Rural Peru." *Journal of Rural Studies* 44: 143–52.

Chien, S. S. 2008. "The Isomorphism of Local Development Policy: A Case Study of the Formation and Transformation of National Development Zones in Post-Mao China." *Urban Studies* 45(2): 273–94.

Clancey, G. 2004. "Local Memory and Worldly Narrative: The Remote City in America and Japan." *Urban Studies* 41(12): 2335–55.

CTC (Córdoba Technology Cluster). 2017. *Monitor TIC. Resultados del 2do trimester de 2016*. Available at: www.cordobatechnology.com/uploads/wysiwyg/files/JBG%20311016.pdf (accessed April 1, 2017).

Cuervo González, L. M. 2010. "Desarrollo económico y primacía urbana en América Latina. Una visión histórico-comparativa." *Contribuciones a las Ciencias Sociales*. Available at: www.eumed.net/rev/cccss/09/lmcg.htm (accessed August 10, 2016).

Daughters, R. 2012. "The IDB/MIF Perspective on Governance and Local Economic Development." Unpublished document.

Davoudi, S., N. Evans, F. Governa, and M. Santangelo. 2008. "Territorial Governance in the Making: Approaches, Methodologies, Practices." *Boletín de la Asociación de Geografos Españoles* 46: 33–52.

Dobbs, R., J. Remes, J. Manyika, C. Roxburgh, S. Smit, and F. Schaer. 2012. *Urban World: Cities and the Rise of the Consuming Class*. New York: McKinsey Global Institute.

Dureau, F., T. Lulle, S. Souchald, and Y. Contreras. 2015. *Movilidades y Cambio Urbano: Bogotá, Santiago y Sao Paulo*. Bogotá: Universidad Externado de Colombia.

Falleti, T. 2010. *Decentralization and Subnational Politics in Latin America*. New York: Cambridge University Press.

Ferré, C., F. H. Ferreira, and P. Lanjouw. 2012. "Is There a Metropolitan Bias? The Relationship between Poverty and City Size in a Selection of Developing Countries." *The World Bank Economic Review* 26(3): 351–82.

Florida, R. 2002. *The Rise of the Creative Class*. New York: Basic Books.

Frick, S., and A. Rodríguez-Pose. 2017. "Big or Small Cities? On City Size and Economic Growth." Papers in Evolutionary Economic Geography #17.25. Retrieved from: http://econ.geo.uu.nl/peeg/peeg1725.pdf (accessed September 24, 2017).

Friedmann, J. 1986. "The World City Hypothesis." *Development and Change* 17(1): 69–83.

Grindle, M. S. 2007. *Going Local: Decentralization, Democratization, and the Promise of Good Governance*. Princeton, NJ: Princeton University Press.

Hardoy, J., and D. Satterthwaite. 1986. *Small and Intermediate Urban Centres: Their Role in National and Regional Development in the Third World*. London: Hodder and Stoughton.

Harvey, D. 1975. "The Geography of Capitalist Accumulation: A Reconstruction of the Maxian Theory." *Antipode* 7(2): 9–21.

Hirschman, A. 1958. *The Strategy of Economic Development*. New Haven, CT: Yale University Press.

Ibáñez, A. M., and C. E. Vélez. 2008. "Civil Conflict and Forced Migration: The Micro Determinants and Welfare Losses of Displacement in Colombia." *World Development* 36(4): 659–76.

Jessop, B. 1998. "The Rise of Governance and the Risks of Failure: The Case of Economic Development." *International Social Science Journal* 155: 29–46.

Jordan, R., and D. Simioni, eds. 1998. *Ciudades intermedias de América Latina y el Caribe: propuestas para la gestión urbana*. Santiago de Chile: CEPAL/Ministero degli Affari Esteri – Cooperazione Italiana.

Kaufmann, D., A. Kraay, and P. Zoido-Lobatón. 2000. "Governance Matters: From Measurement to Action." *Finance and Development* 37(2): 10.

Keating, M. 2001. "Governing Cities and Regions: Territorial Restructuring in a Global Age." In A. Scott, ed., *Global City-Regions: Trends, Theory, Policy*. Oxford, UK: Oxford University Press.

Ketels, C. 2013. "Recent Research on Competitiveness and Clusters: What Are the Implications for Regional Policy?" *Cambridge Journal of Regions, Economy and Society* 6(2): 269–84.

Krugman, P. 1991. "Increasing Returns and Economic Geography." *Journal of Political Economy* 99(3): 483–99.

Lang, T., S. Henn, W. Sgibnev, and K. Ehrlich, eds. 2015. *Understanding Geographies of Polarization and Peripheralization: Perspectives from Central and Eastern Europe and Beyond*. London: Palgrave Macmillan.

Machado, A. 2000. "El papel de las organizaciones en el desarrollo rural." *En La Nueva Ruralidad en América Latina: Memorias Maestría en Desarrollo Rural 20 años*. Tomo II, Bogotá: Pontificia Universidad Javeriana.

Méndez, R., J. J. Michelini, and P. Romero. 2006. "Redes socio-institucionales e innovaciones para el desarrollo de las ciudades intermedias." *Ciudad y Territorio, Estudios Territoriales* 38(148): 377–95.

Michelini, J. J., and C. Davies. 2009. "Ciudades intermedias y desarrollo territorial: Un análisis exploratorio del caso argentino." *Documentos de trabajo GEDEUR*, núm. 5, Grupo de Estudios sobre Desarrollo Urbano, Madrid, pp. 1–26.

Montero, A., and D. Samuels. 2004. *Decentralization and Democratization in Latin America*. Notre Dame, IN: University of Notre Dame Press.

Montero, S. 2009. "Beyond Global Competitiveness: The Construction of the Bogotá City-Region." *Regional Development Dialogue* 30(2): 122–36.

Montero, S. 2015. "Gobernanza y planeación regional en América Latina." *Estudios Jaliscienses* 101: 6–19.

Morgan, K. 1997. "The Learning Region: Institutions, Innovation and Regional Renewal." *Regional Studies* 31: 491–503.

MTEySS. 2017. Observatorio de Empleo y Dinámica Empresarial. Available at: www.trabajo.gov.ar/left/estadisticas/oede/?id_seccion=59 (accessed January 4, 2017).

Murdoch, J. 2000. "Networks: A New Paradigm of Rural Development?" *Journal of Rural Studies* 16: 407–19.

Ostrom, E. 2002. "Reformulating the Commons." In J. Burger, R. Norgaard, E. Ostrom, D. Policansky, and B. Goldstein, eds., *The Commons Revisited: An Americas Perspective*. Washington, DC: Island Press.

Ostrom, E., J. Burger, C. B. Field, R. B. Norgaard, and D. Policansky. 1999. "Revisiting the Commons: Local Lessons, Global Challenges." *Science* 284(5412): 278–82.

Parthasarathy, B. 2004. "India's Silicon Valley or Silicon Valley's India? Socially Embedding the Computer Software Industry in Bangalore." *International Journal of Urban and Regional Research* 28(3): 664–85.

Pike, A., A. Rodríguez-Pose, and J. Tomaney, eds. 2006. *Local and Regional Development*. London: Routledge.

Piscione, D. P. 2013. *Secrets of Silicon Valley: What Everyone Else Can Learn from the Innovation Capital of the World*. London: Palgrave-Macmillan.

Porter, M. E. 1998. "Clusters and the New Economics of Competition." *Harvard Business Review* (November–December): 77–90.

Post, A. E. 2014. *Foreign and Domestic Investment in Argentina: The Politics of Privatized Infrastructure*. Cambridge, UK: Cambridge University Press.

Prebisch, R. 1976. "A Critique of Peripheral Capitalism." *CEPAL Review* 1: 9–76

Roberts, B. 2015. *Gestionando Sistemas de Ciudades Intermedias*. Washington, DC: Inter-American Development Bank/Cities Alliance.

Robinson, J. 2002. "Global and World Cities: A View from off the Map." *International Journal of Urban and Regional Research* 26: 531–54.

Rodríguez-Pose, A. 2013. "Do Institutions Matter for Regional Development?" *Regional Studies* 47(7): 1034–47.

Roy, A. 2009. "The 21st-century Metropolis: New Geographies of Theory." *Regional Studies* 43(6): 819–30.

Santiso, C. 2001. "World Bank and Good Governance: Good Governance and Aid Effectiveness: The World Bank and Conditionality." *The Georgetown Public Policy Review* 7: 1–137.

Sassone, S. M. 2000. Reestructuración territorial y ciudades intermedias en la Argentina. Ciudad y Territorio: *Estudios Territoriales* 32(123): 57–92.

Saxenian, A. 1996. *Regional Advantage*. Cambridge, MA: Harvard University Press.

Saxenian, A. 2007. *The New Argonauts: Regional Advantage in a Global Economy*. Cambridge, MA: Harvard University Press.

Scott, A., and M. Storper. 2003. "Regions, Globalization, Development." *Regional Studies* 37: 579–93.

Soja, E., and M. Kanai. 2007. "The Urbanization of the World." In R. Burdett and D. Sudjic, eds., *The Endless City*. London: Phaidon.

Sotarauta, M., L. Horlings, and M. Liddle, eds. 2012. *Leadership and Change in Sustainable Regional Development*. London: Routledge.

Storper, M. 2013. *Keys to the City: How Economics, Institutions, Social Interaction, and Politics Shape Development*. Princeton, NJ: Princeton University Press.

Storper, M., and R. Walker. 1989. *The Capitalist Imperative: Territory, Technology, and Industrial Growth*. London: Blackwell.

Stren, R. 2001. "Local Governance and Social Diversity in the Developing World: New Challenges for Globalizing City-Regions." In A. Scott, ed., *Global City-Regions: Trends, Theory, Policy*. New York: Oxford University Press.

Teitz, M. B. 1993. "Changes in Economic Development Theory and Practice." *International Regional Science Review* 16(1–2): 101–6.

Uyarra, E., K. Flanagan, E. Magro, J. R. Wilson, and M. Sotarauta. 2017. "Understanding Regional Innovation Policy Dynamics: Actors, Agency and Learning." *Environment and Planning C* 35(4): 559–68.

Vázquez Barquero, A. 2010. "Diversidad territorial y desarrollo endógeno en Argentina." *Cultura Económica* 77: 46–72.

Wallerstein, I. 1979. *The Capitalist World-Economy*. Cambridge: Cambridge University Press.

Ward, P. M., R. H. Wilson, and P. K. Spink. 2010. "Decentralization, Democracy and Sub-national Governance: Comparative Reflections for Policy-making in Brazil, Mexico and the US." *Regional Science Policy & Practice* 2(1): 51–62.

Wilson, R. H., P. M. Ward, P. K. Spink, and V. E. Rodríguez. 2008. *Governance in the Americas: Decentralization, Democracy, and Subnational Government in Brazil, Mexico, and the USA*. Notre Dame, IN: University of Notre Dame Press.

Woods, M. 2009. "Rural Geography: Blurring Boundaries and Making Connections." *Progress in Human Geography* 33: 849–58.

2 Governing local economic development in Latin America

Situating the debate

Karen Chapple and Sergio Montero

We build the idea of fragile governance based on a rich literature in geography, development, and planning, and it is important to acknowledge those precedents. This chapter thus begins with a review of recent literature on peripheries, local economic development (LED), and governance connecting relevant debates in the Anglophone and Spanish-speaking worlds. The review helps us conceptualize the relationship between governance and LED from the perspective of peripheral regions in Latin America. Following that literature review, we present a description of the institutional context of our six Latin American cases that shows their different economic development paths in the three areas of transformation described in the previous chapter: (1) networks and associations, (2) learning processes, and (3) leadership and conflict management.

Understanding peripheries

In Latin America, the concept of periphery has a long academic trajectory and is often associated with dependency theory, which emerged during the mid-twentieth century to criticize the optimistic development possibilities espoused by modernization theory. Drawing upon Marxist ideas and putting them to work in the uneven geography of Latin America, dependency theorists argue that primary resources flowed from a periphery of poor states, including most Latin American countries, to a core of wealthy and industrialized states (Cardoso and Faletto 1979; Prebisch 1976). According to dependency theory, the ways in which developing countries were integrated into the world capitalist system maintain and reinforce their poverty and impede any hope of development unless Latin American countries develop their own industries. These ideas became the theoretical base of the many import-substitution policies and strategies that Latin American countries adopted during the 1960s.

At the local and regional level, dependency theory and the work of several urban and regional economists that emphasized the circular causation dynamics of world capitalism (Hirschman 1958; Myrdal 1957) gave birth to "growth pole" strategies based on the ideas of French economist Francois Perroux (1970). A key assumption of this regional development paradigm was that state-supported industrialization of a few poles in a country – which were often located in intermediate cities – would eventually benefit the national territory through trickle-down effects. During the late 1970s and 1980s these strategies were rejected after many studies showed that financial benefits failed to trickle down (Conroy 1973). In the 1980s, dependency theory lost credibility as free trade theories and neoliberal policies took hold in several Latin American countries. But critiques of dependency theory came not only from free-trade theorists but also from scholars of development, who saw it as a simplified meta-theory of the world system that obscured other dynamics taking place in Latin America (Kay 2010). For instance, the core-periphery duality of the world capitalist system could not explain what some authors called "internal colonialism" (González Casanova 1963; Stavenhagen 1981), that is, how dominant and criollo classes that lived in the capital cities of the newly independent countries of Latin America reproduced a relation of colonial domination with populations living in smaller cities and rural areas (Kay 2010).

There is, however, currently space to rethink the idea of periphery in the context of globalization. Indeed, in recent years the concepts of periphery and peripheralization have experienced a sort of renaissance to explain processes happening at the subnational level, particularly, urban processes. In contrast to dependency theorists (Cardoso and Faletto 1979) and world system theorists (Wallerstein 1979), several authors have argued that peripheralization processes produce inequalities at not only the global scale but all scales. For example, authors writing about shrinking cities in post-socialist Eastern Europe have used the idea of peripheralization in an attempt to explain the wider, multidimensional processes that are affecting these cities beyond the phenomenon of population shrinkage (Lang 2012; Lang et al. 2015; Weck and Beißwenger 2014). They also argue that processes of peripheralization are multidimensional; that is, they are caused not only by economic forces but also by social, political and cultural forces. Processes of peripheralization are also produced discursively, for instance, through the production and circulation of certain regional images and discourses inside and outside the country. From this angle, the generalization among economic development policy makers that global city-regions are the key locomotives of economic growth and global competitiveness (Scott and Storper 2003) is a factor making smaller cities a periphery for LED initiatives as much as the actual forces of globalization. Finally, in this book we also concur with recent conceptualizations of peripheries as a dynamic and socially constructed process rather than a geographical or structural characteristic of a particular space (Lang et al. 2015; Caldeira 2017). As we mentioned in Chapter 1, a key characteristic that the cities and regions in this book share is that much of their young population are moving to larger cities, either within their country or other countries, in search of better job opportunities and livelihoods but also of the urban amenities, diversity and consumption patterns of our increasingly urban-centered representations of culture. This represents for us an important marker of whether a city or region is peripheral in LED terms, more so than its size.

The territorial aspects of economic development

In recent decades, Latin American cities and regions, particularly local governments and their collaborators in governance, have assumed increasing importance in designing and implementing LED policy (Borja 2001). Such an understanding of LED has coincided with a widespread devolution, particularly in Latin America, of political, administrative, and financial powers from national to municipal and other subnational governments (Falleti 2010; Grindle 2007; Montero and Samuels 2004). There has been an unprecedented structural transformation of subnational governments from a mere administrative subdivision of the nation-state, run by appointed mayors and governors, to a new and more sophisticated entity run by elected officials. Subnational governance structures have become capable of making decisions and administering resources with relative autonomy from national desires and interests, although they are rarely given fiscal independence and often depend on fiscal transfers from the national government. In any case, the project of governing and planning in Latin America has become less *grandiose*; less about large national plans, comprehensive planning, and macro-economic data, and more about local and regional concerns, participatory techniques, and strategic planning. Yet the lack of institutional capacity, skills, and resources among many local officials and agencies, as well as the lack of clarity about how local governance structures should be organized to promote economic development, obstruct efforts to achieve clear and positive results in this area (Montero 2015). This has especially been the case in smaller Latin American cities and rural areas, where decentralization reforms have been met with high hopes from local communities and NGOs but also with remarkable institutional deficiencies (Jordan and Simioni 1998; Bebbington 1997). Governing LED has proven particularly challenging due to the long dominance of the national government in industrial policy. Even as localities have assumed increasing responsibilities for developing and attracting private sector activity, most funding for economic development activities, such as business loans, remains centralized (Montero and Samuels 2004).

In contrast to large cities and metropolitan regions, rural regions and smaller cities have attracted little attention so far in LED and innovation literature, even though these debates are experiencing a renaissance, particularly in Latin America (Berdegué et al. 2015; Méndez, Michelini, and Romero 2006; Vázquez Barquero 2010). Economic development in rural settings has traditionally encountered particular challenges such as persistently high poverty rates, the role of agriculture as dominant economic activity, the pull of nearby cities, the weakness of the private sector, and the lack of specialized human capital (De Janvry and Sadoulet 1993). In this context, many rural development scholars agree on the need for a renewed rural development approach in which agriculture is one among many options to improve the lives of the rural poor (De Janvry et al. 1989; De Janvry and Sadoulet 1993;

Ellis and Biggs 2001; Woods 2009). The successes and failures of recent years have made it clear that local economic development in rural areas is not only a matter of improving agriculture and connecting farmers to markets and global value chains, it is also about understanding how governance dynamics and informal institutions such as social capital that make certain development initiatives thrive in some regions and not others (Murdoch 2000; Chapple and Montero 2016). Similarly, recent debates about LED in Spain and Latin America emphasize that while globalization might reinforce the economic position of large urban agglomerations, it can also bring new possibilities of connection to the global economy for small and intermediate cities (Méndez et al. 2006; Michelini and Davies 2009; Vázquez Barquero 2010). For instance, Méndez et al. (2006) have argued that intermediate cities have strong social networks of cooperation that could be used to create new economic development possibilities. This is important, they argue, not only for intermediate cities themselves but also for the role they can play in catalyzing regional development and facilitating the diffusion of innovations to more peripheral areas of a country. Berdegué et al. (2015) have empirically explored this relation, showing how the presence of small and intermediate cities in Chile and Colombia is beneficial for the development potential of rural areas.

Governing local and regional economic development

As decentralization has resulted in more autonomy for peripheral regions and secondary cities, they have innovated new approaches to the governance of economic development. Governance refers to a new way of governing space in which NGOs, the private sector, and other non-state actors are given a more significant and active role in public decisions, policy making, and planning (Rhodes 1997). Unlike many advanced industrialized countries, in most Latin American countries, economic development had traditionally been subsumed under national industrial policy, with a focus on international trade. Despite the diversity of regions within each country, few national governments prepared economic development strategies specific to different parts of the country. Latin American regions are thus not only learning how to deal with authority over their own territories for the first time but also preparing new strategies for economic development. Many are exploring different forms of territorial governance, or ways of governing space in which NGOs, the private sector, and other non-state actors are given a more significant and active role in public decisions, policy making, and planning. This governance process among these state and non-state actors, who are autonomous but mutually dependent, functions as "self-organized steering" (Jessop 1998, 29).

For this complex governance process to work, certain practices need to be in place, according to Jessop (1998). First, local and regional actors need to simplify governance models and practices, so that roles and responsibilities can be easily understood and assumed. Second, actors need to develop a dynamic capacity for interactive learning. Third, the governance process must help to establish a common worldview among actors. Governance thus means linking self-coordinating networks (in an economic sector, spatial territory, or other system), which develop a common language and vision around an issue, and continuously adapt their behavior. Joint action may occur either horizontally – between stakeholders in equivalent positions (such as associations) – or vertically, in hierarchies (as between levels of government).

Another way of conceptualizing this approach is as organizing the "conditions for governance" or metagovernance (Jessop 1998). These conditions (or design principles) may be established by public or private actors, or some combination, but must be based on local values, norms, and principles (Kooiman and Jentoft 2009). In the case of peripheral regions or secondary cities in Latin America, values about community and place are embodied in what Friedmann (2007) calls assets – human, social, cultural, intellectual, natural, environmental, and urban – or what Bebbington (1999) describes as capitals "(natural, produced, human, social and cultural) that are at once the resources (or inputs) that make livelihood strategies possible, the assets that give people capability, and the outputs that make livelihoods meaningful and viable" (Bebbington, 1999, 2029). The underlying norm is the preservation and sustainability of these assets or capitals. The final condition is the economic development strategy, endogenous development. These then shape how the regions develop networks and learning mechanisms.

Filling the gap: networks and associations, learning processes, and leadership

Taken together, this book's six cases illustrate the challenges and opportunities of building governance for local economic development from peripheral regions in Latin America. Three key elements of governance that are developed throughout the book are explored in the following sections: (1) networks and associations, (2) learning processes, and (3) leadership and conflict management.

Networks and associations

The role of social capital in regional economic development is near legendary, thanks in part to the story of the Third Italy (Piore and Sabel 1984; Putnam, Leonardi, and Nanetti 1993). Social capital facilitates both *bonding* among like actors and *bridging* to the external world, thereby supporting action (Putnam et al. 1993). Networks of trust and collaboration not only facilitate joint action but can also span private and public worlds to bring the state and society into a synergy that can then become a developmental asset (Evans 1996). Local actors can construct synergy – or permeable social capital that spans public–private boundaries – by transforming social identities, innovating organizational design, or redefining problems (Evans 1996). Shaping the development of both social and human capital are informal institutional arrangements that govern behavior and thus also shape the capacity to design and implement effective local and regional economic development strategies (Rodríguez-Pose 2013). Institutional arrangements are always linked to specific places, and they can create barriers to intervention, for instance as local customs result in lock-in, or reinforce patterns of inequality, according to Rodríguez-Pose (2013). This suggests that rather than designing institutions from the top down, altering local institutions, we should tailor economic development strategies to acknowledge and engage with local institutional arrangements and "institutional bottlenecks" (Rodríguez-Pose 2013, 1044).

In medium-sized cities such as Córdoba, network contacts ranging from close friends to business acquaintances form networks that become the basis of associations. Associations improve productivity by helping firms learn from customers, competitors, suppliers, employees, and public institutions (Cooke and Morgan 1998). They also mediate relations between the public sector and specific industries, providing information to the public sector about the needs of producers, while helping members comply with regulations and access state assistance (Sabel 1993; Tendler and Amorim 1996). In rural areas like Arauco and Lurín, new growth networks emerge from traditional structures such as small farm systems or artisanal workshops, with their high levels of trust and sociocultural cohesion (Murdoch 2000).

The cases in this book illustrate the complexity of activating social capital that penetrates entrenched power structures. For instance, in Quetzaltenango (Chapter 4), dense networks of civil society and private actors struggle to interact meaningfully with the public sector both in local municipalities and in Guatemala City. Yet the Córdoba, Linhares, and Mompox cases (Chapters 5, 6, and 8) illustrate different ways of constructing connections that will leverage local developmental assets. Córdoba shows the potential of associations of small and medium-sized companies to influence LED policy and moved from an "industrial complex" or "growth pole" approach that benefits large and multinational companies through tax subsidies to another approach more aligned with the more endogenous idea of local economic development. In Linhares, private sector collaboration ultimately mobilizes state resources to improve productive conditions and economic development in the region. In Mompox, a new collective of independent artisans is innovating new forms of association based on informal collaboration systems with specific and well-defined roles for each member, as well as horizontal mechanisms of reciprocity that seek to build trust among members before formalization.

Learning processes

Many economic development theorists influenced by evolutionary economics have begun to examine the role of learning in local economic development. To conceptualize learning, it is important to revisit Polanyi's ([1958] 1998) distinction between tacit and explicit knowledge. Explicit – or codified – knowledge is typically transferred verbally or in writing, acquired in educational institutions, and considered a key part of an individual's human capital. But some knowledge cannot be conveyed symbolically, either because it is unconscious (e.g., knowing how to ride a bicycle) or because available codes are inadequate. Since it is built of personal experience, often context-specific, and difficult to pass on to others, networks of associations are key to its transmission (Von Hippel 1994). Tacit knowledge may best be acquired through demonstration, imitation, and practice, often in a master–apprentice relationship. A common social context, in the form of shared language, values, and culture, can facilitate the transfer of tacit knowledge (Lundvall and Johnson 1994). It thus acts as social learning, or a change in practical activity that occurs through social practices (Friedmann 1987). Schön (1973) uses the analogy of agricultural extension services, or demonstration farms, that shatter fixed boundaries, creating a new organizational format. We refer to this particular form of tacit knowledge as *experiential* knowledge.

The process of sharing tacit knowledge, recombining it into new knowledge, and overcoming the organizational inertia that creates resistance to change creates collective learning. Collective learning can be understood as the territorial equivalent of the type of learning that happens within firms (Lawson and Lorenz 1999). Collective learning can therefore generate new forms of local economic governance and, more importantly, it can also lead "to the development of new tailor-made institutions which in turn enhance local capabilities" (Helmsing 2001, 304). At the local governance level, it can create new "regional competence" (Helmsing 2001, 302); specifically, the ability to spot change, create and communicate awareness, and spur the mobilizing of resources. The debates on learning regions can help clarify how learning occurs in places. Learning regions are flexible networks of public and private actors, embedded in specific regions, who facilitate learning and adaptation, thereby fostering innovation (Morgan 1997; Hassink 2005). They are premised upon the localized nature of tacit knowledge, specifically, the difficulty of articulating such knowledge over long distance, the need for learning experientially, and the role of common social context in effective knowledge sharing (Florida 1995; Lundvall and Johnson 1994).

Yet with its narrow focus on technology and knowledge transfers between industry and universities in urban centers, the learning region model may fail to address the diversity of actors, unique problems, and cultural context of rural regions (Wellbrock et al. 2013). Likewise, the idea of regional systems of innovation (Doloreux 2002) – where new knowledge is created jointly between firms and institutions based on interaction with each other and their environment – seems to exclude rural areas, where the innovation may be simple access to markets rather than new products per se. Latin America's peripheral regions often function as "communities of practice," where knowledge is acquired not through the simple transfer from one person to another but rather socially constructed out of environmental context, social relations, and historic paths. Learning is two-way, changing both how a learner sees the world and how the world sees the learner (Brown and Duguid 2001). It often takes the form of a "living curriculum," encompassing storytelling, conversation, coaching, and apprenticeship (Wenger 1998). And because communities of practice are organized by social relations – whether organizations, networks, or occupational groups – tacit knowledge flows within them across geographic borders, regardless of spatial proximity, in an "extra-localization of cultural 'closeness'" (Amin 1999; Bunnell and Coe 2001, 583). Learning might also be understood as the capability to engage meaningfully in the world and act as an agent of change (Sen 1999). Most effective in activating this transformation are soft mechanisms of learning like storytelling and experiential knowledge, which can transmit best practices and thus create new aspirations about what can be achieved through collaboration efforts (Sorensen 2006; Sorensen and Torfing 2009). Networks can institutionalize these fragile, local forms of governance into regional economic development when they connect across multiple levels of the public and private sectors.

But how is learning related to economic development? According to Lundvall and Johnson (1994), various types of knowledge shape the capacity for local economic development:

- know-what: broad knowledge about facts
- know-why: an understanding of scientific principles
- know-how: specific skills, including not just the knowledge of how to produce goods and services but also to bring them to market, and
- know-who: the density and strength of social networks.

While the transfer of know-what and know-why can be done by local or external technical experts, the know-how and know-who tend to be transmitted tacitly and depend on local context. However, considerable uncertainty remains over the role of spatial proximity in providing this social context (Gertler 2003). Learning might best be understood not as the possession of human capital but the capability to engage meaningfully in the world and act as an agent of change (Sen 1999). This capability comes from both assets – what Bebbington (1999) refers to as the five capitals – natural, produced, human, social and cultural – and the ongoing transformation of assets into income or improved quality of life. To the extent that these assets are grounded in space, learning is as well. In this context, storytelling and experiential knowledge can be helpful ways to situate learning about know-how and know-who. The power of storytelling has been rediscovered in the last decades in urban and regional planning (Throgmorton 1996; Sandercock 2003). For example, Sandercock has shown how stories can act as a catalyzer of change "partly by inspirational example, and partly by shaping a new imagination of alternatives" (Sandercock 2003, 18). However, not every story can act as a catalyzer of change. Stories need to be persuasively told (Throgmorton 1996), and will eventually require the availability of financial means and/or political will. What makes storytelling different from transmitting knowledge through technical expertise? A story has a chronological logic (a beginning and an end), a clear plot and protagonists, a kind of moral tension, and also a "potential for generalizability" (Sandercock 2003, 13) or, in other words, the ability to apply a story to similar situations in other places and times. Storytelling to disseminate best practices can also be an effective tool to align the goals of network actors and convince them of the urgent need for coordination and joint action (Sorensen 2006; Sorensen and Torfing 2009).

The Lurín case (Chapter 3) illustrates how learning works in peripheral regions. Three types of learning – technical expertise, storytelling (via study tours, or *pasantías*), and tacit or experiential knowledge (a form of capacity building) – combine to give the region new meaning and a collective vision for the future. The three types of learning work together to motivate new collaborations among local and regional actors: the storytelling and experiential knowledge legitimate the technical expertise. Combined, this learning has aligned the goals of network actors in the region and convinced them of the urgent need for coordination and joint action around water issues. All three types of learning do not necessarily have to be present, but engaging meaningfully requires more than just formal human capital. At its most powerful, the learning process is two-way and collective. These innovations in the Lurín River Basin have led higher levels of government to successfully institutionalize these bottom-up initiatives nationally in partnership with NGOs. The Quetzaltenango case (Chapter 4) chronicles the emergence, spread, and current challenges of Grupos Gestores in Guatemala, a model of associations of private sector and civil society actors, illustrating a process of governance and learning embedded in territory. The chapter shows the opportunities and limits of the spread of models and "best practices" to promote local economic development and public-private collaboration.

Leadership and conflict management

Key to governance processes are catalytic actors who can influence others through processes of individual and shared leadership (Uyarra et al. 2017; Sotarauta, Horlings, and Liddle 2012; Stimson, Stough, and Salazar 2009; Storper et al. 2015). Several leadership scholars (Beer 2014; Davies 2009; Purdue 2001) distinguish between transactional and transformational leaders. Transactional leaders are those who take the initiative to make contacts to exchange something of value (Peters 2012). This kind of leadership assigns or agrees on what needs to be done, usually in exchange for recognition of the successful completion of their work. Transactional leadership is considered a top-down process with a specific orientation towards management or administration. It is considered to be especially useful in corporate and institutional environments with defined operational parameters, but it has a limited scope and may not be as effective in complex networks or socioeconomic systems (Davies 2009).

In rural development, there is a tendency to promote the transformational leadership model, which involves leaders and followers working together to develop common goals (Rada 1999). Transformational leaders go beyond conformity and create change in the beliefs, needs, and values of followers (Peters 2012). The main purpose of this kind of leadership is to guide followers to levels where they can achieve tasks associated with a project or take charge of it without the direct involvement of the leader (Davies 2009). Consequently, transformational leaders in rural development aim to build capabilities so that rural actors are able to respond to new challenges (Davies 2009). Taking into consideration the importance of leaders in the success of local associations, Beer (2014) identifies a set of characteristics that define an effective leader in a rural and community environment. An effective leader (1) forms a realistic vision of economic and social development of the community; (2) is endorsed by the great majority of the community or, failing that, actively engages to achieve it; (3) motivates people to achieve a common vision; and (4) preaches by example. Beer (2014) also suggests that in rural communities, effective local leaders build community resilience and can contribute to ensuring the economic future of its people.

Leadership is less about formal authority than collective processes in which interdependent actors must collaborate in order to achieve an objective that otherwise could not be achieved (Karlsen and Larrea 2012). Shared leadership facilitates the development of "collective" capabilities that reduce dependency and promote the institutionalization of collaborative processes between local actors. Once rooted in the territory, collaborative processes remain in place even as actors rotate in and out of governance networks. To develop shared leadership, networks and associations must build ways of working based on shared values and procedures (Haga 2007). In early stages, perhaps just one or two key actors catalyze the process, but over time, more leaders emerge. Often, actors have different positions, interests, and views, necessitating conflict management. To build consensus, actors must explain their positions, making explicit their differences (Karlsen and Larrea 2012). Ultimately, via this dialogue they will need to find a space of agreement just large enough to move forward with action. The existence of common values, vision, and commitment can motivate actors across a region to collaborate (Horlings and Padt 2013).

One example of an emerging process of shared leadership is in Arauco (Chapter 7), where the loss of the association's president forced stakeholders to actively assume responsibility for leadership. In a process of collective decision-making, the organization restructured, redefining the rules and roles of the participants in order to develop new strategies. In Mompox (Chapter 8), a group of young filigree artisans that emerged in 2015 offers an interesting example of a new kind of associativity that breaks with the old model of associations built around traditional older male leaders and provides a renewed force for collective action among younger generations. While still new and quite fragile, the analysis of this new association shows the importance of including factors such as intergenerational leadership to better conceptualize the relationship between association, leadership, and LED.

Extending the debate

Even as our understanding of governance and economic development has evolved, bolstered by the discussion of the role of networks, learning, and leadership, theory and evidence on economic development governance in Latin American regions remains weak. The Anglo-dominated discussion of governance largely derives its insights from advanced industrial economies with strong federalist traditions – conditions that seem remote from the Latin American continent, with its gradual and fragile recovery from centralist statism. Similarly, conceptions of networks and learning in the LED literature often seem to relate more to the context of large urban agglomerations than to peripheral regions. In the chapters that follow, we use six Latin American cases to describe the distinctive local attempts to develop and sustain local economic development processes in a context of emergent, even if fragile, governance. As we stressed in the previous chapter, in using the term fragile as opposed to weak, we seek to emphasize the possibilities of governance transformation in these areas through soft mechanisms such as network creation, learning processes, and shared and inclusive leadership. In doing so, we stress the evolutionary possibilities of these peripheral economies. Fragile governance is thus about emergent processes rather than a static structure that frames all the actions of actors in these territories.

References

Amin, A. 1999. "An Institutionalist Perspective on Regional Economic Development." *International Journal of Urban and Regional Research* 23(2): 365–78.

Bebbington, A. 1997. "New States, New NGOs? Crises and Transitions among Rural Development NGOs in the Andean Region." *World Development* 25(11): 1755–65.

Bebbington, A. 1999. "Capitals and Capabilities: A Framework for Analyzing Peasant Viability, Rural Livelihoods and Poverty." *World Development* 27(12): 2021–44.

Beer, A. 2014. "Leadership and the Governance of Rural Communities." *Journal of Rural Studies* 34: 254–62.

Berdegué, J. A., F. Carriazo, B. Jara, F. Modrego, and I. Soloaga. 2015. "Cities, Territories, and Inclusive Growth: Unraveling Urban–Rural Linkages in Chile, Colombia, and Mexico." *World Development* 73: 56–71.

Borja, J. 2001. "El gobierno del territorio de las ciudades latinoamericanas." *Revista Instituciones y desarrollo* 8: 83–142.

Brown, J. S., and P. Duguid. 2001. "Knowledge and Organization: A Social-Practice Perspective." *Organization Science* 12(2): 198–213.

Bunnell, T. G., and N. Coe. 2001. "Spaces and Scales of Innovation." *Progress in Human Geography* 25(4): 569–89.

Caldeira, T. P. 2017. "Peripheral Urbanization: Autoconstruction, Transversal Logics, and Politics in Cities of the Global South." *Environment and Planning D: Society and Space* 35(1): 3–20.

Cardoso, F. H., and E. Faletto. 1979. *Dependency and Development in Latin America*. Berkeley, CA: University of California Press.

Chapple, K., and S. Montero. 2016. "From Learning to Fragile Governance: Regional Economic Development in Rural Peru." *Journal of Rural Studies* 44: 143–52.

Conroy, M. E. 1973. "Rejection of Growth Center Strategy in Latin American Regional Development Planning." *Land Economics* 49(4): 371–80.

Cooke, P., and K. Morgan. 1998. *The Associational Economy: Firms, Regions, and Innovation*. Oxford, UK: Oxford University Press.

Davies, A. 2009. "Understanding Local Leadership in Building the Capacity of Rural Communities in Australia." *Geographical Research* 47(4): 380–9.

De Janvry, A., and E. Sadoulet. 1993. "Market, State, and Civil Organizations in Latin America beyond the Debt Crisis: The Context for Rural Development." *World Development* 21(4): 659–74.

De Janvry, A., R. Marsh, D. Runsten, E. Sadoulet, and C. Zabin. 1989. *Rural Development in Latin America: An Evaluation and a Proposal*. San José, Costa Rica: Inter-American Institute for Cooperation on Agriculture.

Doloreux, D. 2002. "What We Should Know about Regional Systems of Innovation." *Technology in Society* 24(3): 243–63.

Ellis, F., and S. Biggs. 2001. "Evolving Themes in Rural Development 1950s–2000s." *Development Policy Review* 19(4): 437–48.

Evans, P. 1996. "Government Action, Social Capital and Development: Reviewing the Evidence on Synergy." *World Development* 24(6): 1119–32.

Falleti, T. 2010. *Decentralization and Subnational Politics in Latin America*. New York: Cambridge University Press.

Florida, R. 1995. "Toward the Learning Region." *Futures* 27(5): 527–36.

Friedmann, J. 1987. *Planning in the Public Domain: From Knowledge to Action*. Princeton, NJ: Princeton University Press.

Friedmann, J. 2007. "The Wealth of Cities: Towards an Assets-Based Development of Newly Urbanizing Regions." *Development and Change* 38(6): 987–98.

Gertler, M. S. 2003. "Tacit Knowledge and the Economic Geography of Context, or the Undefinable Tacitness of Being (There)." *Journal of Economic Geography* 3(1): 75–99.

González Casanova, P. 1963. "Sociedad plural, colonialismo interno y desarrollo." *América Latina* 6(3): 15–32.

Grindle, M. S. 2007. *Going Local: Decentralization, Democratization, and the Promise of Good Governance*. Princeton, NJ: Princeton University Press.

Haga, T. 2007. *Orchestration of Networking Processes*. Trondheim, Norway: Norwegian University of Science and Technology.

Hassink, R. 2005. "How to Unlock Regional Economies from Path Dependency? From Learning Region to Learning Cluster." *European Planning Studies* 13(4): 521–35.

Helmsing, A. H. J. 2001. "Externalities, Learning and Governance: New Perspectives on Local Economic Development." *Development and Change* 32(2): 277–308.

Hirschman, A. 1958. *The Strategy of Economic Development*. New Haven, CT: Yale University Press.

Horlings, I., and F. Padt. 2013. "Leadership for Sustainable Regional Development in Rural Areas: Bridging Personal and Institutional Aspects." *Sustainable Development* 21(6): 413–24.

Jessop, B. 1998. "The Rise of Governance and the Risks of Failure: The Case of Economic Development." *International Social Science Journal* 155: 29–46.

Jordan, R., and D. Simioni, eds. 1998. *Ciudades intermedias de América Latina y el Caribe: Propuestas para la gestión urbana*. Santiago de Chile: CEPAL/Ministero degli Affari Esteri – Cooperazione Italiana.

Karlsen, J., and M. Larrea. 2012. "Emergence of Shared Leadership in the Basque Country." In *Leadership and Change in Sustainable Regional Development*, edited by M. Sotarauta, L. Horlings, and J. Liddle, 212–33. London: Routledge.

Kay, C. 2010. *Latin American Theories of Development and Underdevelopment*. London: Routledge.

Kooiman, J., and S. Jentoft. 2009. "Meta-Governance: Values, Norms and Principles, and the Making of Hard Choices." *Public Administration* 87(4): 818–36.

Lang, T. 2012. "Shrinkage, Metropolization and Peripheralization in East Germany." *European Planning Studies* 20(10): 1747–54.

Lang, T., S. Henn, W. Sgibnev, and K. Ehrlich, eds. 2015. *Understanding Geographies of Polarization and Peripheralization: Perspectives from Central and Eastern Europe and Beyond*. London: Palgrave Macmillan.

Lawson, C., and E. Lorenz. 1999. "Collective Learning, Tacit Knowledge and Regional Innovative Capacity." *Regional Studies* 33: 305–17.

Lundvall, B. A., and B. Johnson. 1994. "The Learning Economy." *Journal of Industry Studies* 1(2): 23–43.

Méndez, R., J. J. Michelini, and P. Romero. 2006. "Redes socio-institucionales e innovaciones para el desarrollo de las ciudades intermedias." *Ciudad y Territorio, Estudios Territoriales* 38(148): 377–95.

Michelini, J. J., and C. Davies. 2009. Ciudades intermedias y desarrollo territorial: un análisis exploratorio del caso argentino. *Documento de trabajo 5. Madrid: Grupo de Estudios sobre Desarrollo Urbano, Consejo Superior de Investigaciones Científicas.*

Montero, A., and D. Samuels. 2004. *Decentralization and Democratization in Latin America*. Notre Dame, IN: University of Notre Dame Press.

Montero, S. 2015. "Gobernanza y Planeación Regional en América Latina." *Estudios Jaliscienses* 101: 6–19.

Morgan, K. 1997. "The Learning Region: Institutions, Innovation and Regional Renewal." *Regional Studies* 31: 491–503.

Murdoch, J. 2000. "Networks: A New Paradigm of Rural Development?" *Journal of Rural Studies* 16: 407–19.

Myrdal, G. 1957. *Economic Theory and Underdeveloped Regions*. London: Gerald Duckworth & Co.

Perroux, F. 1970. "Note on the Concept of Growth Poles." In *Regional Economics: Theory and Practice*, edited by D. L. McKee, 93–103. New York: Free Press.

Peters, K. 2012. "Socially Embedded Leadership." In *Leadership and Change in Sustainable Regional Development*, edited by M. Sotarauta, L. Horlings, and M. Liddle, 145–63. London: Routledge.

Piore, M. J., and C. F. Sabel. 1984. *The Second Industrial Divide: Possibilities for Prosperity*. New York: Basic Books.

Polanyi, M. (1958) 1998. *Personal Knowledge. Towards a Post Critical Philosophy*. Reprint, London: Routledge.

Prebisch, R. 1976. "A Critique of Peripheral Capitalism." *CEPAL Review* 1: 9–76.

Purdue, D. 2001. "Neighbourhood Governance: Leadership, Trust and Social Capital." *Urban Studies* 38(12): 2211–24.

Putnam, R. D., R. Leonardi, and R. Y. Nanetti, 1993. *Making Democracy Work: Civic Traditions in Modern Italy*. Princeton, NJ: Princeton University Press.

Rada, D. R. 1999. "Transformational Leadership and Urban Renewal." *Journal of Leadership & Organizational Studies* 6(3–4): 18–33.

Rhodes, R. A. W. 1997. *Understanding Governance: Policy Networks, Governance, Reflexivity, and Accountability*. Buckingham, UK: Open University Press.

Rodríguez-Pose, A. 2013. "Do Institutions Matter for Regional Development?" *Regional Studies* 47(7): 1034–47.

Sabel, C. F. 1993. *Learning by Monitoring: The Institutions of Economic Development.* Center for Law and Economic Studies, Columbia School of Law, New York.

Sandercock, L. 2003. "Out of the Closet: The Importance of Stories and Storytelling in Planning Practice." *Planning Theory & Practice* 4(1): 11–28.

Schön, D. A. 1973. *Beyond the Stable State: Public and Private Learning in a Changing Society.* Harmondsworth: Penguin.

Scott, A., and M. Storper. 2003. "Regions, Globalization, Development." *Regional Studies* 37: 579–93.

Sen, A. 1999. *Development as Freedom.* New York: Anchor Books.

Sorensen, E. 2006. "Metagovernance: The Changing Role of Politicians in Processes of Democratic Governance." *The American Review of Public Administration* 36(1): 98–114.

Sorensen, E., and J. Torfing, 2009. "Making Governance Networks Effective and Democratic through Metagovernance." *Public Administration* 87: 234–58.

Sotarauta, M., L. Horlings, and M. Liddle, eds. 2012. *Leadership and Change in Sustainable Regional Development.* London: Routledge.

Stavenhagen, R. 1981. *Siete tesis equivocadas sobre América Latina. Sociología y Subdesarrollo.* México, DF: Nuestro Tiempo.

Stimson, R., R. Stough, and M. Salazar. 2009. *Leadership and Institutions in Regional Endogenous Development.* Cheltenham, UK: Edward Elgar Publishing.

Storper, M., T. Kemeny, N. Makarem, and T. Osman. 2015. *The Rise and Fall of Urban Economies: Lessons from San Francisco and Los Angeles.* Stanford, CA: Stanford University Press.

Tendler, J., and M. A. Amorim. 1996. "Small Firms and Their Helpers: Lessons on Demand." *World Development* 24(3): 407–26.

Throgmorton, J. A. 1996. *Planning as Persuasive Storytelling: The Rhetorical Construction of Chicago's Electric Future.* Chicago, IL: University of Chicago Press.

Uyarra, E., K. Flanagan, E. Magro, J. R. Wilson, and M. Sotarauta. 2017. "Understanding Regional Innovation Policy Dynamics: Actors, Agency and Learning." *Environment and Planning C* 35(4): 559–68.

Vázquez Barquero, A. 2010. "Diversidad territorial y desarrollo endógeno en Argentina." *Cultura Económica* 77: 46–72.

Von Hippel, E. 1994. "'Sticky Information' and the Locus of Problem Solving: Implications for Innovation." *Management Science* 40(4): 429–39.

Wallerstein, I. 1979. *The Capitalist World-Economy.* Cambridge, UK: Cambridge University Press.

Weck, S., and S. Beißwenger. 2014. "Coping with Peripheralization: Governance Response in Two German Small Cities." *European Planning Studies* 22(10): 2156–71.

Wellbrock, W., D. Roep, M. Mahon, E. Kairyte, B. Nienaber, L. Dominguez Garcia, M. Kriszan, and M. Farrell. 2013. "Arranging Public Support to Unfold Collaborative Modes of Governance in Rural Areas." *Journal of Rural Studies* 32: 420–9.

Wenger, E. 1998. *Communities of Practice: Learning, Meaning, and Identity. Learning in Doing.* Cambridge, UK; New York, NY: Cambridge University Press.

Woods, M. 2009. "Rural Geography: Blurring Boundaries and Making Connections." *Progress in Human Geography* 33(6): 849–58.

3 From learning to fragile governance in Lurín

Rural economic development in rural Peru

Karen Chapple and Sergio Montero

Introduction

As small cities and rural areas in Latin America take on new responsibilities for economic development, the process of learning becomes critical. Thus far, the lively debate about learning and regional development has largely focused on innovation and high-tech industries in the urbanized context, often governed by public–private partnerships (Asheim 2012; Cooke and Morgan 1998; Doloreux 2002). Yet, lacking the "soft" infrastructure that enables governance, and with a weak private sector, rural areas benefit little from traditional economic development strategies and instead must devise new approaches via local learning. Using the case of the Lurín River Basin in Peru, in this chapter we analyze the tangible and intangible governance factors that are key in translating these collective learning processes into local economic development outcomes.

The Lurín River Basin is the southernmost of three river basins in the metropolitan region of Lima. Though considered part of the periphery of the metropolitan region, poor transportation infrastructure keeps Lima at a distance (two to five hours' drive). This poor accessibility has hindered the economic integration of the region into Lima and insulated many of its producers from globalization (both the benefits and costs). Most districts of the Basin have lost population in the last two decades due to migration to Lima; however, Lurín has retained much more of its nonurban land than nearby river basins. Nongovernmental organizations (NGOs) have worked for over two decades to improve conditions and build local capacity in the valley with little impact: poverty persists for as much as half of the local population. Yet the past 20 years have brought significant economic transformations to the rural villages of Lurín. These include increased agricultural productivity due to the building of several water reservoirs in the village of San Andrés de Tupicocha, the emergence of tourism as a new economic activity in Antioquía after the implementation of a community-led program that painted many of the village buildings, and the building and operation of a factory to produce marmalade with the region's fruits in Cochahuayco. The region around the basin is currently struggling to develop effective territorial governance institutions for economic development. In recent years, local and regional actors have created several institutional arrangements that seek to coordinate environmental and economic development strategies at the regional level. NGOs in Lurín have focused on building institutional capacity and governance structures as a way to coordinate and promote regional economic development. In this chapter we focus on the emergent governance of economic development processes and collective action in the region.

Based on over 30 interviews with key actors in the area and the observation of meetings of NGOs, local officials, and peasants in several villages in Lurín, we examine how economic development initiatives have occurred in the region. In this chapter we understand governance as self-organizing networks of actors that facilitate collective action initiatives (Jessop 1998). While public actors can be part of governance initiatives, they do not always have to be present (ibid.). We look at governance dimensions that are both *horizontal*, i.e., coordination across municipalities, peasant communities or families, and *vertical*, engaging the multiple levels of government from community to municipality to district to region to the nation-state. The mechanism that activates both of these governance dimensions is *learning*, which in rural Lurín occurs in many different forms, from the transmission of technical expertise by agricultural engineers to the building of confidence in community members through storytelling to the experience of different techniques through fact-finding missions to other regions. In particular, we analyze three community-led processes of economic development in irrigation, tourism, and agro-food industry. We argue that in Lurín's successful economic development projects, three different types of learning – technical expertise, storytelling, and tacit or experiential knowledge – combined to create new meaning for its territorial assets and collective vision for the future, which together may form the basis for an economic development strategy. When these learning processes activated governance along both vertical and horizontal dimensions, actors in the region created the potential for institutionalizing these emergent economic development processes in the long term.

We begin with a review of relevant literature on territorial economic development, governance, and learning. After presenting a framework for conceptualizing learning and governance in a rural context, we provide a brief historical overview of the socioeconomic conditions and governance dynamics in Lurín. We then look at the success and failures of local and regional economic development strategies in irrigation, tourism, and fruit processing in light of the role of learning and governance. The conclusion discusses implications for policy and institution-building efforts to promote local and regional economic development in rural contexts in Latin America.

Economic development, governance, and learning: a theoretical framework

To develop a relevant theoretical framework that allows us to study economic development in the Lurín River Basin in Peru considering governance and learning as critical variables, in the following sections we briefly review three academic debates: (1) the territorial aspects of economic development, with a focus on rural development; (2) the rise of governance and the role of networks and social capital; and (3) the role of learning in regional economic development.

The territorial aspects of economic development

In recent decades, cities and regions have assumed increasing importance in the design and implementation of economic development strategies, placing new emphasis on their capacity for governance and collective learning (Amin 1999; Chapple, Montero, and Sosa 2012; Lawson and Lorentz 1999; Scott and Storper 2003). However, villages and rural regions have attracted little attention in the local economic development and innovation literatures. Instead, most of these debates have taken place in the field of rural development, which has recently moved towards a more territorial focus while maintaining its key preoccupation with the dynamics of agriculture and its impact on peasants' income and welfare (Murdoch 2000; Marsden and Bristow 2000; Ellis and Biggs 2001). A new paradigm of sustainable rural livelihoods is emerging that consists in broadening income sources beyond subsistence farming to a variety of rural and nonrural activities, such as crafts production, housing investment, and remittances (Bebbington 1999; Ellis and Biggs 2001). Rural livelihoods develop via the existence (and accessibility) of diverse assets that can be transformed into income or Bebbington's five capitals (natural, produced, human, social, and cultural), which are at the same time inputs, capabilities, and outputs (Bebbington 1999, 2029). Rural development authors have increasingly appealed to the need to better understand the role of governance, networks, and social capital (Murdoch 2000).

Governance, networks, and social capital in rural areas

Effective governance by self-organized networks entails collective action and leadership, facilitated by social capital (Putnam, Leonardi, and Nanetti 1993; Woolcock 1998). The state may play a role here as a facilitator: "the state can help most by providing inputs that local people cannot provide for themselves and then maintaining a 'hands-off' stance with regard to activities that are within the scope of local action" (Evans 1996, 112). According to Sorensen and Torfing (2009), facilitators (or metagovernors) should combine hands-on and hands-off methods, stepping back from network design but offering a more hands-on approach in terms of network management and participation. Yet rural areas tend to be socially heterogeneous, creating a particular need for collective leadership to coordinate across multiple networks embedded in place (Collinge and Gibney 2010). In rural areas, the availability and form of social capital is often structured by the political economy of development, which may either limit or grant local capacity for action (Bebbington et al. 2006).

A network perspective can also be useful for studying the economy of rural areas. The networks are twofold: (1) vertical agro-food networks, in which farmers and rural areas are linked to broader supply and production chains, in part because of the market value of their proximity to nature; and (2) horizontal networks, or what Murdoch calls "the new rural networks of innovation and learning" (Murdoch 2000, 412). The "old structures" of rural areas, such as small farm systems or artisanal workshops, with their high levels of trust and sociocultural cohesion, are well equipped to form the new horizontal networks of rural economic growth – though they may also lead to resistance to change (Murdoch 2000, 414). These networks also prove key to mobilizing assets, with the activation of social capital occurring either by rural communities reaching from the inside out or external organizations connecting from the outside in (Bebbington 1999).

Learning and local economic development in rural areas

While many authors have noted the importance of understanding rural development through the language of governance, networks, and learning (Murdoch 2000; Wellbrock and Roep 2015), less is known about how learning can generate new local and regional networks and, therefore, new forms of governance. Asheim (2012) argues that policy makers have adopted the idea of a learning region as an answer for regions with weak territorial competence. This offers the potential for regional development coalitions, a more broadly defined regional innovation system that includes a variety of organizations involved with competence building (ibid.). Arguing for conceptualizing learning as happening in space rather than in a particular place, Hassink and Klaerding (2012) point out the role of different types of knowledge (analytical, synthetic, and arts-based) – not all of which are based upon proximity to an urban or regional agglomeration – in the process of learning, Yet, as Lundvall and Johnson (1994) point out, the "know-how" and "know-who" forms of knowledge tend to be transmitted tacitly and depend on local context.

The idea of communities of practice offers a different way of understanding learning that may be more appropriate for rural regions. In this view, knowledge is acquired not through the simple transfer from one person to another, but as socially constructed out of environmental context, social relations, and historic paths. Tacit knowledge thus flows via social relations across geographies (Amin 1999). However, transmission of practice occurs most powerfully in forms such as apprenticeship and common experience, grounded in place.

Conceptual framework: from learning to governance in a rural context

We develop our conceptual framework based on Jessop's (1998) definition of governance as self-organizing networks, adding in the notion of learning across space. Different self-coordinating networks exist in an economic sector, spatial territory, or other system (in Lurín typically small family associations, NGOs, and local government) (Figure 3.1). They are reflexively self-organized, meaning that they develop a common language and vision around an issue, but also that they learn from failure and continuously attempt to adapt their behavior. This may create joint action either horizontally – between stakeholders in equivalent positions (such as associations) – or vertically, in hierarchies (as between levels of government). Where coordination and learning across these networks is occurring, there is metagovernance.

In this study we focus on one key governance mechanism in the rural context: learning. Recognizing the role of "know-how" and "know-who" in addition to technical expertise ("know-what" and "know-why"), we show how individuals transmitting knowledge via their networks can lead to new forms of governance. In our analysis of economic development processes taking place in Lurín (irrigation, tourism develepment, and fruit processing), we find three different modes of learning: technical expertise, storytelling, and experiential knowledge. As these three types of learning converge, villagers are able to construct new meanings for their livelihood, which in turn gives them the capability to act and develop shared leadership. When these learning processes are able to activate governance along both vertical and horizontal dimensions, actors in the region create the potential for institutionalizing economic development processes in the long term. This facilitates two-way learning: not only do locals learn about new ways of doing things, but also government officials become familiar with their practices, giving them legitimacy and access to resources.

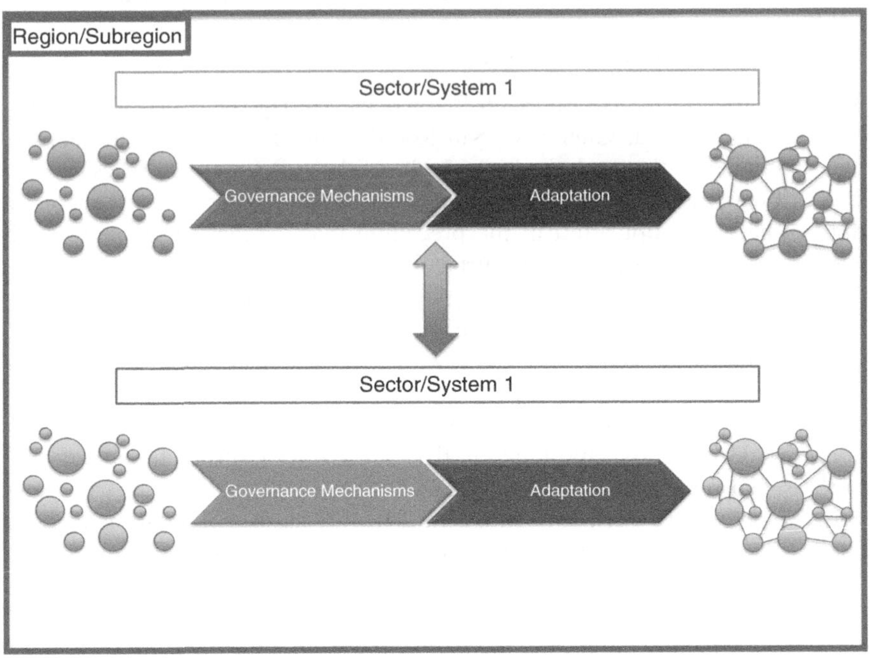

Figure 3.1 Metagovernance framework

Methods

This research relies on both extensive interviews and field observations over a period of six months in 2012. Over 30 interviews took place with actors in two different areas of the Lurín River Basin, Antioquía and Tupicocha, as well as with NGOs and government agencies in Lima. The study was initially commissioned by the Multilateral Investment Fund of the Inter-American Development Bank, which sought to better understand the relationship between governance and local economic development, drawing from the experience of the many projects they have funded in Latin America. Because of this, we were able to work closely with NGOs in the region to develop a list and make contact with key informants. This initial list snowballed into about a dozen more interviews with locals, which ensured that we heard voices from outside the IAD Bank and the Global Center for Development and Democracy's influence. Interviews took place in Spanish and were semi-structured, covering a large range of issues from the changes in the community over time to the key actors involved in specific economic development initiatives. Because the research project occurred concurrently with a series of economic development workshops for local residents, we were able to observe six community meetings as well, each in different communities of the basin.

Socioeconomic and institutional context of the region

Overview of the Lurín River Basin

The districts in Lurín (San Andrés de Tupicocha, Santiago de Tuna, San Damián, Lahuaytambo, Langa, Cuenca or San José de Chorrillos, and Antioquía) that were included in the study had just 7,239 of the valley's 165,000 residents in 2007, concentrated in the upper part of the basin (Figure 3.2). Most of the districts had lost population in the preceding two decades. In general, Lurín has retained much more of its nonurban land than the other river basins serving Lima; however, locals are abandoning much agricultural land as they seek livelihoods in the city. Approximately half of local land is in community ownership and guided by community rules, while the other half is held by individual landowners, who may lack property titles.

The population of the middle and upper Lurín River Basin is generally poorer, older, and less educated than that in the rest of Peru. The poverty rate in the seven municipalities ranged from 50 to 75 percent in 2007 (compared with 31 percent in Peru as a whole in 2010). Educational attainment at the college level is low (ranging from 5 to 14 percent) compared to Peru, where 31 percent have some higher education.

The dominant means of support in the seven municipalities (based on 2007 data) are agriculture, hunting, cattle, and forestry, generally employing over 70 percent of the workers. Tourism provides minimal employment except in

Figure 3.2 The Lurín Region

the municipality of Antioquía, where it has grown in recent years and currently accounts for about 3 percent of employment. There are a few family-based SMEs, accounting generally for 5 to 10 percent of overall employment in the municipalities. Particularly in the upper basin, locals have had access to electricity, sanitation, television, and the internet for just a few years. Moreover, it is only since the development of reservoirs that agricultural production has been possible throughout the year (particularly in the upper basin), rather than just the three rainy months. These investments are likely altering the sectoral composition of the region.

Proximity to Lima

Lurín differs from other rural Andean regions because of its geographical proximity to Lima, which is from two to five hours away (depending on the road). This proximity facilitates both economic and social connections, giving the region a dual identity as both a rural enclave and part of the country's largest metropolitan region. The debate about the role of spatial proximity in the transmission of knowledge, i.e., learning regions or organizational communities of practice, presents an interesting framework in which to view the Lurín case. Much closer to Lima than other Andean communities, the region has benefited from this proximity, which fosters vertical connections and two-way communication, while also permitting many locals to live dual lives, as *comuneros* and Lima residents. The local economy is closely tied to Lima, with most agricultural products sent to the metropolitan markets. Local livelihoods depend on Lima also through migration; there is a constant outflow of youth to the city and only a few return, even though, reportedly, life in Lima is itself challenging. Lurín inhabitants are divided between those who think of themselves as *comuneros* (local peasants, legally defined as those that have lived in the area for more than four years) or *proprietarios* (landowners). Many members of either group are essentially dual citizens of Lurín and Lima, holding jobs in Lima but maintaining land in the valley. Most local leaders, including elected officials such as the mayors and the leaders of the *comunidades campesinas*, live in Lima most of the time and commute to the basin several times per week. The rootedness of the mayors in Lima helps facilitate connections to higher levels of government.

Proximity thus enables both the acquisition of formal knowledge or technical expertise and stories about different ways of acting. At the same time, many of the region's successes come from knowledge transmitted through rural communities of practice, i.e., learning about innovations in other regions through experiencing it firsthand home in the village. This is a form of experiential knowledge that must be grounded in space in order for locals to engage in it.

Lurín's proximity to Lima has also brought it more attention and resources from outsiders. Many NGOs choose to work there because of its convenient location close to Lima; working in the area allows them to maintain offices in both locations. Many refer to Lurín as the "last green valley" in Lima, highlighting its potential role as a local vacation spot. This visibility has put Lurín on the map but also places it under more pressure to establish endogenous development approaches.

Institutional context and key actors in the basin

Governing economic development in the basin are a number of public sector, civil society, and private sector actors at different levels. Multiple different politico-administrative divisions in Peru, all elected bodies, have jurisdiction over the basin: the regional and provincial governments of the Metropolitan Municipality of Lima, the provincial municipality of Huarochirí, and its seven district municipalities – each also made up of multiple divisions called *comunidades campesinas* (autonomous organizations with legal authority, typically consisting of families or groups tied together by place or economic or property interest). Since 2007, two or more district municipalities are allowed to enter into a voluntary agreement to become a joint *mancomunidad* and provide services and promote local development jointly; in Lurín, the Mancomunidad comprises the seven district municipalities and the provincial municipality of Huarochirí. In addition to the comunidades campesinas, NGOs play a powerful role in local governance. In contrast, the private sector, consisting mostly of associations of local producers, is minimally represented.

NGOs have been involved in the Lurín River Basin for two decades, although their presence became more important and visible after decentralization reforms took place in Peru after the 1990s. In 2003, thanks to the collaboration between the NGO platform and ten mayors in the basin, an Association of Municipal Authorities (AAM) was established, a form of regional cooperation addressing the cyclical scarcity of water and the discontinuity of the transportation infrastructure within the basin, which seriously limited intra-basin movements (Governa 2012). In 2004, the national government enacted the "Pro-Cuenca" program to improve natural resource management, choosing the Lurín River Basin as its first pilot program due in part to the relationships between NGO staff and the national president Alejandro Toledo. In 2009, two NGOs, the Global Center for Development and Democracy (CGDD) and the Research, Education and Development Center (CIED) started a territorial development project in Lurín with the technical and financial support of the Inter-American Development Bank to improve the competitiveness of the Lurín River Basin through the joint action of the region's public and private entities.

These actors organize themselves in networks with both horizontal and vertical dimensions. Working primarily horizontally are the comunidades campesinas, which play an important role in terms of governing communal property and water usage, as well as fostering civic participation. Associations often grow out of family ties; as one NGO leader explained, "Andean development begins with the family and then gives work to others." Families form building blocks for business networks that go beyond the traditional community interests in water and land management to conduct economic development. Associations range from the irrigation committees governing water usage that have existed for hundreds of years to the more recent local tourism and producers' associations (now 16 in total) for specific products such as cider vinegar processing and guinea pig farming.

Another horizontally organized association is the Mancomunidad Municipal de la Cuenca Valle de Lurín, which has focused on infrastructure development, particularly water and sanitation, but is increasingly involved in economic development governance, due to the strength of its vertical connections with higher levels of government. Although there are other examples of mancomunidades across Peru, many consider this Mancomunidad, which grew out of the territorial governance effort of the AAM, a model of combined environmental and economic governance, worthy of replication (Jurado 2012). However, it grew in part out of vertical interventions of NGOs in the basin, particularly the support of CGDD and CIED.

In a rural river basin such as Lurín, it is critical to secure resources for development from higher levels of government. This may occur via competitive processes with other regions or through personal connections with government officials. Either way, the process results in learning, often two-way, in a vertical dimension, between municipalities and regional and national government agencies. One key player in this vertical knowledge transfer is the intermediary, in this case, the mayor of the provincial government, Dr. Rosa Vásquez. Her awareness of opportunities from national programs, particularly in tourism, has helped keep resources flowing to the basin, and at the same time her influence with the national government has increased awareness of the Mancomunidad and Lurín's potential. Likewise, the regional government and NGOs have played important roles in funding local projects, though some mayors complain that the projects are mostly symbolic, with minimal impact.

Learning, governance, and economic development in Lurín: water reservoirs, tourism, and fruit processing

In this section, we analyze three community-led economic development processes in the region: the building of artificial reservoirs in Tupicocha, the emergence of tourism in Antioquía, and the establishment of a fruit processing factory in Cochahuayco. These cases show how three types of learning – through technical expertise, storytelling, and experiential knowledge – combine to empower communities to act collectively. Through the combination of these three types of learning, each with its own geography, new, albeit fragile, forms of governance and social capital can emerge. The first case, the building of reservoirs and irrigation improvements, illustrates how three different learning mechanisms in combination create a convincing narrative for the area's future, thus activating both horizontal and vertical governance networks and creating capacity for change. The second and third cases, in tourism and food processing, show how the failure to combine the three types of learning results in governance failure.

Water reservoirs and irrigation improvements in Tupicocha

An important year in the agriculture history of San Andrés de Tupicocha was 1983. That year, Teodoro Rojas, a Tupicocha resident who had spent some years working elsewhere as an agricultural technician, came back to the village resolved to build a reservoir to improve agriculture irrigation, based on the Gallito Ciego dam he had seen in Cajamarca. Rojas gathered the community and told them the benefits of the irrigation innovations that he had seen elsewhere. Initially, the *comuneros* were skeptical, particularly of the valve technology he was proposing, as they have traditionally used a stick to control water flow. According to Rojas: "They couldn't imagine it because they had never seen it before."

Eventually, Rojas was able to convince some people in the community to build it, but lack of funding, specifically the rejection of a funding application to Cooperación Popular, a national agency that promotes the creation of small companies and business initiatives in Peru, hampered implementation of the project. Therefore, Rojas had to seek funds among interested families in the Cullpe and Tupicocha communities. Over a period of eight years, each family lent Rojas what they could afford in the form of materials and labor. To coordinate this exchange of materials and work hours, a new "comité de regantes" (an irrigation committee) was created. When the economy of the community improved substantially after the reservoir was eventually built, they decided to build two more. This time, some of the families that had been skeptical were now interested in collaborating, so two more irrigation committees were created in order to coordinate the construction of the reservoirs. The whole of Cullpe community was now involved.

After the first reservoirs were built in 1991, and the irrigation and agricultural productivity improvements became obvious, a positive attitude towards change and innovation emerged in the basin. As peasants in neighboring municipalities saw this success, they became interested in improving their own agricultural production. Seeing these improvements in their own region, according to Rojas, "sort of gave hope to farmers." After the first reservoirs were widely acknowledged as successful, it became easier for peasants to access more sources of funding for this kind of projects. NGOs and different government agencies became very interested in promoting these irrigation innovations and have funded numerous *pasantías*, or brief study tours to outside areas, to try to replicate them in other rural communities in Peru and beyond. Meanwhile, about 70 percent of Cullpe peasants in Tupicocha "have moved from a subsistence economy with food insecurity to a surplus economy with food security" (Alfaro Moreno and Claverías 2010, 40).

The public–private networks created around the building of water reservoirs represent one of the most interesting and effective cases of learning transformed into a governance mechanism in the Lurín River Basin. Under the leadership of Teodoro Rojas, who was elected Tupicocha mayor and later the president of the Mancomunidad, the national government awarded the Mancomunidad funding for two technical studies for reservoirs that will provide 15 million cubic meters of water for the region. Compared with the one million cubic meters of water of the eight reservoirs built in the region, this will represent a significant improvement for peasants in the region.

This case illustrates a successful combination of three forms of learning that created collective action and new governance capabilities in the village of Tupicocha. First, Mayor Rojas leveraged both his technical knowledge about reservoirs and his storytelling about other areas to have members of the community build a reservoir. Both these forms of knowledge come from outside the region, but the construction of the reservoir in the local area then provided the experiential knowledge that built the trust necessary for more collaboration in building other reservoirs. In combination, this learning aligned the goals of network actors in the region and convinced them of the urgent need for coordination and joint action around water issues. Finally, higher levels of government in partnership with NGOs have successfully institutionalized these bottom-up initiatives via pasantías and political leadership from the bottom up. This then has become the first major success of the Mancomunidad: to support and scale up a fragile public–private collaboration around an economic development initiative that was born out of the combination of three processes of learning.

In many ways the story of the reservoirs is reminiscent of the idea of commons governance (Ostrom 1990). The Cullpe farmers adhere to several key design principles for common pool resources: equitable costs and benefits, broad participation, and recognition of management rights by higher authorities. Institutional innovation and new meaning emerge from local assets, particularly cultural endowments and knowledge (Bebbington 1999; Escobal and Valdivia 2004; Ostrom 2002). As we will see in the following sections, this has not always happened with other economic development processes in Lurín. In the cases of both tourism and fruit processing, actors have not succeeded in combining the three types of learning, and they have failed to develop a joint capacity to act and sustain the projects over time.

The emergence of tourism in Antioquía

As the shift to a broader conception of rural livelihoods has occurred in recent decades, tourism has become a booming industry (Desforges 2000) and an increasingly attractive economic activity for many rural communities in Peru (Fuller 2011). Tourism can easily be monopolized by a handful of private actors (such as big hotel chains) and be detrimental to the local environment and culture, but in practice is often fragmented. For instance, in the Cusco-Macchu Picchu area, where Peruvian tourism is highly concentrated, tourism involves many actors and stakeholders and cannot be promoted by a single entity (Ladkin and Martinez Bertramini 2002).

While tourism has been embraced by many local officials and NGOs in Peru, the development of a tourist infrastructure and services (such as roads, restaurants, and hotels) is inconsistent outside the well-known touristic areas.

To address the decrease in agricultural production in the Lurín River Basin in the mid 2000s, CIED researchers started to think of new ways to generate income in the area. Given the presence of rural tourism in the neighboring village of Cieneguilla – where many Limeños go during the weekend looking for better climate and nature – the idea emerged to attract at least part of this tourism to Antioquía. While the close proximity to Lima and Cieneguilla was an advantage in comparision to more isolated villages in the Andes, the town suffered from a poor image.

Working together with CIED, Cementos Lima, the biggest concrete manufacturer in Peru, which is headquartered in the basin, donated the equivalent of USD 2,000 to Antioquía through their social responsibility office to organize an international competition to recruit an artist that would design house painting schemes for the village. About 25 artists participated in the competition; the winner was Peruvian artist Enrique Bustamante, who proposed painting different floral and animal designs on the exterior walls in bright colors. The project was received with enthusiasm by a group of Antioquía residents interested in developing tourism in the village, who formed a local committee under the name "Colores para Antioquía" (Colors for Antioquía). This association, made up of people who already had an economic interest in tourism or were trained in tourism by NGOs, oversaw the implementation process, which started in August 2004.

Colores para Antioquía was also key to building trust among residents and persuading them about the benefits of joining the project. Fuller (2011) has also shown how the tourism project gained legitimacy when the local priest of Antioquía allowed them to paint the town's church, a major event that led to the participation of the rest of the residents. By November 2004, about 30 houses had been fixed and painted (Fuller 2011). At this point, the vertical dimension was activated: the national government became interested and, through the program "Mejorando mi pueblo," funded the second phase of the painting project. The Ministry of Housing provided support for improvements to the main square, while the National Fund for Development Cooperation (or FONCODES, the infrastructure program of the Ministry of Social Inclusion) donated funds for a tourist office and pasantías to learn about tourism initiatives in other places (Fuller, 2011). The Ministry of Foreign Commerce and Tourism, the provincial mayor, and the CGDD have also given them money to train local guides and conduct a tourist census.

This initiative, including the final phase of public-private collaboration, resulted in significant improvements. The number of tourists in Antioquía increased from 2,303 in 2006 to 5,527 in 2008, which in turn has improved the quality of life of Antioquía residents (Alfaro Moreno and Claverías 2010, 33–4; Fuller 2011). Currently, about 200 tourists visit Antioquía every weekend during Lima's winter (July–November) (Fuller 2011). However, the lack of tourist infrastructure such as hotels, restaurants, and roads to the main tourist attractions limits the length of stay of tourists and therefore the economic potential of this new activity.

An additional benefit that the painting project has had for the town has been to improve the residents' self-esteem and local identity, strenghtening women's participation in local economic activities and political issues, and improving houses and public spaces in the village as well as the quality of life of the population in general (Alfaro Moreno and Claverías 2010; Fuller 2011). A distinctive feature of the emergence of tourism in Antioquía is that, as noted by Fuller (2011, 933), in contrast to other rural tourism projects arising from local uniqueness, in Antioquía difference was "produced" through the murals. While this process experienced many obstacles, our interviews confirm that currently the project is seen in a positive light by most Antioquía residents and has also facilitated the emergence of a new generation of young people with interest in developing the tourism sector.

As noted by Fuller (2011), the Antioquía project is in many ways paradigmatic in Peru because it involved the collaboration of a large number of actors, including local residents, the local government, national government agencies, an NGO, and the private sector. Antioquía's painting project has received many national and international prizes and, interestingly, it has become a model of sustainable tourism that has been replicated in neighboring villages such as San Damián and Lahuaytambo and other Peruvian villages far from Lurín such as Sogay (Arequipa) and San Jerónimo de Tunán (Huancayo) (Alfaro Moreno and Claverías 2010, 32). Lima's regional government and the municipality of Huarochirí have also referenced the Antioquía painting project as a successful case of local economic development and public-private collaboration (Alfaro Moreno and Claverías 2010).

However, by 2010 the collaboration around tourism issues in Antioquía had decreased substantially (Fuller 2011). The local government had stopped collaborating with CIED and blamed the NGO for selling the project as its own. On the other hand, members of Colores para Antioquía blamed CIED for intervening too much in the association's "internal issues" and were skeptical of the local government given the mayor's initial disapproval of the project. Colores itself lost participants, and the new mayor was not supportive. Multiple actors – from local associations to NGOs to the various levels of government – continue to battle for leadership of local tourism initiatives, with disagreement over next steps. Thus, local actors have not succeeded in facilitating successful joint action either vertically, across multiple layers of NGOs and government, or horizontally, between associations or sectors.

Storytelling and experiential knowledge played a key role in promoting collaboration around tourism in Antioquía. Hearing about the success of tourism in Cieneguilla built support among villagers, and seeing the initial painting and murals completed bolstered confidence even more. Pasantías aided the learning process. Where the effort has fallen short, however – in addition to the lack of investment in tourism infrastructure – is in technical expertise and support from different government agencies and NGOs to buoy the weak governance structure created around Colores para Antioquía. Lacking a cohesive strategy for moving forward into the complicated arena of tourism development, actors have not been able to create shared meaning. Though the activity has activated some networks, there is no coordination between them, and no metagovernor has stepped forward.

The fruit processing plant in Cochahuayco

During the 1990s, NGOs were mostly focused on improving the lives in the Lurín River Basin by technical "supply" solutions, that is, by sending agricultural engineers to train peasants in improving methods of agricultural production in the area. In the 2000s, however, there was a new focus on diversifying the economic activities of the region and shifting into higher value-added activities. Specifically, CIED supported fruit processing by encouraging an association of farmers and providing financial support in buying food-processing equipment. An example of this effort is the establishment of the Vallelindo association in Cochahuayco to produce apple cider vinegar and fruit marmalade.

Traditionally, local farmers in Lurín only sold harvested apples. CIED gave a group of women a training workshop on how to make cider vinegar and sent engineers to the village first to teach them production techniques and then how to make marmalade. CIED trainers pushed the women to form an association, in part because it was the only way to ask for funds from the philanthropic agency Fundación Katrina. Thus, they created the Valle Lindo association of about 20 farmers, most of them women, to produce a marmalade called Frutsana. A visit by the Minister of Women and Social Development (MIMDES; since renamed to Ministerio de la Mujer y Poblaciones Vulnerables [MIMP]), Virginia Borra, to Cochahuayco resulted in a promise to help them with their business but only if the money was managed by the local comunidad. The processing plant was built in 2010, with training on the equipment. Learning also took place through numerous internships, sponsored by CIED, which were three-day workshops ("módulos") in which women with businesses in other regions (Huancayo province and Ecuador) told them stories about their business and ways of producing, whether marmalade, trout, or other products. However, efforts to build technical expertise have been more focused on how to improve production than how to sell the product. Most of what they produce – cider vinegar and marmalade – is sold either locally in Cochahuayco to tourists who visit the town or in the local festivals of Lurín villages. The association had to rent the machines for their business from the comunidad, making very little profit after paying all the costs. This has resulted in many of the founders leaving the association (only seven are left). Some still prepare the products they learned to make, vinegar and marmalade, but on their own, without using the processing plant and the formal market. The process has left them disillusioned about NGO efforts, as one association leader revealed:

> We don't want more engineers to come and tell us what to do; all the money that CIED and other NGOs are going to spend on engineers they should give it to us, because now we have the capacity to learn by ourselves.

Thus, once again the learning process – and territorial governance – has fallen short. Although storytelling occurred via the intervention of outside actors, as well as pasantías to outside areas, actors never gained the technical expertise in selling that they needed. The biggest gap was the lack of experiential knowledge to build confidence in the farmers. Without a model of successful food processing, farmers remained unsure of what they were to create. This case illustrates how economic development governance can fail at commons governance in the absence of collective learning. The development of the fruit processing plant failed to meet many of the design principles so important to common pool resource management. The design and implementation of the project and its regulatory structure lacked broad participation, there has been little monitoring, no sanctioning system is in place, and costs exceed benefits for many participants. This failure hints at the challenges these communities face in developing governance for territorial economic development.

Conclusion: collective learning and fragile governance in Lurín

The last 20 years have seen catalytic changes in the middle and upper Lurín River Basin. Among the most transformative have been the reservoir projects in Tupicocha, which are being scaled up by a successful public–private collaboration effort. While the emergence of tourism and the establishment of a fruit processing plant have been innovative in providing new sources of economic activity to rural livelihoods in Lurín, they have also been less successful in their sustainability over time. Accompanying these developments is the emergence of new governance mechanisms in the region, including the Mancomunidad, the Council of Water Resources, and a network of NGOs. With a supportive national government as well, these new forms of governance offer hope to leverage even more change.

These examples illustrate how different types of learning enabled new forms of territorial governance for economic development in the region. The most successful cases draw on a combination of three types of learning: technical expertise (whether engineering or painting, both skills acquired from outside the region); storytelling (stories about other places and *pasantías*, or brief learning missions to outside areas); and experiential knowledge (the learning from examples embedded in place). All three types of learning need not be present, but engaging meaningfully requires more than just formal human capital. As one NGO leader explains, "That one farmer sees that which the other is doing is better than having an engineer teach it to him." In the most successful case – the building of water reservoirs – the different types of learning worked together. Learning creates new meaning from assets, which then support the power to act collectively. This then complicates the idea of governance on which we base our conceptual framework. Our findings develop the idea of learning capacity, showing that learning must occur in multiple and reinforcing ways. We also find that coordination must happen across networks and hierarchies, horizontally and vertically, to access not just knowledge but resources. The mechanisms for metagovernance, thus, may need to be defined more broadly.

Although the combination of these three types of learning resulted in different kinds of collaboration among farmers and peasants, the most successful cases also utilized both horizontal and vertical networks for "know-how" and "know-who," creating a space for two-way learning around a common vision. For example, in the reservoir case, local families organized (horizontal) joint action, articulated a clear vision for the future, and gained the attention of higher levels of government. Although the specific institutional arrangements will vary by place, the development of this vision into a new narrative for the area is key to motivating collective action and leadership there. This narrative also differentiates it from the Lima metro, making it less a periphery than a locus in its own right.

In all three cases, proximity to Lima has facilitated the transfer of knowledge, but proximity cannot be understood as the replication of the primary city's economic development model. Thus, local economic development in Lurín can be best understood by analyzing the various sociospatial contexts throughout the world where learning activated governance mechanisms rather than conceptualizing it as a single "learning region." We suggest it would be helpful to broaden the idea of the regional innovation system to regional development coalition (Asheim 2012), and conceive of the relevance of learning – and acquiring different types of knowledge – in place-based networks (Hassink and Klaerding 2012). This learning system extends from Lurín to Cajamarca to Lima to Washington, DC, making Lurín less of a periphery than a node in an enlarged network.

The Lurín case has some important lessons for other rural regions with economic development needs. "Soft" mechanisms of learning such as storytelling and experiential knowledge can create collective action or governance, even if weak at the initial stages. Local, regional, and national governments can institutionalize these fragile forms of governance into regional economic development when they take a hands-on approach to vertically and horizontally coordinate actors. It suggests that while joint action or governance mechanisms around a problem or need might emerge relatively easily through processes of learning, the development of a shared vision among public and private actors is key in order to scale up public–private projects to the regional level. It is by building and supporting different types of learning that territorial projects can become part of a regional narrative, which may eventually serve as the basis of new institutions. This, then, is another path towards the "constructability" of synergy, or social capital that reaches from public to private (Evans 1996).

The failures in governance – specifically, the challenges in economic development in agroindustry and tourism – seem to occur when these dynamics of learning and networks, and the leadership that grows out of these dynamics, are absent. For instance, lack of technical expertise and experiential knowledge doomed the process of constructing meaning around the cider vinegar plant, an asset imposed largely from outside. Similarly, in the case of tourism, there is a collective action failure along both vertical and horizontal dimensions due to the inability of local government, NGOs and local residents to construct shared meaning about touristic assets around which to organize collective action.

Thus, the successes in the basin are not yet about economic development. Specific economic development interventions may need to wait until they become part of a vision shared by locals. Instead, policy makers might best focus on ways of fostering different types of learning, not just within the basin but also at higher levels of government. Obviously, *pasantías* can play a catalytic role, but ideally their participants will not just sight-see but also gain some technical expertise and practice (for instance, in teaching themselves how to market their agricultural products).

Future research in this valley and similar rural regions should seek to understand how learning and new institutional arrangements shape economic development over the long term. In a sense, enabling this process of mutual learning is itself a sustainable development strategy, one that can support rural communities by diversifying its economy into different sectors and slow the pull of youth migration to cities. This new regional competence (Helmsing 2001) evens the playing field, reducing the power of the city as a magnet for the rural poor. Even if Lurín is not yet ready to join the market, it may be playing a vital role in the metropolitan region.

References

Alfaro Moreno, J., and R. Claverías. 2010. *Socio-Economic Diagnostic Report for the Lurín River Basin*. Lima: CGDD/CIED.

Amin, A. 1999. "An Institutionalist Perspective on Regional Economic Development." *International Journal of Urban and Regional Research* 23: 365–78.

Asheim, B. 2012. "The Changing Role of Learning Regions in the Globalizing Knowledge Economy: A Theoretical Re-Examination." *Regional Studies* 46(8): 993–1004.

Bebbington, A. 1999. "Capitals and Capabilities: A Framework for Analyzing Peasant Viability, Rural Livelihoods and Poverty." *World Development* 27(12): 2021–44.

Bebbington, A., L. Dharmawan, E. Fahmi, and S. Guggenheim. 2006. "Local Capacity, Village Governance, and the Political Economy of Rural Development in Indonesia." *World Development* 34(11): 1958–76.

Chapple, K., S. Montero, and O. Sosa. 2012. "Evolving Regionalismos: Latin American Regions in the 21st Century." *Regional Development Dialogue* 33(1): iii–xv.

Collinge, C., and J. Gibney. 2010. "Connecting Place, Policy and Leadership." *Policy Studies* 31(4): 379–91.

Cooke, P., and K. Morgan. 1998. *The Associational Economy: Firms, Regions, and Innovation*. Oxford: Oxford University Press.

Desforges, L. 2000. "Travelling the World: Identity and Travel Biography." *Annals of Tourism Research* 27(4): 929–45.

Doloreux, D. 2002. "What We Should Know about Regional Systems of Innovation." *Technology in Society* 24(3): 243–63.

Ellis, F., and S. Biggs. 2001. "Evolving Themes in Rural Development 1950s–2000s." *Development Policy Review* 19(4): 437–48.

Escobal, J., and M. Valdivia. 2004. *Perú: Hacia una estrategia de desarrollo para la sierra rural*. Washington, DC: Inter-American Development Bank.

Evans, P. 1996. "Government Action, Social Capital and Development: Reviewing the Evidence on Synergy." *World Development* 24(6): 1119–32.

Fuller, N. 2011. "Reflexiones sobre el turismo rural como vía de desarrollo: El caso de la comunidad de Antioquía, Perú." *Estudios y perspectivas en turismo* 20(4): 929–42.

Governa. 2012. Boletín Institucional e-governa 19(March): 7–11.

Hassink, R., and C. Klaerding. 2012. "The End of the Learning Region as We Knew It: Towards Learning in Space." *Regional Studies* 46(8): 1055–66.

Helmsing, A. H. J. 2001. "Externalities, Learning and Governance: New Perspectives on Local Economic Development." *Development and Change* 32(2): 277–308.

Jessop, B. 1998. "The Rise of Governance and the Risks of Failure: The Case of Economic Development." *International Social Science Journal* 155: 29–46.

Jurado, A. R. 2012. *Programa de desarrollo territorial y generación de empleo en la cuenca del río Lurín, Lima*. (ATN/ME-11652-PE): Evaluación Intermedia. Lima and Buenos Aires: Inter-American Development Bank.

Ladkin, A., and A. Martínez Bertramini. 2002. "Collaborative Tourism Planning: A Case Study of Cusco, Peru." *Current Issues in Tourism* 5(2): 71–93.

Lawson, C., and E. Lorenz. 1999. "Collective Learning, Tacit Knowledge and Regional Innovative Capacity." *Regional Studies* 33: 305–17.

Lundvall, B. A., and B. Johnson. 1994. "The Learning Economy." *Journal of Industry Studies* 1(2): 23–43.

Marsden, T., and G. Bristow. 2000. "Progressing Integrated Rural Development: A Framework for Assessing the Integrative Potential of Sectoral Policies." *Regional Studies* 34(5): 455–69.

Murdoch, J. 2000. "Networks: A New Paradigm of Rural Development?" *Journal of Rural Studies* 16: 407–19.

Ostrom, E. 1990. *Governing the Commons: The Evolution of Institutions for Collective Action*. Cambridge, UK: Cambridge University Press.

Ostrom, E. 2002. "Reformulating the Commons." *Ambiente & Sociedade* 10: 5–25.

Putnam, R. D., R. Leonardi, and R. Y. Nanetti. 1993. *Making Democracy Work: Civic Traditions in Modern Italy*. Princeton, NJ: Princeton University Press.

Scott, A. J., and M. Storper. 2003. "Regions, Globalization and Development." *Regional Studies* 37(6&7): 579–93.

Sorensen, E., and J. Torfing. 2009. "Making Governance Networks Effective and Democratic through Metagovernance." *Public Administration* 87: 234–58.

Wellbrock, W., and D. Roep. 2015. "The Learning Rural Area Framework: A Heuristic Tool to Investigate Institutional Arrangements which Support Collaboration in Rural Areas." *Sociologica Ruralis* 55(1): 106–24.

Woolcock, M. 1998. "Social Capital and Economic Development: Toward a Theoretical Synthesis and Policy Framework." *Theory and Society* 27(2): 151–208.

4 Learning via communities of practice

The experience of Grupos Gestores in Guatemala

Karen Chapple, Sergio Montero, and Pedro Peterson

Introduction

Beginning in the 1990s, several local associations of private sector and civil society actors emerged around Guatemala to tackle some of the country's most urgent local economic development challenges. In a national context of widespread poverty, economic instability, centralized government, and fresh scars from the country's protracted Civil War, Grupos Gestores sought to build local initiatives for economic development. Grupos Gestores are civil society entities born out of efforts of local members of the private sector to associate themselves to promote local economic development. From their origins in 1996 in the Guatemalan highland city of Quetzaltenango, the Grupos Gestores model has since expanded throughout the national territory. There are currently 102 Grupos Gestores in 18 of Guatemala's 22 departments, as shown below in Figure 4.1.

Although Grupos Gestores leaders in Quetzaltenango were not initially planning for expansion and replication, many leaders from other Guatemalan cities became interested in the Grupos Gestores model and the national government has promoted the model in other areas of the country. The creation of a National Network of Grupos Gestores (*Red Nacional de Grupos Gestores*, or RNGG) enabled the widespread replication of the model across the country through a "community of practice," a network that facilitates rapid and transformational learning across regions. As Grupos Gestores form, they learn from each other and adapt, continually innovating new approaches. Yet, lack of public infrastructure investment and poor coordination across public and private actors at the local level hinder their economic development efforts. Moreover, as this chapter shows, the very cohesiveness of the community has created challenges in developing a public–private mechanism for regional governance.

Based on almost 80 interviews conducted in 2014, this chapter examines how Grupos Gestores work to promote local economic development in the context of an increasingly decentralized Guatemala. A case study of efforts to develop tourism illustrates the challenges to integrate the interests and views of private sector associations (Grupos Gestores) and the public sector (local and national government). The chapter begins with a discussion of

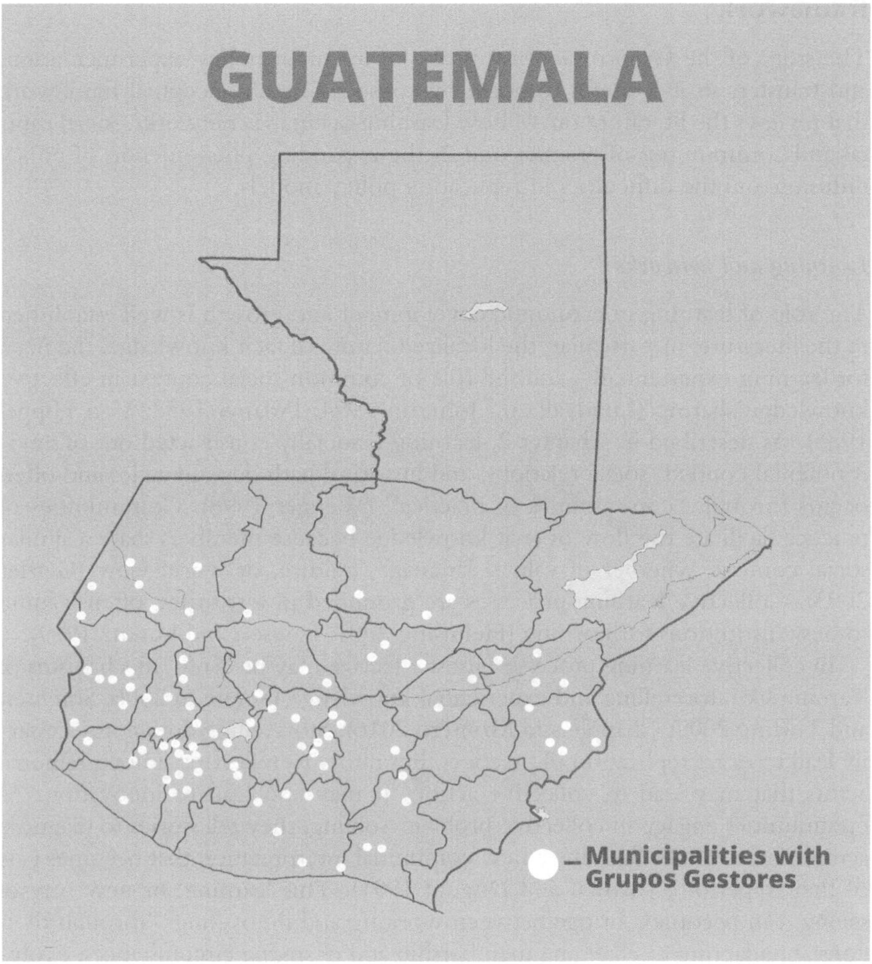

Figure 4.1 Municipalities in Guatemala with Grupos Gestores as of 2014

Source: Gutiérrez 2011

the challenges of learning, governance, and replication of local economic development models. After an overview of the local environmental, socio-economic, and institutional context in Guatemala, it then describes how the Grupos Gestores model works, using the case of tourism in two municipalities in Guatemala's Region VI: Quetzaltenango and Totonicapán. Based on the accumulated experience of Grupos Gestores in promoting public–private collaborations in Guatemala, a conclusion offers suggestions for how better to integrate the private and public sector governance of economic development in Guatemala.

Learning, policy models and governance: a theoretical framework

The story of the Grupos Gestores is one of learning, policy experimentation, and transfer, so it is useful to begin by constructing a conceptual framework that reviews the literature on: 1) how learning occurs via networks, social capital and communities of practice and 2) the expanding phenomenon of policy diffusion and the difficulties in replicating policy models.

Learning and networks

The role of learning in economic development and growth is well established in the literature, in particular, the localized nature of tacit knowledge, the need for learning experientially, and the role of common social context in effective knowledge sharing (Lundvall and Johnson 1994; Polanyi 1958; Von Hippel 1988). As described in Chapter 2, learning is socially constructed out of environmental context, social relations, and historical path dependencies and often occurs through "communities of practice" (Wenger 1998). Communities of practice facilitate the flow of tacit knowledge because members share a similar social context, whether of values, language, culture, or world view (Gertler 2003). Collective learning processes are grounded in territories, often leading to new institutions for learning (Helmsing 2001; Lawson and Lorenz 1999).

In collective learning processes, most effective may be "soft" mechanisms of learning like storytelling and experiential knowledge (Sorensen 2006; Sorensen and Torfing 2009; Chapple and Montero 2016). Storytelling does not necessarily lead to exact replication of practices, but rather to reflection among regional actors that may lead to collective action. It may also lead to innovation. As communities engage in collective problem-solving, they tell stories to diagnose symptoms, together building a new communal interpretation that becomes part of their repertoire (Brown and Duguid 1991). This learning, or new way of seeing, can become a bridge between working and innovating: "through their constant adapting to changing membership and changing circumstances, evolving communities-of-practice are significant sites of innovating" (ibid., 41).

Social capital – both the bonding among like actors that forges strong ties, and the bridging to the external world that creates weak ties – can also facilitate learning (Piore and Sabel 1984; Putnam et al. 1993). Network contacts ranging from close friends to business acquaintances form networks that become the basis of associations, ideally creating the synergy that spans the boundaries between public and private (Evans 1996). Networks mobilize assets in an endogenous process, with the activation of social capital occurring either by rural communities reaching from the inside out, or external organizations connecting from the outside in (Bebbington 1999). However, existing power dynamics, and the insularity of strong tie networks, may hinder economic development governance (Bebbington et al. 2006), creating a need for new models of public–private cooperation.

Policy replication and the difficulties of scaling up models

Many theorists and practitioners have sought to understand better the processes by which certain policies become models and are replicated in other places. Known in the academic literature by various terms such as policy diffusion (Dobbin et al. 2007; Shipan and Volden 2008), policy transfer (Dolowitz and Marsh 2000; Stone 2001), lesson-drawing (Rose 1993; Radaelli 2004) or policy mobilities (Peck and Theodore 2010; McCann and Ward 2011), this is generally understood as a process by which "knowledge about policies, administrative arrangements, institutions and ideas in one political setting past or present is used in the development of policies, administrative arrangements, institutions and ideas in another political setting" (Dolowitz and Marsh 2000, 5).

The learning process is always shaped by domestic politics and governance dynamics (Stone 2001; Meseguer and Gilardi 2009; Montero 2017). Similarly, policy ideas are constantly transformed as they travel, as policy makers in other places will always adapt them according to the needs and socio-political and economic contexts in their particular geographic locations (Peck and Theodore 2010). One concept that may be particularly useful for understanding policy diffusion is Mintrom's (1997) discussion of the role of policy entrepreneurs. Mintrom describes how critical the relationship between policy entrepreneurs is for the successful instatement of new and innovative policies, but he also notes the challenges to this relationship posed by election cycles and politics within the public sector.

Another way to understand how policy models are replicated across jurisdictions is the notion of scaling-up. Where scaling processes work, they are likely to include strong political commitment; a lively civil society; sophisticated, context-specific procedures; realistic assessment of financial resources, needs, and institutional realities; strong systems for sharing knowledge; proper incentives for different stakeholders; and best practice context from previous experiences (Hancock 2003). Yet, scaling up policies as a strategy of action is not easy task. For example, writing about the difficulties to scale up community-driven development schemes, Binswanger and Aiyar (2003) highlight several key obstacles including prohibitive fiscal costs, hostile institutional settings, inexperience with models involving co-production, lack of adaptation to the local context, and improper scaling-up logistics (Binswanger and Aiyar 2003). In this context, the public sector role remains critical:

> communities and local governments can be truly empowered only by giving them *an assured flow of funds from the central government* . . . Untied funds are crucial to enable communities / local governments to choose their own priorities, and create skills through learning by doing.
>
> (Binswanger and Aiyar 2003, 10; original emphasis)

Before examining the ways in which Grupos Gestores have tried to influence the governance of local economic development in Guatemala, we provide first an overview of economic development governance in Guatemala, and then background information about the region where the Grupos Gestores first emerged, Quetzaltenango.

Decentralization, territorial planning and economic development in Guatemala

Guatemala has been highly centralized since colonial times, with most of the country's political and economic power concentrated in the capital: Guatemala City. Quetzaltenango, which emerged as a potential second node in Guatemala at the turn of the twentieth century, suffered a series of setbacks in subsequent decades, from natural disasters to the collapse of the coffee economy during the Great Depression of the 1930s in the United States, which prevented its growth as another economic pole. The import substitution industrialization policies of the 1960s cemented the economic power of Guatemala City as the national government undertook a program to promote industrial development around the capital, further eroding the political and economic base of secondary cities like Quetzaltenango (Gutiérrez 2011).

Although decentralization reforms in Guatemala have not been as deep as in many Latin American countries (Falleti 2005), the national government has taken steps in recent decades to devolve fiscal, political, and administrative power toward subnational governing units, particularly municipalities. The Constitution promulgated in 1985 slowly began the process of decentralization by creating eight regional administrative units that combine several departments. However, during this time the country was still embroiled in its tragic Civil War and so the next major decentralization effort was the Decentralization Law of 2002, which created departmental councils to promote infrastructure development.

Traditionally, municipal governments in Guatemala did not have a clear mandate to promote LED, and their primary responsibilities were generally limited to the provision of basic services and land use planning, which may not be seen as key components of territorial development (Rodríguez and Orantes 2013).[1] To take a more territorial approach to economic development, the 2002 reforms created municipal Commissions for Development, Tourism, Environment, and Natural Resources (FETARN Commissions), which are the sole subnational public agencies with a mandate to promote local economic development. In practice, however, FETARN Commissions generally focused on environmental issues, and in any case lack the funding and technical support to have an impact in local economic development.

In order to implement these policies, many municipalities have created Municipal Offices for Local Economic Development (OMDELs). OMDELs play a key coordinating role among various economic development institutions. In some cases, they have served as key intermediaries between Grupos Gestores and elected officials, helping to get funding and implement ideas from the Grupos Gestores by giving the politicians greater ownership of projects.

In other cases, however, there have been conflicts and duplication of efforts between OMDELs and Grupos Gestores.

Despite these tentative steps towards establishing a subnational institutional framework to promote local economic development, most local administrations in Guatemala are underfunded and without the capacity to increase their revenues.[2] For instance, although municipal governments receive funds from property and value-added taxes, only the National Congress can authorize tax increases, which they have been hesitant to do under the argument that municipalities would be at risk of taking on excessive debt (Gutiérrez 2011). As a result, a municipality like Quetzaltenango remains highly dependent on transfers from the central government to perform even its basic functions: fiscal decentralization has not been closely linked to political and administrative decentralization. Local tools for economic development are quite limited, including a weak enterprise zone program, programs to waive minimum salaries, and some subsidy programs for agricultural inputs such as fertilizers, Therefore, the ability to engage in meaningful and potentially transformative LED processes is severely restricted.

About Quetzaltenango and Region VI

Region VI, in the southwest of the country, includes six departments – Quetzaltenango, Retalhuleu, San Marcos, Suchitepéquez, Sololá, and Totonicapán – with a population of about three million. At 225,000 residents, Quetzaltenango (also known by its Mayan name Xelajú, or Xela) is the second largest city in Guatemala, and the biggest outside the capital's metropolitan area. It is the capital of Quetzaltenango department and the main economic center of Region VI. The historical and economic formation of Guatemala, however, has led to highly centralized and uneven geographic development patterns with a disproportionate amount of the country's productive capabilities concentrated in Region I (the location of the national capital), while other regions have much higher incidences of poverty and its attendant consequences. For example, although Region I has 22 percent of the country's population, it accounts for 48 percent of the GDP. The poverty rate in Region I is 16 percent, compared with almost 60 percent in Region VI (Gutiérrez 2011).

Region VI in general, and Quetzaltenango in particular, have both opportunities and challenges. The economy of the region remains largely dependent on a variety of agricultural products, ranging from leaf vegetables, fruits, and grains. Coffee and cocoa are some of the more profitable agricultural products of the region, although much of the production is still dedicated to more basic, low value staples. A small manufacturing sector has emerged in recent decades, particularly in wood and wood products, which employs 650 carpenters in almost 300 firms, almost all of which are small and medium enterprises (SMEs). One of the strongest economic drivers of the region has been the services sector, particularly healthcare, education, and tourism.

The city of Quetzaltenango has a public university and seven private colleges (among almost 800 total educational institutions), all of which attract thousands of students from throughout Guatemala. The city has a relatively high adult literacy rate (93 percent) and enrollment in schools is high among all age groups. A growing tourism sector benefits from the local education infrastructure, and the city has carved itself a distinctive niche in attracting Spanish language students from the United States and Europe to its 35 Spanish schools, which contribute roughly $2.4 million to the economy each year (Banco Interamericano de Desarrollo 2014).

Yet, Quetzaltenango faces serious challenges that threaten its ability to grow and generate employment and income opportunities for its citizens. Its territorial master plan has not been updated in at least ten years and as a result, the city's urban perimeter has grown without proper controls. The precarious public transportation network relies on an old and unsafe fleet, which does not have any dedicated lanes for easy mobility and the city does not have adequate infrastructure for bicycle travel. Only 40 percent of households within the city have access to properly treated water and the municipal water company is unable to account and properly charge users (which hinders the expansion of the system).

The City's business environment is also quite unfavorable. The municipal government has no streamlined platform for business licensing, leading to a delay of close to one month to attain a simple business license. Although unemployment is low (only 2.3 percent), most workers (70 percent) operate informally, perhaps partially as a response to the difficulties of legalizing business activities. The local GDP per capita (USD 2,900) is therefore much lower in Quetzaltenango than in comparable cities in Mexico and El Salvador (Banco Interamericano de Desarrollo 2014). The lack of employment opportunities in Quetzaltenango has driven qualified young people – including skilled graduates of the region's learning institutions – away from the region to Guatemala City, Mexico, or the United States.

The Grupos Gestores model

The case of the Grupos Gestores illustrates how a community of practice develops and expands. Groups form out of strong ties and learn by doing, working through problems together by sharing stories. But to deal with the unforeseen challenges of territorial governance, they must adapt the model. After an overview of the Grupos Gestores model, this section turns to a case study of how the Grupos Gestores have tried to develop tourism in Quetzaltenango.

Grupos Gestores emerged in 1996 in Quetzaltenango as a local vehicle to promote LED activities. According to Roberto Gutiérrez, one of the founders and current President of the Board of Directors of the National Network of Grupos Gestores (RNGG), private and civil society actors formed the original Grupo Gestor in Quetzaltenango in 1996 in response to the excessive centralization of the Guatemalan state. Dozens of associated groups have formed in other cities since then to address the same issue (Gutiérrez 2011).

With international assistance, the Quetzaltenango municipality undertook a strategic planning process in 1996 along with private sector and civil society representatives in order to address the lack of the economic opportunities in the region, particularly for young people. The plan called for promoting the strong services sector in the region (such as tourism and education) as well as for investments in urban development and mobility infrastructure. At the end of the strategic planning process, six of the participants from the municipal government; cooperatives; the commercial, industrial, and construction sectors; and the association of managers decided to form the first Grupo Gestor. The group was established as a formal not-for-profit entity.

A Grupo Gestor is an association of local leaders and professionals, serving voluntarily, to promote economic development projects in their municipalities. Grupos Gestores form from groups of business associates, often based on personal relationships (attendance of the same schools or university programs, membership in social clubs, etc.) rather than sector-specific affinities. Once formed, most Grupos limit membership in order to focus on targeted projects, and open themselves to new membership only periodically. They thus differ from grassroots organizing projects, which try to expand membership continually.

Each Grupo Gestor can establish its own set of by-laws regarding membership, procedural rules, and other regulations, but a common set of standards applies to many of the groups interviewed for this study. Although the membership of Grupos Gestores nominally include representatives from municipal government agencies, the group dynamics are generally dominated by actors from the local private sector. The various Grupos Gestores interviewed adamantly stated that their groups did not engage in partisan politics, and if a member chooses to run for elected office, they are asked to take a leave from group activities. Although Grupos Gestores do not endorse individual candidates for mayor (or other offices), they often meet with candidates during electoral periods to voice their concerns and hear the candidates' positions on important topics. The groups are self-run and autonomous, its members are unpaid and participate by invitation, and each group's Board of Directors (*Junta Directiva*) is elected every two years.

In general, Grupos Gestores projects must be tied to territorial development, financially viable, innovative, and collaborative in nature. A typical project undertaken by Grupos Gestores is to improve market access for local firms, entrepreneurs, and artisans. The Quetzaltenango Grupo Gestor, for example, has been studying the idea of launching a "sales agency" (*comercializadora*) for local products since 2008. In 2013, they launched the *Comercializadora de Negocios Solidarios* (Social Business Sales Agency, or COMERS) with the goal of improving conditions for exporting high-quality artisan products. To this end, they hired a designer trained in New York City and targeted new markets such as the large Guatemalan communities in cities like Los Angeles. Another effort attempts to help local carpenters improve their products to sell in more demanding tourist markets like Antigua. The Grupo

Gestor in Quetzaltenango also engaged in a process in 2005 to develop a "Competitiveness Agenda" (*Estudio de Potencialidades y Agenda Departamental de Competitividad – EPAC*), with support from the National Program for Competitiveness (PRONACOM) and the World Bank. The Agenda includes a list of 40 priority projects that has guided the Grupo Gestor's investment proposals to the municipal and departmental governments.

Another type of project that the Grupos Gestores has supported, with considerable success, is the construction of facilities to enhance the productivity of producers. Supported by funding from the IDB and the national government, Grupos Gestores has helped to construct production centers, industrial parks, and greenhouses. International aid agencies have traditionally helped to finance such facilities as well, but many stakeholders argue that the intervention of the Grupos Gestores has helped keep the projects on the municipalities' agenda and accelerate the pace of construction.

Not all projects succeed. Many Grupos Gestores generate ideas for projects, but lack funding and logistical support to follow through. One Grupo Gestor outside of Quetzaltenango told the story of a failed facility for fish farming: the RNGG provided technical support in the form of a consultant, and the fish tanks were built, but there was no follow through about how to get the facility underway. This then discouraged local actors from participating in other efforts.

A recent evaluation of the Grupos Gestores found that Grupos Gestores tended to be formed among communities of family and friends with homogeneous socioeconomic characteristics (Aguirre, Rugani, and Cohn 2016). Overall, the training provided by the Grupos Gestores is effective, and where Grupos Gestores members are strongly committed, initiatives have experienced positive results. Communities that have initiated projects to improve business climate have experienced better quality of life, and projects to foster entrepreneurship have resulted in higher income for members. However, in cases particularly where training is insufficient, local Grupos have remained dependent on the RNGG for both finance and facilitation, leading to a passivity among members.

The challenges of promoting public–private collaborations through the Grupos Gestores model in the tourism sector

In the last decade, many public–private associations have been formed throughout Guatemala as a strategy to promote tourism, particularly in municipalities and regions outside the traditional tourism magnets of the country (Tikal, Antigua, and Guatemala City). Grupos Gestores, local government agencies, NGOs, and many other local actors have been involved in leading these efforts, sometimes resulting in interesting collaborations and learning experiences, and other times in conflict and duplication of efforts. This accumulated experience, therefore, provides valuable opportunity to analyze the strengths and weaknesses of the Grupos Gestores model in practice. In particular, this section analyzes the emergence and development of a number of tourism associations in Quetzaltenango and Totonicapán. Together, they illustrate the challenges in achieving effective collaboration between public and private actors but also the important role that factors such as leadership, learning processes, networks, association types, institutions and conflict management play in associational approaches to local economic development.

Tourism and local economic development

Despite the late incorporation of Guatemala into the global tourism industry due to the civil war that afflicted the country between 1960 and 1994, tourism is becoming an increasingly important source of income and employment for many municipalities and regions in the country. The number of international tourists in Guatemala has increased from about 192,000 in 1984, to 560,000 in 1995, to 2 million in 2013 (INGUAT 2014). Indeed, the income in foreign currency derived from tourism in 2013 (USD 1.48 billion) represented more than the income derived from traditional Guatemalan export commodities such as coffee (USD 691 million), sugar (USD 941 million) or bananas (USD 601 million) (INGUAT 2014).

While the potential economic development and job opportunities of tourism are appealing for local government officials, NGOs, private sector organizations, and international development organizations, there are also major obstacles to sharing the potential economic benefits of tourism across regions. For example, the territorial structure of tourism flows in Guatemala is highly uneven and most of the visitors – as well as tourism facilities – concentrate in just three regions – Guatemala City, Antigua, and Tikal (Sánchez Crispín et al. 2012) – a phenomenon that occurs in other Latin American countries like Peru (Ladkin and Martinez Bertramini 2002). Another important challenge in promoting tourism is the large and diverse number of actors and stakeholders that need to be coordinated to make a place attractive for tourists (including local governments, hotel and restaurant owners, tour guides, etc.), particularly in areas that lack well recognized landmark tourist attractions and facilities (ibid). The large number of actors involved in tourism makes the successful association and collaboration of public and private actors especially important.

Tourism has also been criticized as an economic activity that can be easily monopolized by a handful of private actors (such as big hotel chains) and be eventually detrimental for the local environment and local culture. The blend of actors and the degree of community participation in the design and implementation of a territorial tourism strategy will greatly impact the kind of tourism development outcomes that can be achieved. For instance, Zapata et al. (2011) analyzed several NGO- and donor-initiated tourism projects in Nicaragua in which potential customers and tourists were identified based on the NGO and donors' knowledge, personal networks and values, which, eventually, made the projects target "long-haul" international tourists rather than the domestic market. By targeting the international tourism market, Zapata et al. (2011) argued that decision making was left to imported consultants and experts in international tourism while locals were left executing decisions they didn't understand, thus fostering a culture of dependency and limited local leadership and ownership.

The governance of tourism in Guatemala

The governance of tourism in Guatemala has traditionally been a centralized endeavor largely overseen by the Tourism Secretary of the President, whose task is to monitor the implementation of the President's tourism policies and operating plan together with the national agency Guatemalan Institute of Tourism (INGUAT) as the chief executing entity. However, there has been a push to decentralize this institutional structure in recent years as the new tourism development framework in Guatemala (Política Nacional para el Desarrollo Turístico Sostenible 2012–2022 or PNDTS), at least in rhetoric, increasingly relies on a decentralized governance model with a strong role for local agencies and associations (Gobierno de Guatemala 2012). This new tourism development paradigm also embraced ideas of sustainable tourism and established that for the development of the tourism sector, it is essential to have common agreements between public and private sectors as well as among the three different levels of government (national, department and local).

Currently, INGUAT is responsible for the implementation and execution of the 2012–2022 PNDTS and is in charge of fostering public–private sector cooperation/participation at the local level as well as making sure that local communities are included in tourism promotion initiatives, mostly through the promotion of self-management tourism associations (CATs). Under this new national policy, CATs are regarded as "the base of competitive tourism development planning for the country" and considered "vital instruments for local tourism development through the formation of clusters" (Gobierno de Guatemala 2012, 30). While the importance of public–private collaboration figures prominently in this national plan, the document also establishes that local governments are "the main actors in the process of tourism development planning in their municipalities" (Gobierno de Guatemala 2012, 30).

CATs are governed by a general assembly and led by a board of directors that is normally formed by a president and four or five more members. There could also be special commissions formed for specific topics of interest of CAT members. One of the main advantages of forming a CAT rather than relying on associations formed by private actors is that tourist projects agreed in CATs can receive public funds from INGUAT and other government sources. In collaboration with public and private actors, CATs should formulate a diagnostic report of opportunities and challenges to develop tourism in each municipality, a Master Plan of Sustainable Tourism and, together with INGUAT, coordinate and manage funds to implement the identified strategic tourism projects.

PNDTS specifically states that CATs should look for a strategic collaboration with Grupos Gestores to promote tourism. Yet, as we will see in the cases to follow, several challenges emerged in practice that brought many of these public–private collaborations to lock-in situations. According to a representative of RNGG interviewed in this study, "tourism is a good example of how public–private relationships don't always have shared interests."

In the following sections we will examine the lessons from the experience of the local CAT in Quetzaltengango and Totonicapán.

Quetzaltenango's first CAT: lack of participation of a representative set of local actors

Among small tourism businesses and entrepreneurs in Quetzaltenango (Xela from now on), INGUAT is perceived as a bureaucratic entity more concerned with tourism campaigns at the national and international levels than with the everyday needs of local businesses. This image is reinforced by the perceived failure of the first local CAT in Quetzaltenango. The controversy around the CAT's projects in the Cerro del Baúl hill, a popular hiking place for locals and tourists, illustrates some of the local frustrations with this tourism development framework. In 2006, with funds from INGUAT and other government agencies, the Board of Directors of Xela's local CAT opened some facilities on the top of the Cerro del Baúl hill, including an enclosed overlook, a space for a café/restaurant and bathrooms (Figure 4.2). However, after investing significant government resources in building this infrastructure, CAT members didn't follow up with the project and the facilities currently sit empty and lack maintenance. There were also some planning mistakes that show a disconnection between members of the Board of Directors and the project needs. For instance, they designed bathrooms and bought appliances (sink, toilet, etc.) even though there is no running water in that area.

The lack of involvement of a diverse set of local actors in this first CAT and the perception among businesses in the local tourism industry that members of the CAT Board of Directors were misspending government funding and using the association for their own benefit led to the creation of a parallel tourism association in the city named AQUETUR. As one AQUETUR member recalls: "the origins of AQUETUR are related to the bad management of the local tourism association at the time." AQUETUR brought together different actors in the tourism industry in Quetzaltenango as well as members of other established local associations such as the Association of Tourist Guides and the Association of Spanish Schools. Despite repeated attempts by AQUETUR members to rent the built facilities from the local government and put them to use, they have run into many bureaucratic obstacles and have constantly been denied the right to use them. In the opinion of one of AQUETUR member, their lack of "good connections" with high level officials in the government or INGUAT prevents them from getting the required permit.

This experience illustrates a common issue in local tourism associations and in local economic development efforts more broadly: an overly narrow focus on a small subset of parties rather than casting a wide net to engage a diverse

Figure 4.2 The "mirador" in Cerro del Baúl

Photo credit: Sergio Montero

set of regional actors. While naming a small team of executive directors, a top-down approach, can expedite the establishment of an association, in the medium and long term, the lack of representation can make the association disconnected from the diverse needs and demands of the local tourism industry and local economy. For instance, in the case of the local Quetzaltenango CAT, some of our interviewees point at the fact that the CAT president and other members of the Board of Directors were appointed by INGUAT and the local government as a key reason for the disconnection between the leadership and the rest of the local businesses in the tourism sector and, therefore, the failure of this structure to survive in the long term.

More optimistically, this could also be analyzed as a learning experience. After the failure of this first initiative, in 2014, a new CAT was established in Quetzaltenango with members coming from the public and private sector, including AQUETUR and Grupos Gestores. Because national laws and policies on tourism promotion only allow having one CAT per municipality, the new association was established at the department level. While it is still early to assess the role of this new public-led association, most of our interviewees saw the new CAT in a positive light because of its more horizontal and open approach to including the different actors that are part of the local tourism industry. For an interviewee: "as opposed to before, [the new CAT] has all the actors that need to be present: hotels, restaurants, guides, etc." The current president of the new departmental CAT is, indeed, a member of Grupos Gestores Quetzaltenango.

Totonicapán: Grupos Gestores – local government conflict, governance failure and duplication of efforts

Totonicapán is a small city of about 90,000 inhabitants and the capital of the department of the same name. It is 30 kilometers away from Quetzaltenango. In recent years the city and the department have initiated various tourism initiatives to try to attract more visitors. Grupos Gestores tend to complain about the difficulties they experience in collaborating in LED projects with the local government, and the case of tourism in Totonicapán is illustrative. In 2005, Grupos Gestores created a tourism committee that failed to engage the local government in the long term. After a conflict between the Grupos Gestores and local government leaders, the local government created its own parallel tourism association. The following analyzes key elements of this conflict to understand the strengths and weaknesses of public–private collaboration in practice.

In 2005, a departmental CAT was founded in Totonicapán led by a member of Grupos Gestores with experience in tourism. The association began with members of seven municipalities called *Plataforma Departmental de Turismo* (Departmental Tourism Platform) and eventually became a departmental CAT. The CAT provided an institutional figure with teeth: as the founder (now President of the Board of Directors) said, "the reason of naming it CAT was because this was a condition to receive funding and support from INGUAT." Currently, the association has 40 members including tour guides, a women's chocolate cooperative, weaving artisans and a carpenter that builds artisanal boxes. Five people form the core group, which meets sporadically to discuss urgent issues, but mostly they communicate through phone calls. According to the President, one of the main challenges for this CAT has been finding people who are committed to carrying out tourism initiatives in the long term. He suggests a need for "proactive people that see tourism as something of their own" (CAT president interview); otherwise the initiative will not be sustainable over time.

One of the successes of Totonicapán departmental CAT has been the establishment of a Punto de Atención al Turista (PAT) in San Andrés Xecul. In collaboration with USAID and the international organization Counterpart, the departmental CAT was able to channel funds to build a PAT tourist office in San Andrés with a café and a shop with artisanal regional products. The CAT was also able to fund the design of a website to promote tourism in the municipality and, with the help of the local Grupos Gestores, train youth in tourism. While this is perceived as a successful experience by Grupos Gestores members, San Andrés Xecul's PAT has run into problems in recent years. The main challenge is that tourists come with organized tours to see the city's iconic church and leave without patronizing local small businesses. Grupos Gestores and INTECAP experts have given tourism professionals in San Andrés training and workshops, including courses on interpretation, guiding tours, and other issues related to tourism. However, despite this formal training for locals, tourists tend to come with their own guides, leaving quickly because of the lack of activities and tourist facilities. In other words, more infrastructure and local businesses will be necessary to attract tourists for longer – a problem that requires collaboration across diverse stakeholder groups. Yet, the local government does not participate in this CAT due to a series of unresolved conflicts between Grupos Gestores and members of Totonicapán OMDEL office, which eventually led to the creation of an alternative local CAT led by OMDEL. According to the local government, the Grupos Gestores-led departmental CAT excluded local government leaders in order to take credit for the touristic successes.

From the perspective of Grupos Gestores members, the lack of inclusion stems from an over-emphasis of the state's role by government actors. A disagreement over the organization of tours to the Chajil Siwan Park is illustrative. Chajil Siwan is a community-owned ecological park managed by 90 families and supported by the Swiss NGO Helvetas in collaboration with the local government as a social and economic development project. Although the park managers charge an entrance fee of Q15 (USD 2), the departmental CAT was running tours including a visit to the park, among other attractions, for USD 30. This led the park managers to threaten a group of tourists that arrived through a CAT tour – and ended the collaboration.

This case illustrates that while finding a group of proactive leaders with experience in tourism is important for an association to survive over the years, it is also important to have legitimate representation from the different actors that are part of the industry. In particular, the lack of inclusion of local government representatives in positions of leadership will most likely result in duplication of initiatives as the case of Totonicapán illustrates. Another interesting lesson from this case is that efforts on providing training for members have to be balanced with more structural efforts at improving tourism infrastructure and market access.

Interestingly, as this case suggests, NGOs have largely succeeded in collaborating with local governments. The Swiss NGO Helvetas has been collaborating with Totonicapán municipality for more than ten years. Indeed, after the conflict that led to the creation of an alternative CAT in Totonicapán, they offered their support to the local government to create a new tourism initiative. According to a local representative, the Totonicapán municipality has welcomed Helvetas because they offer "tangible things" to the population such as giving out fertilizers, building roads, and the like. The local representative argues that local citizens "want to see concrete, iron, a road." Visible projects help politicians build support for re-election; since the Grupos Gestores often fail to explain clearly what sort of tangible things the municipality would be able to achieve, politicians are not compelled to collaborate.

Lessons and challenges for the Grupos Gestores

The Grupos Gestores were formed in response to the over-centralization of Guatemala and the weakness of municipal and departmental governments in implementing local economic development policies, as well as the perception among private sector actors that what limited funds did make their way to the local level were likely to be misused. Thus, there has been a strong sense of mistrust among the Grupos, other private sector actors, and local governments. Local actors claim that there is often rivalry between Grupos Gestores and the municipalities in claiming ownership over successful projects, either to establish legitimacy or to gain electoral benefit. Mayors do not want members of Grupos Gestores to be able to take credit for the successes – and then become political rivals. Some also argue that the mayors steer funding towards infrastructure projects rather than local economic development or competitiveness because of their higher visibility and therefore a potential for personal gain to improve electoral changes. Because politicians are perceived as corrupt, the Grupos Gestores do not want their projects to be associated with them. As one leader argued, "To make ourselves political is to kill the movement." Grupos Gestores leaders argue that they can only maintain their neutrality by staying separate from the public sector.

However, municipal governments work much more closely with international aid agencies that fund many LED efforts, due in part to agency mandates. One international aid agency suggested in an interview that the Grupos Gestores would be more effective if they promoted the benefits of projects more aggressively to the mayors and tried to form partnerships, rather than viewing the municipality as a rival or obstacle. Another common critique of the Grupos Gestores model, one that even members of the Grupos share, is that the lack of meaningful engagement with the public sector, particularly local governments, severely limits the ability of Grupos Gestores to undertake projects that may have stronger territorial impacts. While the projects the Grupos Gestores have promoted in several cities (market studies, launching the *comercializadora*, etc.) may have helped a targeted group of producers, their scope and reach is narrow. Even when the government responds positively to projects proposed by the Grupos, they often fail to follow through. Broader territorial projects require a closer engagement with an empowered local government apparatus. The strength of the Grupos Gestores – its cohesive, strong-tie networks – has also been its weakness, as it has failed to form bridging ties with public sector actors.

Synergy spanning public and private boundaries (Evans 1996) has yet to emerge in this case. Due to the weakness of municipal governments in Guatemala, especially with regards to promoting economic development, as well as the perception among the private sector that government officials are inefficient and corrupt, Grupos Gestores are slow to engage with the public sector in their activities. As a result, the communication between the Grupos and municipal governments tends to be one-way: Grupos Gestores make policy recommendations that they believe will improve the business climate in their regions, and the municipal governments ignores them, creates duplicative efforts, or is incapable of carrying them through. Without an empowered local government apparatus, it is unlikely that projects proposed or initiated by Grupos Gestores can be scaled to achieve broader territorial impact.

Despite these shortcomings, the Grupos Gestores has functioned as a community of practice. Bonds form due to shared values, language, and world views. In each community, its members diagnose problems and share stories about solutions. As they actively engage in projects, not only do individual capabilities grow, but also collective learning occurs, in the form of a new shared understanding about what works. Proximity fosters learning: stories pass readily from community to community due to their shared social contexts. Thus an ongoing process of adaptation and innovation occurs. This is illustrated by the case of tourism, where repeated efforts demonstrated the need for more inclusive approaches – and the ability of the Grupos Gestores to adapt and change its membership when necessary. Yet, the many different experiments in tourism development have also provided evidence that without significant investment in tourist infrastructure, these smaller efforts may be doomed. This, in turn, points to the need for a more territorial approach to economic development governance.

Over the years it has become clear that the Grupos Gestores needed to expand and involve the public sector to have a significant and durable impact. Thus, the RNGG launched a new program, the *Mesas de Competitividad*, in Region VI departments in 2009 with the understanding that "systemic competitiveness" requires the active participation of public sector actors and the mobilization of the state's resources and political capital. At these roundtables, the Grupos Gestores and other important stakeholders in local economic development policy such as business chambers, universities, NGOs, and municipal and departmental governments engage in dialogue about their local and regional economies. Subsequently, the national government has begun to encourage the replication of the Mesas de Competitividad model across the country and the participation of departmental governors in their activities. However, the Mesas do not yet have any dedicated funding sources to implement projects.

Conclusion

In one sense, the development of a public–private governance model like the Grupos Gestores as an alternative to the highly centralized structure for economic development policy of the Guatemalan state is a remarkable success. This model, based on the strengthening of social capital and civic participation among non-governmental actors, emerged only a few years after the end of Guatemala's protracted civil war, which had created deep societal divisions and suspicion among social groups. The development of partnerships geared towards creating economic opportunities in peripheral regions is therefore an achievement in and of itself, especially as the model has expanded throughout the country (and recently to Honduras).

The sustainability – and expansion – of the Grupos over time is testimony to the strengths of its social networks, even though the local economic development benefits model itself remains unproven. Tied together by the "love of the land," inspired by dedicated leadership, and sharing a common concern about the outmigration of youth, the majority of Grupos Gestores members have stayed involved. The structure of the organization is one key to its success: for instance, it works through committees that include members motivated to work on particular issues, and the RNGG provides institutional continuity and connections with international funders. The ongoing cultivation of new leadership by the Grupos has developed a counterforce to established politicians and political parties.

Most importantly, both the Grupos Gestores and the RNGG engage in a process of continuous learning, creating multiple opportunities for knowledge sharing (such as the annual congresses). As circumstances and membership change, the Grupos Gestores adapt and innovate. Although the RNGG initiates the replication process from the top down, and the new Grupos often lack the tools to yield quick outcomes, they learn by doing, rather than trying to replicate by rote.

Our interviews with many of the actors involved in LED issues revealed some limitations with the model, however, and the tourism cases illustrate many of the challenges of public–private collaboration, participation, and leadership. The Grupos Gestores often suffer from poor internal dynamics. Participants burn out and the Board of Directors does not always share leadership democratically. Even though internal conflicts are rare, the members often do not manage conflicts with outside entities well (particularly the local government). The model also faces the challenges of narrow engagement with a small number of firms, when local economic development in peripheral regions such as Quetzaltenango requires a broad territorial engagement and improving the productive capacities of many actors in the local economy. Improving a region's tourism industry, for example, involves upgrading specific visitor attractions, but also local restaurants, tour guides, crafts, and the like, otherwise those tourist dollars will spill out to outside vendors.

Actors from both Guatemala's national government and local areas have worked for decades to create a new, decentralized governance system for local economic development. Remarkably, one local innovation, the Grupos Gestores, has spread throughout the country. The continuous engagement of civil society and the private sector has sustained the Grupos Gestores, which continue to learn and evolve. The challenge that remains is how to strengthen and empower the public–private collaboration in the Mesas from the top down, while still fostering this learning and innovation from below.

Notes

1 We do not agree with this, and, in fact, Peterson in Chapter 6 argues that land use planning is indeed an important element of territorial development strategies

2 As political scientist Tulia Falleti (2005) highlights, the *sequencing* of decentralization reforms is crucial, and in Guatemala, in the context of LED responsibilities, administrative duties have been devolved to subnational governments ahead of political and fiscal powers.

Bibliography

Aguirre, M. A., M. Rugani, and E. Cohn. 2016. *Evaluation of the Integral Impact of the Grupos Gestores in the South-West Region of Guatemala.* Washington, DC: The Catholic University of America.

Alex, R., T. Eng, and L. Rudis. 2014. "Water Governance in Quetzaltenango, Guatemala." Unpublished studio report, University of California-Berkeley.

Banco Interamericano de Desarrollo. 2014. Xelajú Sostenible: Las Cuentas Claras, El Agua Viva, La Ciudad Limpia Y El Territorio En Orden. Washington, DC: Inter-American Development Bank.

Bebbington, A. 1999. "Capitals and Capabilities: A Framework for Analyzing Peasant Viability, Rural Livelihoods and Poverty." *World Development* 27(12): 2021–44.

Bebbington, A., L. Dharmawan, E. Fahmi, and S. Guggenheim. 2006. "Local Capacity, Village Governance, and the Political Economy of Rural Development in Indonesia." *World Development* 34(11): 1958–76.

Binswanger, H. P., and S. S. Aiyar. 2003. "Scaling up Community-driven Development: Theoretical Underpinnings and Program Design Implications." Washington DC: World Bank policy research working paper 3039.

Brown, J. S., and P. Duguid. "Organizational Learning and Communities-of-practice: Toward a Unified View of Working, Learning, and Innovation." *Organization Science* 2.1(1991): 40–57.

Chapple, K., and S. Montero. 2016. "From Learning to Fragile Governance: Regional Economic Development in Rural Peru." *Journal of Rural Studies* 44: 143–52.

Dobbin, F., B. Simmons, and G. Garrett. 2007. "The Global Diffusion of Public Policies: Social Construction, Coercion, Competition, or Learning?" *Annual Review of Sociology* 33(1): 449–72.

Dolowitz, D. P., and D. Marsh. 2000. "Learning from Abroad: The Role of Policy Transfer in Contemporary Policy-Making." *Governance* 13(1): 5–23.

Evans, P., 1996. "Government Action, Social Capital and Development: Reviewing the Evidence on Synergy." *World Development* 24(6): 1119–32.

Falleti, T. G. 2005. "A Sequential Theory of Decentralization: Latin American Cases in Comparative Perspective." *American Political Science Review* 99(03): 327–46.

Gertler, M. S. 2003. "Tacit Knowledge and the Economic Geography of Context, or The Undefinable Tacitness of Being (There)." *Journal of Economic Geography* 3(1): 75–99.

Gobierno de Guatemala. 2012. Política Nacional Para el Desarrollo Turístico Sostenible de Guatemala, 2012–2022. Retrieved from www.segeplan.gob.gt/downloads/clearinghouse/politicas_publicas/Turismo/Politica_Nacional_DTS_Guatemala_2012_2022.pdf (accessed Jan 10, 2015).

Gutiérrez, R. 2011. De Movimiento Social a Política Pública. *La Propuesta de La Red Nacional de Grupos Gestores Para El Desarrollo Económico de Guatemala.* Quetzaltenango, Guatemala: Red Nacional de Grupos Gestores.

Hancock, J. 2003. "Scaling Up Issues and Options: Supporting Good Practices and Innovation." *AGR* Working Paper, World Bank. Washington, DC.

Helmsing, A. H. J. 2001. "Externalities, Learning and Governance: New Perspectives on Local Economic Development." *Development and Change* 32(2): 277–308.

INGUAT. 2014. Boletín Anual de Estadísticas de Turismo, 2013. Retrieved from www.inguat.gob.gt/media/boletines/boletin-anual-2013.pdf (accessed Jan 10, 2015).

Ladkin, A., and A. M. Bertramini. 2002. "Collaborative Tourism Planning: A Case Study of Cusco, Peru." *Current Issues in Tourism* 5(2): 71–93.

Lawson, C., and E. Lorenz, 1999. "Collective Learning, Tacit Knowledge and Regional Innovative Capacity." *Regional Studies* 33: 305–17.

Lundvall, B. A., and B. Johnson. 1994. "The Learning Economy." *Journal of Industry Studies* 1(2): 23–43.

McCann, E., and K. Ward (eds.) 2011. *Mobile Urbanism: Cities and Policy-Making in the Global Age.* Minnesota: University of Minnesota Press.

Meseguer, C., and F. Gilardi. 2009. "'What' in the Study of Policy Diffusion?" *Review of International Political Economy* 16(3): 527–43.

Mintrom, M. 1997. "Policy Entrepreneurs and the Diffusion of Innovation." *American Journal of Political Science*: 738–70.

Montero, S. 2017. "Study Tours and Inter-city Policy Learning: Mobilizing Bogotá's Transportation Policies in Guadalajara." *Environment and Planning A* 49(2): 332–50.

Multilateral Investment Fund of the Inter-American Development Bank. 2009. "Support for Competitiveness in Guatemala's Southwest Region: Donors' Memo." Washington, DC: Inter-American Development Bank.

Peck, J., and N. Theodore. 2010. "Mobilizing Policy: Models, Methods, and Mutations." *Geoforum* 41: 169–74.

Peterson, P. 2018. "Against the Grain: Networked Governance and Local Economic Development in Linhares, Brazil." In S. Montero and K. Chapple (eds.), *Fragile Governance and Local Economic Development.* London: Routledge.

Piore, M. J., and C. F. Sabel. 1984. *The Second Industrial Divide: Possibilities for Prosperity.* New York: Basic Books.

Polanyi, M. 1958 [1998]. *Personal Knowledge: Towards a Post Critical Philosophy.* London: Routledge.

PRONACOM. 2015. Mesas de Competitividad: Institucionalidad Territorial Para La Competitividad Y El Desarrollo Económico Local. Guatemala City: PRONACOM.

Putnam, R. D., R. Leonardi, and R. Y. Nanetti. 1993. *Making Democracy Work: Civic Traditions in Modern Italy.* Princeton, NJ: Princeton University Press.

Radaelli, C. 2004. "The Diffusion of Regulatory Impact Analysis: Best Practice or Lesson-Drawing?" *European Journal of Political Research* 43(5): 723–47.

Rodríguez, F., and L. Orantes. 2013. Estudio Temático de Desarrollo Económico Local. *Estudio País: Guatemala.* Washington, DC: FOMIN.

Rose, R. 1993. *Lesson-Drawing in Public Policy: A Guide to Learning across Time and Space.* New Jersey: Chatham House.

Rose, R. 2002. "When All Other Conditions Are Not Equal: The Context for Drawing Lessons." In C. Jones Finer (ed.), *Social Policy Reform in Socialist Market China: Lessons for and from Abroad.* Aldershot: Ashgate.

Sánchez Crispín, Á., G. Mollinedo Beltrán, and E. Propin Frejomil. 2012. "Estructura territorial del turismo en Guatemala." *Investigaciones geográficas* 78: 104–21.
Shipan, C. R., and C. Volden. 2008. "The Mechanisms of Policy Diffusion." *American Journal of Political Science* 52(4): 840–57.
Sorensen, E. 2006. "Metagovernance: The Changing Role of Politicians in Processes of Democratic Governance." *The American Review of Public Administration* 36(1): 98–114.
Sørensen, E., and J. Torfing. 2009. "Making Governance Networks Effective and Democratic through Metagovernance." *Public Administration* 87(2): 234–58.
Stone, D. 2001. *Learning Lessons, Policy Transfer and the International Diffusion of Policy Ideas.* Working Paper. Coventry: University of Warwick. Centre for the Study of Globalisation and Regionalisation.
Von Hippel, E. 1988. *The Sources of Innovation.* New York: Oxford University Press.
Wenger, E. 1998. *Communities of Practice: Learning, Meaning, and Identity.* Cambridge: Cambridge University Press.
Zapata, M. J., C. M. Hall, P. Lindo, and M. Vanderschaeghe. 2011. "Can Community-based Tourism Contribute to Development and Poverty Alleviation? Lessons from Nicaragua." *Current Issues in Tourism* 14(8): 725–49.

5 Córdoba, the Argentinian Silicon Valley?

Common narratives, institutional experiments, and mutual adjustments to develop a regional innovation system outside Buenos Aires

Andrés Matta and Sergio Montero

Introduction

The information and communications technology (ICT) industry in Córdoba, Argentina, has grown from 1,600 workers in 2001 to more than 10,000 in 2016 (MTEySS 2017; CTC 2017). The automotive industry, which represented 20% of the city's total employment in the 1990s, decreased its share sharply, with only a 3% growth in industrial employment, while ICT industries grew by 82% from only 2.4% of employment to 8.6% of industrial employment (Table 5.1). Something similar can be said about the evolution of the provincial gross domestic product (GDP), considering that while the GDP grew approximately 60% at constant prices between 1993 and 2013, the ICT sector increased in the same period by 180% (Figure 5.1). The ICT industry has become an increasingly important source of employment for the local and regional economy, and it is positioning Córdoba as a key center in Latin America. Small and medium enterprises (SMEs) continue to grow and emerge in the field, while five important multinational companies have established operations in the region in the last 15 years. The fast growth of Córdoba's ICT industry is not, however, a story of individual entrepreneurship or the result of the arrival of foreign multinationals to the region. Even though both elements have played a role, the growth of Córdoba's ICT industry has also benefited from government intervention and the active organization, collaboration, and support of the private and public sectors in the region, particularly associations of SMEs, since the early 2000s.

The ICT sector in Córdoba illustrates how local SME associations have successfully put pressure on the government to change its economic development policy from a focus on attracting foreign multinationals as the key force to develop the region to the promotion of a local economic development strategy that emphasizes territorial processes of learning, social capital, and institutional networks to strengthen the innovative capacity and growth potential of local companies. Córdoba is a good example of the opportunities and difficulties in articulating public and private actors around a local economic development

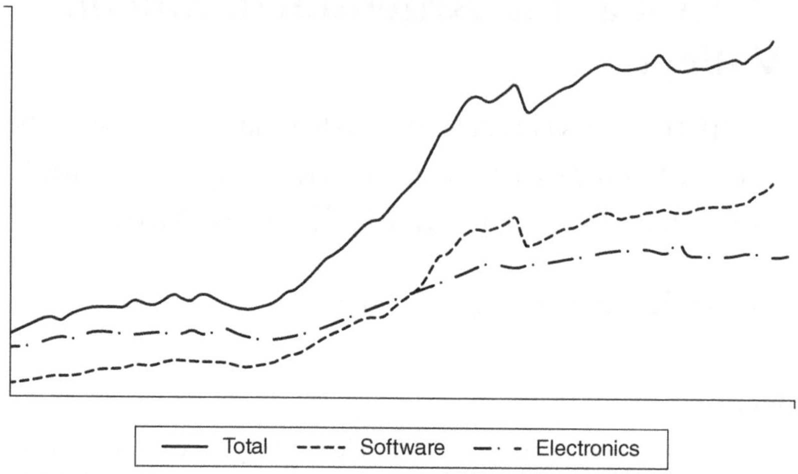

Figure 5.1 Evolution of numbers of employed in the information and communications technology industry in Córdoba, Argentina (1996–2016)

Source: MTEySS (2017)[1]

Table 5.1 Employment growth of the automotive and ICT industries in Córdoba, Argentina (1996–2016)

	Employment growth (1996–2016)	*Percentage industrial employment (1996)*	*Percentage industrial employment (2016)*
Automotive industry	3%	20.9	13.8
ICT industry	82%	2.4	8.6
Industry sector total	36%	–	–

Source: MTEySS (2017)

approach in a new set of economic activities. In Córdoba, this public–private articulation was not achieved through a single or paradigmatic organization. Instead, it has taken place through considerable institutional experimentation and circulation of people between public and private organizations. But if there has been a constant variable in this frenetic process of institutional experimentation, it is the strength and continuity of two associations of local SMEs established in the early 2000s: CIIECCA[2] and CTC.[3]

The case of Córdoba is one of a Latin American city that is trying to reinvent itself to become a regional economy based on technology and innovation-related economic activities. Despite its 1.3 million inhabitants, we consider Córdoba a peripheral city given the primacy that Buenos Aires has traditionally had in the distribution of economic activity and highly skilled workers (see Figure 5.2). Indeed, one of the main obstacles that Córdoba has had to developing a regional innovation system (RIS) is Buenos Aires's pull factor. About 80% of the employment in the ICT industry is concentrated in the metropolitan area of Buenos Aires, leaving Córdoba, the second-largest city of the country, just 5.5%, according to the Ministry of Finance (2016). A businessman we interviewed echoed this with a phrase well known in the country: "God is everywhere, but he attends in Buenos Aires." In considering Córdoba a peripheral region for the ICT industry, we follow the definition of peripheries presented in Chapter 1 as a multidimensional and socially constructed process rather than characterized by its size.

The process developed by Córdoba's ICT industry illustrates also the transition from an economic development strategy based on the idea of "industrial complex" or "growth pole" to another approach aligned with the more endogenous idea of local economic development (LED). While industrial complexes are based primarily on the existence of agglomeration economies, which are often driven by large industries and their vertical supplier networks, LED approaches focus instead on the positive effects of associations and learning generated by horizontal relationships as well as between the agents of an interdependent regional network coordinated by mechanisms that allow both *differentiation* (autonomy, participation, interests) and *integration* (identity and common objectives). Under this interpretation of economic development, innovation is not seen as an exogenous factor brought by large or multinational companies, as the "industrial complex or "growth pole" models suggest. At the heart of the LED model is the idea that innovation is a social process involving increasing levels of learning based on interaction and cooperation (Asheim and Isaksen 1997; Lundvall and Johnson 1994). Therefore, the ways in which local and regional organizations interact with each other are essential for innovation and economic development outcomes (Nelson 1993; Edquist 2001; Freeman 2002). In this process, companies, governments, and universities – the so-called "triple helix" of a region – mutually condition each other's behavior at institutional or structural levels, while at the functional level they conform to expectations (Leydesdorff and Fritsch 2006). This process of mutual shaping is a nonlinear, recursive, and complex path that also includes the possibility of failure, particularly given the potential resistance of certain agents and institutions that are immersed in "path dependence" processes (Dosi 1982). These resistances can be summarized as the limitation of moving from their traditional roles (differentiating, autonomizing) to strategic roles (integrating, synergistic) (Ferreti and Parmentola 2015).

Organization of the chapter

The following sections analyze some of the key factors behind this particular process of horizontal articulation in Córdoba's ICT industry. This chapter draws from nearly 30 in-depth interviews with businessmen, officials from different levels of government, and representatives of different local organizations such as universities and educational centers. Researchers conducted the interviews between 2005 and 2013 in Córdoba in the context of different

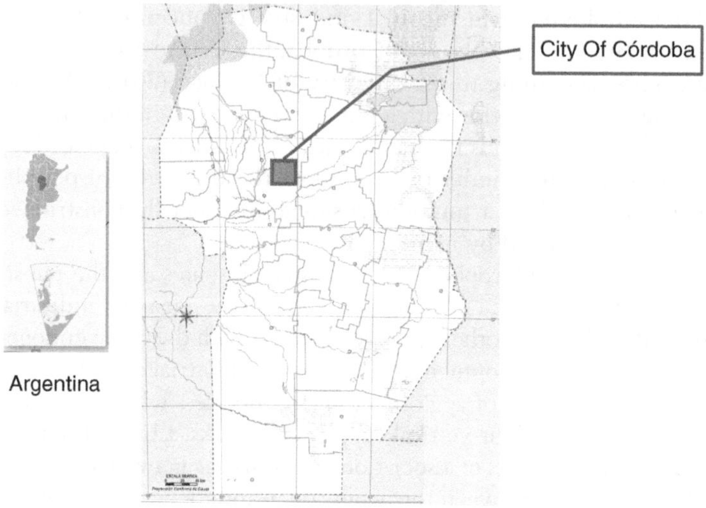

Figure 5.2 Location of the city of Córdoba in Argentina

Source: Instituto Geográfico Nacional de la República Argentina (open source map available at www.ign.gob.ar/content/datos-abiertos)

research projects for the Inter-American Development Bank and the Economic Development Agency of the City of Córdoba (ADEC) (Matta 2011; Giuliani, Matta, and Pietrobelli 2016; Chapple, Peterson, and Montero 2014).[4] The following section briefly describes the project of economic restructuring that has been taking place in the region for at least two decades, in particular the local and state government project in the early 2000s to create a new technological pole, mostly based on attracting foreign multinationals through subsidies and tax exemptions. The subsequent sections discuss several dimensions that are key to understanding the evolutionary process local actors have experienced of modifying this economic development policy approach and moving it towards an LED approach that emphasizes the role of local and regional actors, institutions, and governance dynamics in promoting development and innovation. We identify and analyze three key dimensions in this evolutionary process. First is the creation of a common narrative and a set of related advocacy strategies through which local SMEs aim to influence the public agenda, creating a window of opportunity for the development of an alternative policy. Second, we analyze the importance of institutional experimentation or the creation of new organizations to articulate this common narrative and transform it into a deliberate and consensual strategy. Third, we examine how this co-evolution process involved a "mutual shaping" by providing structural and functional modifications within each of the agents of the triple helix of Córdoba. Finally, we explore the fragility of this process by explaining some of the main limitations that Córdoba faces to become a more successful regional innovation system.

From "Detroit" to "Silicon Valley": Córdoba's project of economic restructuring in the early 2000s

In the last decades, Córdoba has tried to reinvent its economy and move beyond its traditional agricultural and automotive industrial base. Historically, the city has been home to the manufacturing of military aircraft and the automobile industry, which led to the nickname the "Detroit" of Argentina (Servetto 2010). These industries gave the region a particularly local identity, a technologically skilled workforce, and an important network of local suppliers in the car industry. Córdoba's automotive industry emerged and was consolidated in the style of an industrial complex. As the story often goes, it started from the installation of a group of large manufacturing companies (including Kaiser Argentina–Renault, the Military Aircraft Factory [FMA], and some tractor and motorcycle factories) in the 1950s. This was accompanied by national import substitution policies.[5] Despite the ups and downs of globalization and national economic policy, the model has remained in place; currently four large multinational companies dominate the sector. These include Renault (formerly Kaiser), Iveco (established in 1979), Fiat (since 1996), and Volkswagen (since 2001). The sector employed about 10,000 people in 1959, reached a peak of 57,000 employees in 1974, and then fell to 12,000 employees in 2002 (in 2017, the number of workers is close to 15,000) (MTEySS 2017).

Among the main aspects that weakened the automotive economic complex in Córdoba are: (1) the concentration of car-related industries in the industrial periphery of Buenos Aires (in particular since the 1960s), which negatively impacted the establishment of new firms in the rest of the country; and (2) the transformation of global value chains, turning automotive factories into assembly plants of parts that were mostly manufactured abroad. This shift in global value chains has progressively eliminated the classic "rings" of vertical suppliers that characterize a productive pole or industrial complex. To these causes we must add the impact in Córdoba of the national policies implemented during 1991–2002, characterized by a fixed exchange rate called the Convertibility Plan and several neoliberal policies (external trade opening, privatization of goods and public services to transnational capitals, etc.). During this period, the gradual rise in interest rates, high external indebtedness, difficulties in obtaining access to financing, and the loss of competitiveness among the industries contributed to the weakening of SMEs and local value chains. This process also concluded with the economic and institutional crisis of the years 2001 and 2002, in which the national GDP fell by 64% and led to a "mega-devaluation" of the Argentinian peso by 300% (Schorr 2013).

It is therefore not surprising that in 1999 the newly elected government of the province of Córdoba designed an economic development policy oriented to replace the centrality of the automotive industry by the new and still emerging ICT industries. However, in trying to trigger the economic restructuring of the region, the government repeated the same economic development policy model based on tax subsidies to attract large and multinational ICT companies so that they could recreate the supposedly virtuous dynamics of growth poles and industrial complexes. Paradoxically then, for the government, Córdoba had to move from being the Detroit of Argentina to becoming the "Silicon Valley of the South," but with the same kind of industry structure of the previous and dying automobile industrial complex.[6]

With this objective, the government became interested in attracting ICT multinationals and foreign investors through tax exemptions and government subsidies. These policies were based on the assumption that establishing multinationals would create local jobs in the short term and would eventually generate local spillovers in the form of subcontracting and learning processes that would then turn the region into a successful cluster. Indeed, the Córdoba Province Government (CPG) offered generous fiscal incentive packages to several ICT multinational companies, including Motorola (2001), Intel (2006), EDS-HP (2006), Gameloft (2007), and Indra (2008) to establish operations in Córdoba.

The deployment of this policy triggered an unexpected social process led by local SMEs. Through their participation in several associations and networks, local SMEs were able to force the provincial government to modify its original policy approach towards a more participative model based on the strengthening of local institutions and networks of collaboration among local small firms. This policy change was timely, given the poor development outcomes of the newly established ICT multinationals. Indeed, the tax incentives did not have the expected results in terms of income and employment generation. Despite the generous benefits offered by the Córdoba provincial government to IT multinational companies to establish operations, companies have not always honored their promises. While Motorola promised to create 500 jobs in Córdoba, it eventually only created 250 (Borrastero 2013). The Córdoba provincial government also often did not follow up with sanctions on multinationals that did not meet their contractual commitments, even though the government itself has been sanctioned several times for not complying with some of their promises to IT multinationals (Borrastero 2013).[7] Similarly, several local scholars have shown that very few SMEs in Córdoba have been able to achieve spillovers from multinationals in the form of subcontracting opportunities (López and Ramos 2008; Borrastero 2013). For instance, in a study of the relationship between ICT multinational companies and SMEs in Córdoba, López and Ramos (2008) argued that the very scarce spillovers that software multinationals in Córdoba have created are derived from spin-off companies established by local workers previously employed in multinationals, rather than from subcontracting opportunities.

These mixed outcomes are in line with the academic literature on this issue. For example, Altenburg and Meyer-Stamer (1999) have argued that the attraction of multinationals is never a guarantee that spillovers or a regional cluster will be generated or, even if generated, that these will survive for a long time. Indeed, similar regional development strategies, known as "growth-pole" development strategies, were extensively applied in Latin American peripheral regions in the 1960s and 1970s until they were eventually rejected, since many of them did not succeed in promoting local development in the long term (Conroy 1973).[8] Other authors have argued that attracting multinational companies can help bring cutting-edge knowledge and innovation into the local economy but only if enough links and collaborations are created with local firms (Bresnahan, Gambardella, and Saxenian 2001). Indeed, the recent Latin American experience shows mixed results in the relationship between the establishment of IT multinationals and the creation of spillovers at the local level. For instance, Gallagher and Zarsky (2007) have shown that after IT multinationals that came to Guadalajara, the so-called Mexican Silicon Valley, attracted by the NAFTA agreements in the 1990s, significant spillovers for local companies did not result. Instead, the situation created an *enclave economy* in which IT multinationals temporarily benefited from low-wage workers and low environmental regulation and eventually moved to China looking for even lower wages. In contrast, yet other authors have argued that the role of multinationals has been important in creating an international reputation for new emerging IT clusters. For instance, Ciravegna (2011) has argued that the arrival of Intel to San José (Costa Rica) was key in positioning the region "on the map" of IT world clusters, which eventually facilitated the growth of other local and international companies in the region.

Despite this mixed view in the literature, attracting multinationals is a popular strategy among politicians and government officials. Citizens and the local media often see these initiatives in a positive light and as a sign of the success of a government agency in attracting jobs and development opportunities. In the following sections we analyze three key dimensions for local SME companies in Córdoba in the ICT industry to change the "industrial complex" economic development policy approach towards an approach that emphasized horizontal collaboration and a territorial vision of economic development.

Constructing and communicating an alternative narrative of economic development

To change a dominant policy narrative, a powerful alternative has to be created. For this to succeed, two types of strategies must take place: one aimed at generating a common narrative among a group of actors and another aimed at positioning and communicating this narrative at the territorial level. In Córdoba, the construction of a new narrative began defensively, predicated on the arrival of ICT multinational companies. The threat that they would absorb the most talented local labor force served as a powerful narrative to organize local SMEs in associations so that they could gain more negotiation power.

The ICT industry in Córdoba is made up of two main segments: electronics manufacturing and software development. It is estimated that there are about 550 firms in the province (210 electronics companies and 340 software firms), almost all small in size (average number of employees 16). In 1999, five of these small local companies in the electronics sector formed the Central Argentina Chamber of Information, Electronics, and Communication

Industries (CIIECCA). The leaders of these five companies had attended Córdoba's top universities together and had maintained their relationships over the years, which became a crucial factor that facilitated the establishment of CIIECCA in response to the threat of losing their most talented human capital to foreign investors (Berti 2006; Giuliani and Matta 2013). In 2001, a group of 11 local firms in the software sector created another association: the Córdoba Technology Cluster (CTC). Currently, CTC has 180 companies in the Córdoba region. The second step was to consolidate these links through a social process of trust building. Trust among CIIECCA founders was already strong before the association was established. Over the years, the five founding owners have also kept such traditions as regular informal social meetings and barbeques (*asados*) that reinforced trust and eventually resulted in the establishment of CIIECCA (Mitnik and Magnano 2011). By contrast, local SMEs in the software sector were newer to the business and did not have strong ties between them. Indeed, they saw each other as competitors rather than collaborators. In this context of distrust, two factors were key for the creation of CTC: (a) the view of multinationals as a common threat; and (b) the role of a consultant who brought the companies together by teaching them cluster theory and the benefits of associations.[9] Over the years, CTC became a key actor in promoting public–private initiatives and in moving the economic development policy of the Córdoba province government away from attracting foreign companies towards developing the local ecosystem of SMEs. Both CIIECCA and CTC have managed to create a broad common vision that makes them feel they are members and participants of a larger "local and regional development" vision (e.g., in the case of CIIECCA: "to improve the image of Córdoba in the eyes of our country and the world").

In the construction of this alternative common narrative about ICT multinationals, the cluster theory was important in the collaboration of a local and global epistemic community linked to local economic development. A key role in the dissemination of these ideas in Córdoba came from the participation of many CIIECCA and CTC members in a Productive Chain Development Program, organized by the local economic development agency, ADEC, and funded by the Inter-American Development Bank (IADB). Similarly, the IADB also sponsored several conferences in Argentina that brought several international experts in LED and cluster theory to Córdoba. As one ICT entrepreneur pointed out: "At that time everyone was talking about 'clusters' but nobody had previous experience. Participation in this program helped us to have a common identity." Engagement among members of this epistemic community during the first decade of the 2000s aided in the emergence of several "clusterpreneurs" (Kantis et al. 2005) in the Córdoba region. Christensen and Stoerring (2012) have defined "clusterpreneurs" as those individuals with a prominent role in the emergence of a cluster initiative. These authors have highlighted the important role that clusterpreneurs have in creating and helping evolve clusters in peripheral regions. Different actors, both public and private, can play the role of a clusterpreneur. What is crucial is the actor's capacity to create networks and mobilize trust across both public and private sectors. As noted by Christensen and Stoerring (2012, 140), clusterpreneurs are key "to knit regional organizations together, not only in a physical sense by creating networks, equally important by creating social capital."

The role of a clusterpreneur was indeed crucial in the creation of the Córdoba Technology Cluster (CTC) association. The promoter of CTC, an Argentine enthusiast of Porter's (1990) cluster theory, helped articulate a critical mass of local companies that would collaborate and eventually engage with multinational companies so that an innovative software cluster could be developed in the region. He was convinced that social capital had to be built among local SMEs so that they could leverage a better position to negotiate with the government. To build social capital and persuade SMEs of the need to collaborate, he followed what he calls "a technical persuasion process" to move local companies from a situation of distrust and competition to one of collaboration through the establishment of the Córdoba Technology Cluster. As part of that process, association members studied theories and cases from other regions such as Silicon Valley and the Italian industrial districts. As he noted: "a key aspect to create trust among companies was to teach them about why clusters are important for the competitiveness of regions." These readings facilitated the development of a common regional development vision among software companies. "A kind of mythology was created around the idea of making them participants of something important for the region, something beyond their individual business interests," according to the clusterpreneur. The process also included joint visits and study tours of members going together to iconic economic institutions in Córdoba as well as to other ICT centers around the world. Frequently, after a CTC member went to another ICT region outside Argentina, he or she would organize sessions to recount the experience and share conclusions about what worked or not in those places. There were dual objectives of these visits and learning exchanges: to not only learn from what other places were doing but also make CTC members recognize each other as peers in search of a larger objective (regional development) rather than just competitors.

But in addition to building a common and alternative narrative to multinational-centered development policy, an important element that allowed local ICT companies to have a stronger voice in issues of economic development in the province was a carefully designed communication strategy with other local actors in the region. The strategy was based on a series of meetings between ICT representatives with local and provincial government agencies, universities, and the local media. The fact that they were all local companies and that the sector was perceived as innovative and a promising economic activity made their proposal very well received among all local actors. As noted by one of the promoters, the CTC mission "had all the sex appeal" that the media and the government like:

> the companies represented in CTC were diverse and recognized in their field . . . we were from Córdoba but we wanted to work at the global level, [we wanted to create] high-quality jobs, and we had an innovative proposal: the idea of creating a cluster [and not just another Chamber of Commerce].

CTC's objective – to position Córdoba as a global software cluster – was perceived as a "noble cause" by all local actors; it was difficult to deny them a voice in policy decisions. They also regularly invited politicians to speak about innovation and the software industry at their events so that they could feel part of the project. Finally, CTC recognition and strong presence in the local media made them an obligatory stop when new multinational companies wanted to establish operations in Córdoba. After gaining recognition among relevant local actors, CTC started to experiment with different institutional organizations to promote more specific public–private collaborations.

By 2007, the narrative that ICT should be promoted through an LED approach started to become part of the official discourse of the provincial government. Two statements by local Córdoba governors exemplify this change in the economic development policy narrative for the ICT industry. In 2006, when asked in local newspaper *La Voz* about local ICT entrepreneurs who demanded greater participation in ICT policy, Governor de la Sota said:

> Who? The ICT entrepreneurs? They also walk with a lookout tower trying to see where they can put up an easy business. We have pampered them with the industrial promotion. . . . They are *fallutos* (two faced) and *chantas* (scoundrels). All day they are crying and begging. They want to grow with the subsidy of the State. I will not give them what they do not know how to win.
>
> (Bocco and Turello 2006)

Only four years later, in 2010, Governor Schiaretti (from the same political party as the previous one) referred to

> the conditions that the Province has to produce high technology, since it not only has numerous public and private universities that train professionals but also a quantity of small companies with the pioneering spirit of our Córdoba and the will of the provincial State. This combination of joint work allows Córdoba to be seen as a place to invest and develop high technology in the country.
>
> (Cadena 3 2010)

It cannot be overlooked, however, that the change in the provincial government strategy also had to do with the fact that large companies began to slowly migrate their production to other regions. In 2010 Gameloft closed its facilities in Córdoba. EDS was sold to Hewlett Packard and then began a divestiture process, taking its services to India, Philippines, and Panama, letting go of 600 workers. Motorola followed suit and by 2016, they had already fired the last 50 professionals. Interestingly, the mega-devaluation in 2002 generated favorable conditions for foreign investment, mainly because of the relative decline of wages. These conditions gradually changed as rising inflation and unfavorable exchange rates set in, combined with restructuring initiated by large transnational corporations following the global financial crisis of 2008. All these factors, however, became more prominent after the change in perspective adopted by the provincial government in 2007, evidenced by the arrival of new foreign investments that year (EDS, Gameloft) and in 2008 (Indra).

Institutional experimentation around public–private collaboration

Once local ICT companies formed CIIECCA and CTC, they gained a stronger voice and negotiating power to participate in government decisions about economic development policy. Gaining this voice and power was not an automatic outcome but rather the result of a continuous experimental process of public–private collaboration. This section analyzes the most important aspects that allowed these companies to participate and influence economic development policy decisions in Córdoba and how this was done through significant institutional experimentation rather than through a single or paradigmatic public–private organization. One of the first initiatives was the establishment of Instituto Tecnológico Córdoba (ITC) in 2002. ITC was a higher education center jointly founded by CTC and the six universities of Córdoba – both public and private – with the objective of training locals to meet the needs of the local ICT industry. Funding came as a donation from Intel after the multinational company canceled its plans to establish operations in Córdoba after Argentina's 2002 crisis. ITC started as an ambitious project; among its accomplishments was a formal agreement between public and private universities in Córdoba to collaborate on technology-related educational programs for locals.

Another celebrated achievement that brought together local actors in the ICT industry was the passage of a law that made local SMEs in the software industry able to access the same benefits and subsidies as multinational companies. This was the *Ley de Promoción Industrial 9121*, passed by the provincial government in 2003. This law extended five-year subsidies to local SMEs that hired new employees or that experienced energy consumption increases. It also included the possibility of exempting new local SMEs in the ICT industry from provincial taxes for up to ten years. This law benefited about 50 ICT small and medium companies in Córdoba. The passage of these laws required an active process of lobbying senators in the Córdoba provincial government, organized by CTC in training sessions on the role of SMEs in local and regional development. Later, in 2004, the Córdoba provincial government and ADEC, with funds from the MIF and the Ministry of Science and Technology (MINCYT), launched a Supply Chain Promotion program that defined ICT as one key link in the value chain of the regional economy. The project sought to strengthen the linkages and cooperation among private actors in the region as well as between private and public actors, in order to improve local production and exports. The idea was to provide technical assistance to SMEs, particularly those associated under CTC and CIIECCA. In 2005, thanks to the collaboration between ADEC and CTC, the PROFOCO program was launched in Córdoba. PROFOCO (Programa de Competencias Laborales) aimed at training unemployed people in the ICT skills that local SMEs in Córdoba needed. In supporting these projects, the government sought to promote the associativity of local SMEs and contribute to their upgrading efforts.

In 2007, the provincial government increased its efforts to support local ICT SMEs with two new programs that sought to support human capital in the region: Programa de Subsidio al Empleo en Empresas Tecnológicas, which provides funding to train existing and new employees in the ICT industry; and Centro de Residencias en Informática y Electrónica (COMCAL), which started training an average of seven hundred young students per year in ICT skills. CTC and CIIECCA provided the hardware and the administration expenses needed to run the COMCAL program. In 2008, the Córdoba provincial government also launched a series of new funding mechanisms to support the creation and development of new SMEs in Córdoba. Perhaps the most important institutional achievement was the establishment in 2007 of the Córdoba ICT Board, known as Mesa TIC, an abbreviation of Mesa Sectorial de Tecnología, Informática y Comunicaciones. The Board included representatives from the Córdoba provincial government, CIIECCA, and CTC, as well as a representative from each of the multinational companies located in Córdoba. At the time of its establishment, the ICT Board was still under the sectorial approach; it was imagined as a space for dialogue between public and private actors rather than an organization with executive power. However, by the end of 2009, the Board started to gain more decision-making power, thanks to the push by CIIECCA and CTC (which were associated with ADEC). Members of Mesa TIC jointly elaborated a software strategic plan for the region, and in 2011 the provincial government approved this plan to guide government efforts to support the ICT sector in the following ten years. Because the different actors in the region identified human capital training as the main challenge for local ICT companies, the law included a series of internships, fellowships, business incubators, and internationalization strategies for local companies.[10] This plan confirmed the transition within the provincial government from the sectorial supply chain approach to an LED strategy. According to Borrastero (2013, 14), this legal reform legally institutionalizes the participation of the private sector in the design and implementation of sectorial policies. After many deliberations, Board members decided to create a more formal institution to move beyond discussing human resources development strategies towards implementing the more comprehensive objectives of the ten-year strategic plan. Based on the experience of Recife, Brazil, Board members decided to create a foundation to lead the project: Fundación Córdoba TIC. The idea was that the foundation would have its own resources so that it would be able to survive changing political administrations and strategies. By having its own budget, the foundation would also be able to promote local start-ups through risk capital investments. While members of the Board were successful in establishing Fundación Córdoba TIC through a law, the return of former Governor José Manuel de la Sota in 2011 was a setback for this initiative. Despite the recent discontinuation of the foundation, events organized by CTC, CIIECCA, multinational companies, and the local and provincial government have continued. For instance, a new and very successful annual weeklong event called Semana TIC (ICT week) has been taking place every year since 2012. Semana TIC brings together different actors in the ICT industry in Córdoba through seminars, workshops, funding events, and a trade fair.

The ICT sector in Córdoba illustrates how local SME associations have been able to put pressure on the government to change the economic development policy and thus modify the institutional field in which they operate. This process would not have been possible without the proper use of a "window of opportunity" and active efforts to influence government policy.[11] For instance, the promulgation of the National Law for the Promotion of the Software Industry in 2004 required an active process of lobbying senators through different training sessions.

The co-evolution of the agents of the "triple helix"

The third and final dimension we analyze in this chapter to explain the change in economic development policy approach in the ICT industry in Córdoba is an institutional co-evolution process. The concept of co-evolution as proposed by the evolutionary literature could be described as the process of change arising from the "mutual adjustment" between agents that interact within the same context (Nelson 1995; Murmann 2013). In this sense, co-evolution is a reciprocal process in which the different organizations modify their strategy, structure, or functions to adapt to a desired territorial development trajectory. This section will analyze several mutual adjustments that the three agents of the triple helix of Córdoba – business associations, universities, and the state – carried out in order to move from a traditional "industrial complex" perspective (passive, sectorial, rigid, very limited cooperation among agents of the triple helix) to a more strategic one aligned with an LED approach (see a synthesis in Figure 5.3). These adjustments involved two types of changes: (1) changes in organizational structures (a greater openness to different local agents thanks to the creation within each organization of specific dependencies to facilitate interaction and cooperation as well as the inclusion of external agents, or cross-participation, at the directive level); and (2) changes at the functional level (these involved the realignment of key internal functions and objectives of local actors to the strategy of the rest of the agents, which often involved complex processes of internal legitimation and the creation of incentives to move its members to accompany this process).

In the case of business associations, there has been a transition from a sectoral defensive position to a common territorial economic development strategy. Two aspects are key to understand this transition. The first aspect relates to the institutional opening to collaborate with organizations outside the business community and the participation in spaces of territorial governance and articulation. This dimension is clearer in the case of the CTC, which has embraced since its creation the cluster concept as a guiding institutional structure. While most CIIECCA members are manufacturers within the same industry, CTC has collaborated with other nonbusiness local actors, such as universities. On the other hand, both institutions have worked not only with institutions created to defend their sectoral strategy but also with other institutions with a broader local economic development vision, such as ADEC. The second aspect relates to changes at the functional level, particularly to the main activities developed by the institutions in relation to their social base. In general, the traditional model of business association in Argentina focuses on "sectoral representation," that is, lobbying different state agencies to achieve economic benefits for members. This model has its roots in the corporatist tradition that in different periods has also characterized the unions and has been promoted by the State itself. Nonetheless, both CIIECCA and CTC have been progressively emphasizing project management, service delivery, and the creation of "territorial assets." In addition, the case of the SMT (Surface Mount Technology) Center of CIIECCA stands out as another example. Created in 2006 with the support of ADEC and national funds, the Center is a quasi-public asset at the service of local and regional companies. The collective use of the SMT center has resulted in a significant reduction in manufacturing costs and an improvement to product quality for many electronics companies in Córdoba and the region.

Universities also had to evolve to adapt to this transition process. The traditional position of the six local universities with respect to the ICT sector could be summarized as the creation of a few new programs to train local professionals, some academic research in this emerging field, and the provision of consultancy services to a few ICT companies. As we mentioned earlier, the first reaction of Córdoba universities to support the consolidation of the local ICT sector was the creation of the Instituto de Tecnología de Córdoba (ITC). Over the years, this position has broadened to increase the link with the province as well as the creation of new structures and activities. An example of this is the creation of new specific organizational areas such as the Undersecretariat for Innovation, Transfer and Technological Linkage of the National University of Córdoba (in 2007) and the Catholic University of Córdoba (in 2011); the inauguration of a Technological Park and Incubator of technology-based companies (mostly spin-off companies) in the university environment in the National University of Córdoba (in 2011); and the establishment of a Social Advisory Council, also in the same university (in 2016), with different social and economic local actors including a CTC representative. In addition, Córdoba universities have joined spaces of territorial governance such as ADEC (in 2014)

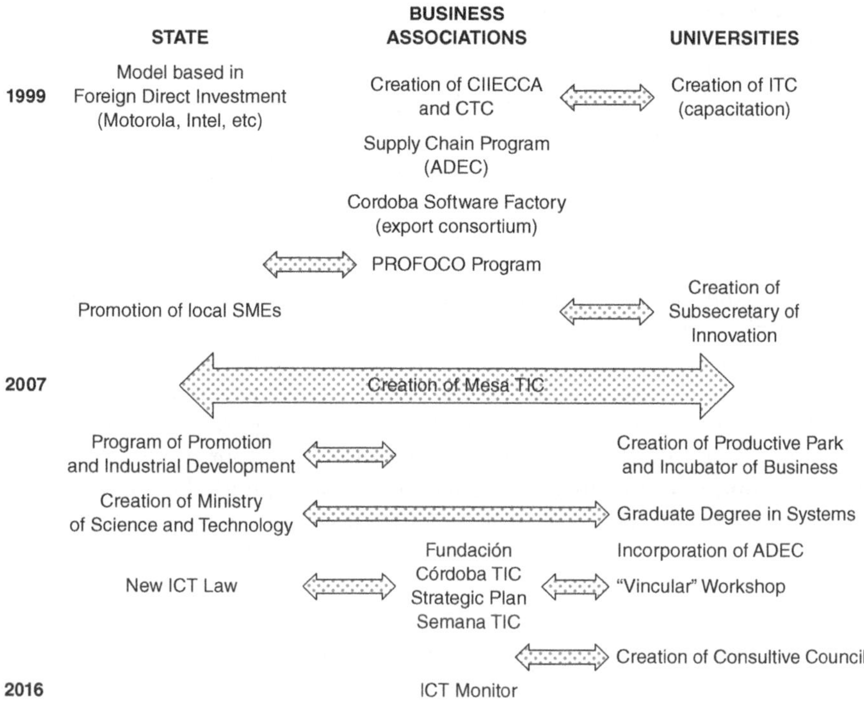

Figure 5.3 Co-evolution in the triple helix in Córdoba

and the Entrepreneurial Ecosystem of Córdoba (in 2013), a space created by the provincial government with more than 60 local institutions to promote a local entrepreneurial culture and stronger university-technology linkages. Following the experience of ITC, in 2008 the National University of Córdoba started a graduate specialization program in Distributed Systems and Services together with the government and Intel. In 2009, the National University of Córdoba created several subsidies and scholarships for innovation and technology transfer. In addition, since 2015 Córdoba universities have actively participated in the organization of Link Córdoba conferences, events aimed at strengthening the public–private articulation and generating links between scientific institutions and companies.

Finally, it is important to note the national government shift from a Keynesian role based on the application of traditional supply side policies (subsidies, tax cuts, etc.) to strategies that intend to generate conditions for the increase of local knowledge, increasing local capacities and the bonds between local actors. These strategies included the creation of new institutional structures such as the Ministry of Science and Technology (in 2007) and the promotion of inter-institutional spaces such as Mesa TIC (2007). The new agreements made with ICT multinational companies located in Córdoba since 2007 included training and transfer and technical cooperation tasks that prioritized interaction with local companies. Similarly, the 2009 Industrial Promotion and Development Program guided tax exemptions, subsidies, and credit lines to processes with a high territorial impact such as promoting innovation, environmental care, or forming partnerships. The incorporation in the governing bodies of important private actors of the local ICT ecosystem. For instance, the clusterpreneur behind the creation of CTC became advisor to several high-ranking officials in charge of economic development in Córdoba, whereas a former CTC director was previously Secretary of Industry in the Córdoba provincial government. Despite the fact that the State never ceased to appeal to passive policies (extending the subsidies granted to multinationals to SMEs), from a functional point of view, the State became oriented to two priority activities related to the generation of territorial resources: the training of human resources and the provision of infra-structure. In the first case, programs such as the "500 × 500" and "500 × 300" were invested in the Software Qualification Program (a continuation of PROFOCO), aspiring to train more than four thousand workers. In the second case, the provincial government has supported the construction of an airport business park, a private enterprise supported by companies of the CTC and CIIECCA to which the State offered AR$30 million in subsidies. Finally, key to this process has been not only the alignment of the provincial government, but also the national government, which also started to develop a more active and territory-based economic development policy for ICT. For instance, in 2003, software development was declared an industrial activity and in 2004 a Strategic Plan of the Software Services Industry (SPSSI) was announced. In addition, in this period the Ministry of Science and Technology was created and the funding of national programs oriented to ICT sectors was considerably increased (FONSOFT and FONTAR in particular).

On the fragility of Córdoba's governance: limitations of Córdoba's local economic development approach

Despite the impressive numbers in ICT employment growth and the advances of Córdoba's local actors and institutions in the ICT industry towards the promotion and implementation of a more territorial vision of economic development, it is questionable whether the institutional mechanisms developed in the region are enough to consider Córdoba a true regional innovation system (RIS). Recent data show that although companies in the sector have managed to demonstrate high levels of resilience, in most cases they have not achieved levels of innovation and competitiveness that allow them to export and cope with international competition (CTC 2017).

A number of constraints impede the strengthening of the ICT industry in Córdoba. There is persistent logic demonstrating the influence of institutional path dependence processes that prevent or delay the impact of the institutional innovations described earlier. In the case of the State, for example, its weakness or inability to comply and enforce the rules and agreements reached has become evident in several instances. This can be seen in the main achievement of the sector: the adoption by law of the ICT strategic plan and the Fundación Córdoba TIC in 2011 as previously discussed. And while the Mesa TIC meetings continue, they have also lost momentum compared to previous years. According to an ICT entrepreneur, the governor did not perceive it as his own project and that the organization never obtained its own funding sources: "the problem with the Board is that it relied too much on the Córdoba government budget . . . And further, it did not have the same self-discipline as the CTC." This shows that the key role that business associations and civil society can play in creating agendas and in the continuity of territorial processes requires certain institutional conditions (such as mutual respect of agreements) and a State (not only a particular government) designed to generate processes of articulation, as has been widely reported in the literature (Evans 1995; Chibber 2006, among others).

In addition, the government was not able to enforce the agreements with the different multinational companies located in Córdoba, which calls into question its capacity to do so in the future. Motorola, Intel, Indra, or Gameloft did not create the employment agreed upon. Many of them failed also to maintain operations in the city during the agreed period, and most did not generate the links with the universities or other local firms they promised after 2007. Similarly, in spite of the policies developed in favor of SMEs, the State has not considered the request to promote "buy local" as a way of encouraging niches where the final product can still compete with the foreign products. As one local businessman pointed out: "We do not want subsidies, we want to be able to sell our products to the state, instead of buying it from foreign companies."

In the case of universities, they have not succeeded in generating a sustained and dynamic relationship with the local productive sector and have not even been able to efficiently execute some initiatives that required articulation between them. The ITC has run into difficulties mostly related to day-to-day management. Some of our interviewees pointed to the different cultures of collaboration between public and private universities as a challenge that would be impossible to overcome in the long term.

In the case of business associations, despite the numerous successful articulations at the territorial level described, they have not been able to escape completely from their sectoral logic, and on many occasions, it has become evident that the regional objectives supported by their leaders are subordinated to the short-term benefits to its associates. As one leader of the ICT sector mentioned when being consulted on a project relevant for the territory but of low impact among technological companies: "We are convinced that the project is important but should be the responsibility of the government. Our associates need to see that the benefits come directly to them." In addition, these "traditional" institutional forms appear to be insufficient to generate interactions and cooperation beyond associations, as evidenced by the difficulties of different initiatives carried out between CTC and CIIECCA with the aim of generating effective linkages between companies in the electronics sector and the software firms.

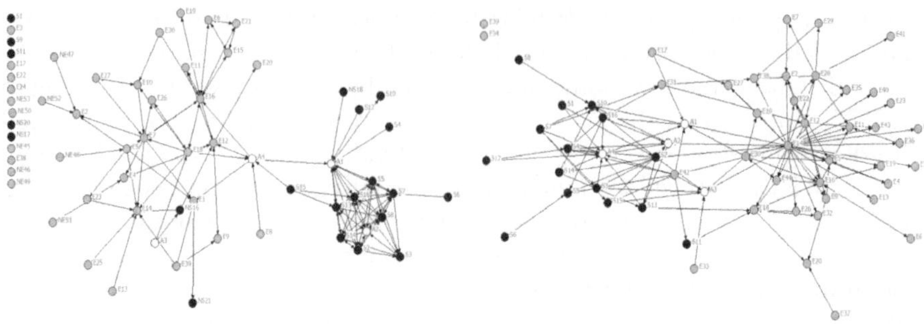

Figure 5.4 Communication networks among CTC and CIIECCA before and after the Productive Chain Development program

References: Gray dots indicate CIIECCA, Black and white dots indicate CTC

Source: Matta, 2011

It is possible to see an example of this dynamic in Figure 5.4, which graphs the communication networks between firms of the two associations at two moments: before and after the intervention of the Productive Chain Development program, which for four years tried to increase cooperation in the ICT industry. In the first graph, we see that relations between CIIECCA and CTC companies were very scarce at the beginning, with only one firm linking both groups. The second graph shows how after the execution of the program, the relations increased significantly.[12]

Finally, although several innovative instances of local articulation and governance such as Mesa TIC were very useful for creating a collective discourse and general agreements, they do not seem to have the capacity to articulate the efforts in a really systemic way, ensuring results at operational levels (for example, by achieving greater cooperation in specific projects, articulating or creating more territorial collective resources, or reaching better economic results in terms of innovation or exports). These new structures also carry with them the logic of other public–private institutions in the economic field; only the position of the State and companies is taken into account, universities have a complementary role, and other local and regional organizations are simply not invited to participate. The most evident is the lack of representation of ICT unions, which are not taken into account in any of the institutional constructions mentioned in this analysis.

Conclusions

Since 2000, local and regional governments have promoted the ICT industry in Córdoba using two approaches: an "industrial complex" (2001–6) and a local economic development (LED) approach (2007–16). The fast growth of the ICT industry in Córdoba during the last 20 years has benefited from the active organization, collaboration, and support of the private and public sectors in the region. Organized local ICT companies have not only achieved better conditions for their members, they have also become active participants in the design and implementation of economic development policies and planning decisions undertaken by the local and provincial governments.

There are some interesting lessons and conclusions that can be drawn from the Córdoba experience. First, the emphasis on associations and public–private partnerships promoted by local and regional governments has worked better when public–private collaboration "build over what has already been constructed," as one outside expert framed it. In other words, linkages have worked better when the new approach builds on initiatives already started/identified by local organizations such as CTC or CIIECCA, rather than starting from scratch based on some new model of LED. In this context, it is important that collaboration centers on particular projects or common worldviews shared by the local actors. For example, the creation of CTC or CIIECCA would have been much more difficult if the actors did not share a common narrative about competing with multinationals to attract human capital or the perception of the need to collaborate to improve human resources, educational policy, etc. Second, in the case of CTC, consultants and intermediaries such as ADEC and the Córdoba provincial government have had important roles not just as knowledge transfer agents or network facilitators but actually as ITC network builders. In other words, these were not just actors within networks; they actively helped produce networks such as CTC.

The Argentinian institutional and economic context is unique among Latin American countries, but the Córdoba case offers general lessons from which other regions can benefit. For example, a couple decades ago, Córdoba's economic development policy was focused on attracting multinational corporations. Now, it is clearly diversifying. This shift in trajectory is based in part on the competitiveness of emerging sectors like ICT, but also due to changes in the tone of the conversation about the local economy, led by its LED agencies and SME associations. The ICT industry in Córdoba is an interesting example of a shift in economic development policy that has been pushed by associations of local SMEs. The success of Córdoba's local SMEs in participating and integrating their demands into government policies has been achieved not just because of the existence of a particular public–private structure but rather through a series of collaborative and institutional experiments between public and private actors.

While there have been encouraging outcomes to the public–private experimentation in Córdoba's ICT industry, difficulties remain in terms of how to sustain these institutional experiments over time, given high levels of political volatility. However, if there has been one constant in this process of institutional experimentation, it is the continuity of two associations of local SMEs established in the early 2000s: CIIECCA and CTC. The experience of Córdoba shows that the construction of a regional system of innovation in peripheral regions is no easy task, but it is also one that is not impossible.

Notes

1 The data obtained by this source have some limitations in that its survey only considered registered employment and used a restrictive criterion to classify the ICT firms, whereas other reports estimate that the sector currently has more than 10,000 workers (CTC 2017).
2 CIIECCA stands for Cámara de Industrias Informáticas, Electrónicas y de Comunicaciones del Centro de Argentina [central Argentina's chamber of information, electronic, and communications industries].
3 CTC stands for Córdoba Technology Cluster (Córdoba's association of small and medium software enterprises).
4 Chapple et al. (2014) included 20 in-depth interviews conducted by Karen Chapple and Sergio Montero in 2011 with government officials, representatives of the main local ICT industry associations CIIECCA and CTC, and key members of Córdoba's LED agency ADEC.

   Matta (2011) included 125 interviews conducted by Andrés Matta in 2005 and 2006 with entrepreneurs using a semi-structured questionnaire. It also used in-depth interviews with members of the "directive commission" of CIIECCA and CTC, and ten program and government officials.

   Giuliani, Matta and Pietrobelli (2016) included 38 interviews conducted by Andrés Matta and Elisa Giuliani in 2012 with entrepreneurs using a semi-structured questionnaire and two focus groups with the executive board of CIIECCA. Also included are interviews with eight government and university officials.
5 The policy known as import substitution industrialization (ISI) occurred in Argentina in different stages and forms between 1930 and 1974. In particular, during 1958–74 a protectionist scheme was in force based on exchange restrictions, high duty levels and the State actively transferring income to the industrial sector (subsidies, credits, provision of services) and to regulate redistributive conflicts. This policy caused gradual growth in industrial GDP, employment, wages, and productivity (Kosacoff 2010).
6 That was the name that international news agencies like Bloomberg gave Córdoba in the early years of the twenty-first century (see, for instance, www.bloomberg.com/news/articles/2005-10-06/c-rdoba-silicon-valley-south, accessed April 17, 2017), which the members of the government themselves repeated in the media (Ramos 2001).
7 The "agreement acts" and the "contracts" became Provincial Laws such as No. 8905 and 9214 (Motorola), 9295 (Intel), 9394 (EDS), 9432 (Gameloft), and 9473 (Indra).
8 These findings do not deny that there are also limitations to policies that seek industrial development within the framework of an ISI strategy. In the context of this debate, different authors point out that the success of these strategies in terms of development must be given certain institutional conditions such as the articulating role of the State, an organized civil society, and the existence of an entrepreneurial class (Evans 1995); the existence of institutionalized R&D policies (Lee 2000); the existence of virtuous meso-economic processes combining innovation and the existence of networks of (Ocampo 2003); or certain capacities of cohesion and leadership of the State (Chibber 2006).
9 Many of the CEOs had, in fact, studied together with that consultant at a private university, and many of them had also been clients of his company.
10 The plan foresees the creation of 27,000 new jobs and increasing sales within the sector fivefold by 2020, requiring an annual budget close to USD 10 million (40% contributed by the State, 45% by companies, and 15% by universities) administered by the Córdoba ICT foundation.

11 This "window of opportunity" is also related to the development of a national policy implemented since 2003 by the governments of Néstor and Cristina Kirchner, who sought to favor national industrial development (the law of 2004 is one of the milestones that follow that line). It should be noted that the governments of Córdoba (despite belonging to the same political party) in general did not ideologically share this position and in many ways were "against the flow." Therefore, the change of strategy in 2007 is even more relevant.

12 The communication network was analyzed via "Social network analysis" as part of an evaluation process undertaken by the Córdoba provincial government and funded by the IADB (Matta 2011).

References

Altenburg, T., and J. Meyer-Stamer. 1999. "How to Promote Clusters: Policy Experiences from Latin America." *World Development* 27 (9): 1693–713.

Asheim, B., and A. Isaksen. 1997. "Location, Agglomeration and Innovation: Towards Regional Innovation Systems in Norway?" *European Planning Studies* 5 (3): 299–330.

Berti, N. 2006. "Del combinado al satélite. Trayectorias, redes y estrategias empresariales del complejo electrónico cordobés." UNLP, unpublished.

Bocco, E., and J. Turello. 2006. "*De la Sota, sin anestesia.*" *La Voz*. http://archivo.lavoz.com.ar/2006/0108/politica/nota383502_1.htm (accessed August 9, 2017).

Borrastero, C. 2013. "Intervención estatal, transformaciones en los vínculos con el sector privado y crecimiento económico sectorial. El caso del sector de software y servicios informáticos de la ciudad de Córdoba, 2000–2010.' *H-industri@: Revista de Historia de la Industria, los Servicios y las Empresas en América Latina* 8: 1–35.

Bresnahan, T., A. Gambardella, and A. Saxenian. 2001. "'Old Economy' Inputs for 'New Economy' Outcomes: Cluster Formation in the New Silicon Valleys." *Industrial and Corporate Change* 10 (4): 835–60.

Cadena 3. 2010. "*La Provincia aportará $110 millones para el Parque Empresarial Aeropuerto.*" http://cadena3.com/contenido/2010/11/02/64858.asp.

Chapple, K., P. Peterson, and S. Montero. 2014. *Collaborating in Córdoba: Towards More Territorial Governance for Local Economic Development.* Report prepared for the Inter-American Development Bank.

Chibber, V. 2006. *Locked in Place: State-Building and Late Industrialization in India.* Princeton, NJ: Princeton University Press.

Christensen, J. L., and D. Stoerring. 2012. "Facilitating Cluster Evolution in Peripheral Regions: The Role of Clusterpreneurs." In *Interactive Learning for Innovation: A Key Driver within Clusters and Innovation Systems*, edited by B. Asheim and M. D. Parrilli, 137–60. London: Palgrave Macmillan.

Ciravegna, L. 2011. "FDI, Social Ties and Technological Learning in New Silicon Valley Clones. Evidence from the Costa Rican ICT Cluster." *Journal of Development Studies* 47 (8): 1178–98.

Conroy, M. E. 1973. "Rejection of Growth Center Strategy in Latin American Regional Development Planning." *Land Economics* 49 (4): 371–80.

Córdoba Technology Cluster (CTC). 2017. *Monitor TIC. Resultados 2do trimestre 2016.* www.cordobatechnology.com/uploads/wysiwyg/files/JBG%20311016.pdf (accessed April 1, 2017).

Dosi, G. 1982. "Technological Paradigms and Technological Trajectories: A Suggested Interpretation of the Determinants and Directions of Technical Change." *Research Policy* 11 (3): 147–62.

Edquist, C. 2001. "Systems of Innovation for Development." *Background Paper for Chapter I: "Competitiveness, Innovation and Learning: Analytical Framework" for the Unido World Industrial Development Report*. www.researchgate.net/publication/237322788_Systems_of_Innovation_for_Development_SID_Background_Paper_for_Chapter_I_Competitiveness_Innovation_and_Learning_Analytical_Framework_for_the_UNIDO_World_Industrial_Development_Report_WIDR_2001.

Evans, P. 1995. *Embedded Autonomy—States and Industrial Transformation*. Princeton, NJ: Princeton University Press.

Ferreti, M., and A. Parmentola. 2015. *The Creation of Local Innovation Systems in Emerging Countries. The Role of Governments, Firms and Universities*. Heidelberg, Germany: Springer.

Freeman, C. 2002. "Continental, National and Sub-National Innovation Systems – Complementarity and Economic Growth." *Research Policy* 31 (2): 191–211.

Gallagher, K. P., and L. Zarsky. 2007. *The Enclave Economy: Foreign Investment and Sustainable Development in Mexico's Silicon Valley*. Cambridge, MA: MIT Press.

Giuliani, E., and A. Matta. 2013. *Impact Evaluation with Social Network Analysis Methods: Program for Supply Chain Development in the Province of Córdoba, Argentina*. Washington, DC: Inter-American Development Bank.

Giuliani, E., A. Matta, and C. Pietrobelli. 2016. "Networks, Cluster Development Programs and Performance: The Electronics Cluster in Cordoba, Argentina." In *The Impact Evaluation of Cluster Development Programs*, edited by A. Maffioli, C. Pietrobelli, and R. Stucchi, 117–50. Washington, DC: Inter-American Development Bank.

Kantis, H., J. Federico, S. Drucaroff, and A. C. Martinez. 2005. "*Clusters y nuevos polos emprendedores intensivos en conocimiento en Argentina*." http://sgpwe.izt.uam.mx/files/users/uami/sppc/Cluster/Kantis_Hugo_2005_Clusters_intensivos_en_conocimiento_Argentina.pdf (accessed October 6, 2015).

Kosacoff, B. 2010. *Marchas y contramarchas de la industria Argentina (1958–2008)*. Santiago de Chile: CEPAL.

Lee, W.-Y. 2000. "The Role of Science and Technology Policy in Korea's Industrial Development." In *Technology, Learning, And Innovation: Experiences of Newly Industrializing Economies*, edited by L. Kim and R. Nelson, 269–90. New York: Cambridge University Press.

Leydesdorff, L., and M. Fritsch. 2006. "Measuring the Knowledge Base of Regional Innovation Systems in Germany in Terms of a Triple Helix Dynamics." *Research Policy* 35 (10): 1538–53.

López, A., and D. Ramos. 2008. "*La industria de software y servicios informáticos argentina. Tendencias, factores de competitividad y clusters*." Working Paper 31, 227–57.

Lundvall, B. Å., and B. Johnson. 1994. "The Learning Economy." *Journal of Industry Studies* 1 (2): 23–42.

Matta, A. 2011. "*Reconstruyendo la trama asociativa*." In *Desarrollo de cadenas productivas, clusters y redes empresariales: Herramientas para el desarrollo territorial*, edited by F. Mitnik, 239–86. Córdoba: Multilateral Investment Fund, Inter-American Development Bank, Agencia para el Desarrollo Económico de Córdoba.

Ministry of Finance. 2016. *Informes de Cadenas de Valor. Software y Servicios Informáticos*. www.economia.gob.ar/peconomica/docs/SSPE_Cadenas_de_Valor_Servicios_SSI.pdf (accessed January 4, 2017).

Mitnik, F., and C. Magnano. 2011. "*La ejecución en sectores urbanos*." In *Desarrollo de cadenas productivas, clusters y redes empresariales: Herramientas para el desarrollo territorial*, edited by F. Mitnik, 143–74. Córdoba: Multilateral Investment Fund, Inter-American Development Bank, Agencia para el Desarrollo Económico de Córdoba.

MTEySS. 2017. "*Observatorio de Empleo y Dinámica Empresarial*". www.trabajo.gov.ar/left/estadisticas/oede/?id_seccion=59 (accessed January 4, 2017).

Murmann, J. P. 2013. "The Coevolution of Industries and Important Features of Their Environments." *Organization Science* 24 (1): 58–78.

Nelson, R. R. 1993. *National Innovation Systems: A Comparative Analysis*. Oxford: Oxford University Press.

Nelson, R. R. 1995. "Recent Evolutionary Theorizing about Economic Change." *Journal of Economic Literature* 33 (1): 48–90.

Ocampo, J. A. 2003. "Latin America's Growth Frustrations: The Macro and the Mesoeconomic Links." Seminar on Management of Volatility, Financial Liberalization and Growth in Emerging Economies, 24–25 April, Santiago, Chile.

Porter, M. E. 1990. *The Competitive Advantage of Nations*. New York: Free Press.

Ramos, C. M. 2001. "*Córdoba: el software da empleo casi a la par de las automotrices.*" *La Nación*, February 12, 2001. www.lanacion.com.ar/52036-cordoba-el-software-da-empleo-casi-a-la-par-de-las-automotrices (accessed August 9, 2017).

Schorr, M. 2013. *Argentina en la posconvertibilidad: ¿Desarrollo o crecimiento industrial?* Estudios de economía política. Buenos Aires: Miño y Dávila.

Servetto, A. 2010. "*Tensiones y contradicciones del tercer gobierno peronista en Córdoba,* 1973–1976." In *Córdoba bicentenaria: Claves de su historia contemporánea*, edited by C. Tcach, 389–416. Córdoba: Centro de Estudios Avanzados y Editorial de la Universidad Nacional de Córdoba.

6 Against the grain

Networked governance and local economic development in Linhares, Brazil

Pedro Peterson

Introduction

Policies to support local production systems (*arranjos produtivos locais*, or APLs) emerged in Brazil in the 1990s, as the state (at the federal, state, and municipal levels) scrambled to find new models to promote industrial development and economic growth after the demise of the centralized import substitution model in the 1980s. In a previous generation of industrial policies, the national governments of Latin American countries, including Brazil, implemented strong measures to substitute domestic production for imports, either by large private sector firms closely aligned with the state ("national champions") or state-owned enterprises. In contrast, policies such as those to support APLs are developed and carried out by networks of private sector associations, labor unions, nongovernmental organizations, and a constellation of public sector actors across subnational units of government.

In Chapter 1 of this book, Montero and Chapple define the governance of economic development as a decentralized process featuring a multiplicity of state and nonstate actors engaging in "self-organized steering" (Jessop 1998). The literature on regional agglomerations of firms, such as clusters and industrial districts, stresses the importance of these forms of self-organization in carrying out economic development processes in contexts where the state has retreated from a predominant role, as occurred in many Latin American countries during the 1980s and 1990s (Schmitz 1999; Giuliani, Pietrobelli, and Rabellotti 2005; Sepulveda and Amin 2006; Crespi, Fernández-Arias, and Stein 2014). This literature frames governance as an evolutionary process that successful regions develop as a way to gain competitive advantage in a global economy. Most authors don't identify these productive coordination efforts as "governance," but rather as "collective efficiency," "productive development policies," and the like. This chapter and Peterson (2015) both explore the concept of governance as the coordination of productive activities as it relates to a broader political engagement of firms with the state. Borrowing Block's (2008; Negoita and Block 2012) concept of a "networked developmental state," I explore the ways in which local economic development (LED) efforts in a peripheral region rely on the coordination of private and public actors at multiple scales, from interfirm relationships to the mediation of state interventions in the regional economy.

The case study in this chapter – a furniture APL in the municipality of Linhares in the state of Espírito Santo, in southeastern Brazil – illustrates the relationship between governance networks and a territorial approach to LED. Linhares typifies the concept of a "peripheral region," located as it is hundreds of kilometers from Brazil's main urban centers; its early development was dependent on commodities like coffee and hardwoods. Nevertheless, since the 1990s it has emerged as one of Brazil's most successful furniture producers and has built an industrial infrastructure that has attracted plants from a range of other sectors. The development of the furniture sector in Linhares has generated broader developmental spillovers, such as an improved workforce, a higher capacity for innovation, infrastructure that can be used and appropriated by other economic sectors, and improvements to living standards and reductions in poverty and inequality.

The development of Linhares's furniture sector has been driven by a network of firms and the municipal and state governments continually seeking to upgrade the region's productive capacity in order to compete with more established industrial centers in southern Brazil. The ability of firms to develop intricate collaborative production methods has led to success with furniture manufacture. More importantly, the firms' ability to establish a policy network with key actors at the municipal and state levels has been instrumental in generating public investments in industrial infrastructure and attracting financing to improve the productive conditions of this peripheral region.

Productive upgrading through territorial development in Linhares

The Linhares case exemplifies the ways in which firms and the state can come together in networks to implement territorial intervention for LED. From a classic economic geography perspective, it is easy to see how a regional furniture industry would have emerged in Linhares in the 1960s and 1970s. The nearby hardwood forests provided the primary inputs needed for the production of simple pieces, and a crisis in the coffee industry – the state's main economic activity – in the 1960s freed local workers who could be employed in this labor-intensive activity (Villaschi, Felipe, and Oliveira 2011). The expansion of the country's most important north–south coastal highway, BR 101, connected Linhares to the state capital, Vitória, and other points to the south (where Brazil's biggest markets are), and later to the northeastern state of Bahia and its capital, Salvador, and other states in the northeast.

However, after the loss of much of the local supply of hardwoods through deforestation and the shift in the low-end furniture market towards fiberboard materials, the continued success of Linhares as an industrial region became more of a puzzle. Other regions in southern and southeastern Brazil, such as

Bento Gonçalves in Rio Grande do Sul and Ubá in Minas Gerais, had much longer histories, not just in furniture production but also in a range of other industrial activities. The challenges inherent in developing the local industry in this region required more than targeted interventions in accessing markets or improving managerial practices. The region needed to find ways to dramatically decrease the costs of its inputs, train the local labor force to work with increasingly complex machinery, manage land use conflicts arising from the growth of the industry and a rapidly expanding urban population, and other pressing issues. Some of these challenges were addressed through strictly private interventions by individual firms, but for the most part groups of firms acting informally or formally represented by the local trade association, or working in policy networks with the municipal and state governments, undertook interventions collectively.

Development in a peripheral region

Since the early 2000s, the Linhares region has experienced remarkable economic growth and social development, consolidating itself as one of the most important furniture producers in Brazil while also diversifying its economy by attracting plants from important domestic multinational corporations in machinery and food production. Local furniture firms have been able to adapt to shifting demands in the Brazilian furniture market and remain competitive even while Brazil's industrial sector overall has entered a serious recession. This ability to adapt to exogenous market and political forces is even more impressive in an industry with relatively low barriers to entry and low profit margins that require firms to achieve great economies of scale in order to be competitive.

The growth of the Linhares furniture industry has occurred in a peripheral region, quite distant from major metropolitan areas and from key inputs for furniture production, such as medium density fiberboard (MDF). Several local entrepreneurs likened producing furniture in Linhares to "swimming against the current." I argue that much of the success of the region owes to a highly collaborative governance network made up of the leading entrepreneurs in the sector but also embedded with municipal and statewide policy actors, geared primarily towards addressing productive challenges under difficult conditions.

In recent decades, the Linhares economy has grown rapidly while social indicators have also improved, as shown in Table 6.1. The municipality's gross domestic product (GDP) grew by more than 6% between 2000 and 2010, faster than Espírito Santo (which was one of the fastest growing states in Brazil during this period) and two percentage points faster than the country as a whole. The poverty rate in Linhares, which had been higher than 46% (19% in extreme poverty) in 1991, dropped dramatically to 26% (7% in extreme poverty) in 2000 and 11% (less than 3% in extreme poverty) by 2010. Linhares currently has a lower rate of extreme poverty than Espírito Santo, which also experienced rapid rates of poverty reduction. The Municipal Human Development

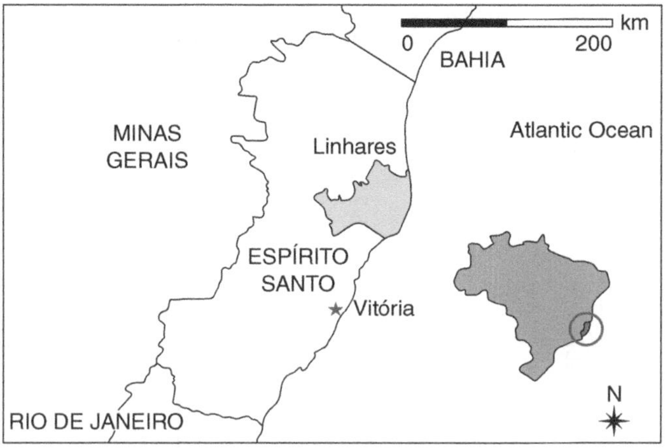

Figure 6.1 The Linhares region in Espírito Santo, Brazil

Index (MHDI), a composite measure of a region's well-being calculated by the United Nations Development Program, shows that Linhares progressed from a score (0.47) that classified it as "low development" in 1991 to a "high development" index (0.72) that is almost equivalent to that of Espírito Santo and Brazil, despite the peripheral location of the region. During this period, the Gini coefficient dropped from 0.60 to 0.52, twice as fast as the decrease in Espírito Santo and similar to the national-level decrease from 0.64 to 0.54. This indicates a less unequal distribution of incomes that, according to the United Nations Development Program, owes to a shift in which lower income groups are able to appropriate greater shares of the wealth generated in Linhares, as well as federal income transfer programs like Bolsa Família.

The Linhares wood and furniture industry

The wood and furniture industry emerged in Linhares in the 1960s, when global markets for the region's main agricultural crop, coffee, entered a prolonged crisis. The region's other main industry, lumber, benefited from an infusion of labor, as workers moved from coffee production to the sawmills that processed the local hardwoods. Some of the sawmills shifted their production to low-quality furniture as the region became more accessible to the country's large metropolitan markets after the construction of the BR 101 highway. In 1979, the Rigoni brothers purchased a fiberboard plant from a national firm, Mobrasa, and opened the first mass production furniture operation in Linhares, called Movelar.

Movelar became the dominant actor in the local furniture industry for the next three decades, until it entered bankruptcy in 2008. The company played a key role in diffusing knowledge about the industry and market demands to

Table 6.1 Demographic and socioeconomic indicators for Brazil, Espírito Santo (ES), and Linhares (1991–2010)

	1991			*2000*			*2010*		
	Brazil	*ES*	*Linhares*	*Brazil*	*ES*	*Linhares*	*Brazil*	*ES*	*Linhares*
Population	146,825,475	2,600,618	119,690	169,872,856	3,097,498	1 12,617	190,755,799	3,514,952	141,306
Annual population growth (%)				1.74%	2.12%	–0.66%	1.09%	1.19%	2.03%
Urban population (% of total)	76%	74%	72%	81%	79%	83%	81%	83%	86%
GDP (in millions BRT)				1,179,482,000	23,248,586	742,490	1,682,208,371	36,642,686	1,209,369
Annual GDP growth							4.3%	5.76%	6.29%
Human Development Index	0.61	0.51	0.47	0.68	0.64	0.62	0.73	0.74	0.72
Poverty rate	36.0%	39.3%	45.4%	28.7%	22.8%	25.6%	14.0%	9.5%	10.8%
Extreme poverty rate	15.6%	16.4%	18.8%	11.4%	7.0%	6.9%	5.3%	2.7%	2.5%
Gini coefficient	0.61	0.60	0.60	0.60	0.60	0.60	0.53	0.56	0.52

Source: IRGF Census, IPFA, United Nations Development Program

Note: Based on RRT value in 2000. GDP and growth rates not calculated for 1991 because IPFA used a different methodology, so results would not be comparable.

local firms. In the 1980s, for example, the Brazilian market for mass-produced furniture shifted from hardwoods to fiberboard materials that could be produced from softer, reforested woods like eucalyptus. Movelar had developed a competency in furniture pieces featuring linear, right-angled designs and was easily able to replace hardwoods with fiberboard in its production lines. Throughout the 1980s, the company developed a local network of suppliers and subcontractors, many of whom were started by former Movelar employees who ventured into business for themselves, which helped to spread knowledge about the industry to firms throughout the region (Villaschi and Bueno 2000). The company gained national reach in the 1980s, but most other local firms functioned either as exclusive suppliers to Movelar or had limited reach outside of Espírito Santo and the neighboring state of Bahia.

When Movelar went bankrupt in 2008, it sent a strong shock to the Linhares regional economy.[1] Between 2006 and 2009, the region lost 17% of its jobs in the furniture sector (more than 1% of all jobs). Employment in the furniture industry has recovered since then, increasing by 6% (to 3,800) since the low point in 2009, but still lower than the 2006 peak of 4,300 jobs. However, as the region was shedding jobs in the furniture sector, the number of firms actually increased between 2006 and 2013 by 20%, from 61 to 73, suggesting a form of horizontal fragmentation of the industry. A study by Espírito Santo's development bank, Bandes (Vieira and Barcelos 2014), shows that this process is occurring throughout the state's furniture industry (likely driven by the trend in Linhares, which has close to half of the state's employment in the sector) but not in other states. Employment in the furniture industry has decreased slightly between 2006 and 2012 in Espírito Santo, while it has increased substantially (30–42%) in states like Rio Grande do Sul, São Paulo, and Minas Gerais, where the other major furniture clusters in Brazil are located. During this period, the number of firms in Espírito Santo increased by almost 50%, while the number of firms increased much more slowly in these other states (14–30%). This indicates that the state's furniture industry is reorganizing itself around hierarchical systems of subcontracting relationships rather than vertically integrated firms.

Despite the turmoil in the industry over the past decade, Espírito Santo has been rapidly catching up with more traditional manufacturing regions in southern Brazil in recent years. Between 2007 and 2011, for example, labor productivity[2] in the state's furniture sector grew by 39%, almost double the national average of 21% and faster than even the most advanced states like Rio Grande do Sul and São Paulo (as shown in Table 6.2a). Although its profit margin[3] is still lower than the national average, it has also grown much faster since 2007, as shown in Table 6.2b. Vieira and Barcelos (2014) show that the gross production value in the furniture industry actually increased in the state between 2007 and 2011, to more than BRL 500 million. Several interviewees confirmed this trend and noted that Movelar's bankruptcy may have helped several firms when its skilled employees became unemployed and sought work in the company's competitors and suppliers. Furthermore, other firms filled market niches that became vacant as the region's leading firm gave up its entire market share. For many firms, revenues have returned to their pre-2008 levels.

Table 6.2a Labor productivity in the furniture industry in selected states (2007–2011)

State	*2007*	*2011*	*Variation*
Espírito Santo	**28.9**	**40.0**	**39%**
Rio Grande do Sul	50.4	65.6	30%
Minas Gerais	29.7	36.2	22%
Paraná	43.3	49.6	15%
Santa Catarina	27.4	31.0	13%
São Paulo	45.5	49.7	9%
Brazil	38.2	46.2	21%

Source: Bandes using IBGE data

Note: In thousands BRL (2013) value added per worker.

Table 6.2b Profit margin in the furniture industry in selected states (2007–2011)

State	*2007*	*2011*	*Variation (percentage points)*
Espírito Santo	**9%**	**27%**	**18**
Minas Gerais	17%	31%	14
Rio Grande do Sul	30%	42%	12
Paraná	26%	32%	6
Santa Catarina	20%	22%	2
São Paulo	31%	32%	1
Brazil	27%	34%	7

Source: Bandes using IBGE data

The networked forms of governance that have guided the growth of the furniture APL in Linhares have taken three forms. First, firms have engaged in partnerships with one another to allow for specialization and large economies of scale, while maintaining the ability to manufacture product lines with several pieces of furniture containing matching design qualities. Second, organized around the local trade association, Sindimol, hybrid public/private governance networks have formed that reach beyond the furniture sector and across multiple jurisdictional scales. Finally, Sindimol has helped to articulate the APL's public investment needs to the municipal government and state agencies and attract investments in industrial and urban infrastructure that have played a key role in both maintaining the furniture industry clustered in Linhares and the spillover effects into other industries.

Value chain governance to manage vertical disintegration

One of the clearest keys to the success of the Linhares furniture APL has been the ability of firms to achieve production efficiencies through collaboration with partner firms. Cost competition is fierce in the mass-produced furniture market niche in which the Linhares APL specializes. Therefore, firms that can focus their production on particular furniture pieces through investments in machinery, worker training, and shop-floor organization are able to gain greater economies of scale than if they were required to produce several furniture types on their own. However, this strategy is difficult for small firms because their primary clients, large furniture retailers, prefer to sell furniture in sets targeted to specific environments (living room, bedroom, kids' room, etc.), with matching design, colors, and the like. Therefore, the disintegration of the furniture sector in Espírito Santo, described above, required new arrangements that would allow firms to meet this market demand with smaller firms. This has been achieved through two forms of production chain governance: a hierarchical arrangement between medium and large firms and smaller subcontractors and horizontal partnerships among small firms. This section describes the emergence of these arrangements, originally driven by the production needs of the region's formerly dominant firm, Movelar.

Movelar's specialization in wardrobe manufacturing drove the rest of the region to also specialize in the same niche. As firms grew larger and moved away from being exclusive suppliers to Movelar, they broadened their scope by producing entire living environments with matching colors and designs, such as full bedrooms, bathrooms, and living rooms. Currently, larger firms often subcontract the production of other components of a room collection (say, a nightstand) or components of bigger pieces (such as the drawers or back of a chest of drawers) so that they can specialize in their flagship product and attain production efficiencies. The subcontractors deliver their orders to the leading firm on a specified date and time, and it is assembled or boxed for shipment to the buyers, usually department stores, home furnishing stores, or independent retailers.

These relationships are often set informally, but with a high degree of control from the bigger firm, which must tightly control the timing of deliveries, ensure that all finishes match perfectly, and check that safety and quality standards are met. One owner of a subcontracting firm described his firm's role as "solving the bottlenecks for the large firms." In his case, his firm produces components of furniture pieces that require manual cutting and detailing, such as the feet of armoires and other detailed pieces. This frees the leading firms to focus on more capital-intensive segments of the production chain, where advanced machinery allows for great economies of scale. These relationships allow the leading firms to spread out their production across several factories, such that they do not have to invest as much in machinery, land, or hiring workers, and can increase or decrease their production according to the demands of the market.[4]

Smaller firms have also taken steps to gain economies of scale by producing entire living spaces in partnerships with other small firms, through arrangements called *dobradinhas* (partnerships). In this case, firms jointly hire designers to sketch out a product line for a particular room and divide the production so that each firm specializes in one or two furniture pieces (the bed, bedside table, chest of drawers, or wardrobe). This allows the firm to invest only in those types of machines that they need for that particular piece and arrange their factory floors to achieve maximum economies of scale. These arrangements also require joint sales of products, so firms in *dobradinhas* also hire sales representatives and logistics firms together in order to sell their product lines. *Dobradinhas* require a great degree of coordination. Design and color schemes, safety standards, and product quality need to be closely controlled and matched, without the benefit of a large leading firm to manage the process. The informality of the arrangements requires trust between partner firms to ensure they do not defect from their relationship for any number of reasons, including the decision to cut off *dobradinha* partners without warning and produce the other's piece in house. For small enterprises that work as subcontractors for larger firms, the *dobradinhas* offer a path towards developing their own product lines without the need to invest in the machinery, factory floor space, and workforce necessary to produce the furniture for entire living environments.

Both types of production chain governance arrangements described here, vertical coordination with subcontractors and horizontal partnerships, rely heavily on close proximity among firms and on trust among the actors. The close proximity allows firms to ensure timely delivery of their products, check in on their partners' operations, and even coordinate minute details such as the timing of when furniture pieces are painted, as slight variations in the weather can cause differences in color, rendering furniture pieces in the same set unsellable. The trade association, Sindimol, has been a crucial force in attracting public investments to facilitate the continued clustering of firms in Linhares as well as fostering trust and cooperation among firms, as I discuss in the following sections.

Sindimol as a builder of social capital

The role of trust and cooperation among firms in facilitating economic development processes has been well documented in the economic sociology literature, usually under the rubric of "social capital" (Evans 1996; Putnam 1993; Woolcock 1998), and it has an even longer tradition among scholars of the embeddedness of social relations in markets (Polanyi 1944; Granovetter 1985). In Linhares, the networks that facilitated the development of the furniture APL were largely built through the joint action of firms within Sindimol, which eventually was established as a professionally run association with broad legitimacy among member firms and public-sector actors.

Local furniture entrepreneurs created Sindimol in 1987 with the goal of establishing a collective action body to represent the sector. As is usual with trade associations in Brazil, Sindimol is a legal entity representing local firms in collective bargaining processes with the workers' union and is the voice of the local industry with negotiations with the state and municipal governments on matters ranging from worker safety and environmental licensing to land use. However, its role goes beyond the strict legal requirements for trade associations. Several of the firms I interviewed described their relationships in Sindimol as completely distinct from their commercial practices. The owner of a small firm that supplies parts to some of the large firms explains the relationships within the association in a way that was echoed by several other owners of firms large and small: "Inside Sindimol we are very united, we share a lot of information. But out there, with our clients, we are each trying to take bites from one another." Sindimol has a full-time manager with a master's degree in APL management from the United Nations' Economic Commission for Latin America and the Caribbean. Aside from running the association's monthly meetings, he regularly conducts surveys to evaluate the operations of member firms, focusing on "productivity and product quality," paying particular attention to management practices. "The financial side is a consequence," he argues. "If the production side is all in order, we will consequently have satisfactory results." He uses these surveys to target specific programs for the firms, such as ways to save on energy consumption, how to optimize the use of materials, decrease absenteeism among employees, and meet environmental legislation requirements, all assisted by specialized consultants.

One of the main strengths of Sindimol is that it has built broad legitimacy among all of the segments in the industry and small and large firms alike. The most prominent, larger firms in the region rotate in the leadership of the organization, but smaller firms feel like they are well represented and that membership in the *sindicato* brings them tangible benefits. The owner of a small furniture workshop, for example, argued that their primary bottleneck is the lack of skilled carpenters in the region. Despite the fact that his firm is fairly marginal within the local industry, he spoke positively of a project he has been developing with the Sindimol manager to train carpenters in the local workforce training center. This entrepreneur also spoke of the benefits of attending the meetings and being around the larger firm owners:

> I am trying to learn, so to be near someone who has been in my position makes it much easier. My idea is this: attaching myself at the hip to those guys because a lot of times, whatever business is left over from their big firm, will be very significant for my firm, which is small.

Sindimol's current president, owner of the medium-sized firm Moverama, has moved to strengthen the representation of small and micro enterprises by creating a working group that will be composed solely of owners of suppliers and carpentry workshops.

Sindimol also operates as a venue for creating social capital among the entrepreneurs in the sector. Its headquarters are located in a large wooded lot inside the APL's main industrial park. Aside from the main office building with working spaces and conference room, it also has a large recreation area with a swimming pool, a *churrasqueira* (barbecue pit), a soccer field, and workout facilities. The same entrepreneur who emphasized the cutthroat nature of their commercial relationships described the activities of Sindimol as follows:

> Our *sindicato* is very active: we have lots of courses, meetings, and lectures. We have a recreation area and every Thursday night we have our pick-up soccer game. I am always the grill master. Two weeks ago we started a program with a personal trainer with two sessions. So our group is very united.

Sindimol's manager also uses every opportunity to build trust among the entrepreneurs. For example, he is often searching for funding to take them on trips to trade fairs, where he makes them share hotel rooms and takes them out to restaurants and nights on the town so that they end up building trust and friendships. In addition to furniture firms, other types of businesses that participate in the production chain are also invited and attend the meetings, such as local sawmills and the plant that produces cardboard boxes for firms in the APL.

Sindimol as a coordinator with the state

Sindimol has also played a key role in articulating the needs of the furniture sector with the municipal and state governments. They have been quite strategic in working with the public sector, seeking investments to address long-term challenges of the sector rather than subsidies for short-term needs. For example, they have prioritized ensuring that firms can continue to operate in close proximity to one another and not be driven out by rising rents within a growing city. They have also worked closely with state government agencies to identify improvement opportunities within the furniture industry and the investments necessary for firms to undertake in order to enter these new markets.

Sindimol coordinates the relationships between the furniture sector and the municipal government in order to address many of the productive bottlenecks in the region. This occurs through the direct participation of Sindimol in municipal matters, via planning councils and other activities. One particular example with which Sindimol has been intimately involved is the land use conflicts generated by the location of industrial activities in residential areas. These conflicts arose as the city's residential neighborhoods grew outwards without proper planning and code enforcement, eventually enveloping the many industrial areas. Consequences included negative externalities both for the residences (noise, fumes, and truck circulation from the manufacturing activities) and for the firms, which are unable to expand their operations once they are surrounded by homes. Land values in residential areas are much higher than those in industrial zones, which means higher land taxes for firms, an additional cost that chips away at the ability of firms to operate in a highly competitive sector.

As a result of these land constraints, some local firms have relocated to surrounding municipalities with a greater supply of cheap land parcels, and several others are considering doing so. However, any dispersion of local firms would likely lead to the loss of a key competitive advantage, the ability to engage in activities that require face-to-face interaction and are crucial to the survival of the local industry, such as the *dobradinhas* and the subcontracting relationships.[5] As Schmitz (1999) and others have noted, external economies that arise from agglomeration are a key ingredient to achieving collective efficiencies that allow small enterprises to improve and remain competitive.

Sindimol has worked with the municipal government to find and develop land suitable for industrial activities as a way of maintaining the strong agglomeration economies in Linhares. In 1996, for example, a group of entrepreneurs in the sector bought a one million square meter lot to develop as an industrial park. They subdivided the lot into several parcels, most of which have been occupied by furniture firms, but some by firms in other industries. For decades, the industrial park had poor infrastructure and a deficient circulation network, but following the previous municipal master plan, the city government paved its roads and provided lighting. Firms were able to move from the residential neighborhoods to the industrial park with low interest loans from the state's development bank, Bandes. Land parcels in the industrial district have become very attractive to firms, and land values have increased substantially. As a result, smaller firms are no longer able to move to the industrial park; they remain stuck in the residential areas. Sindimol has taken up the goal of working with the municipal government to create an industrial park devoted specifically to small firms with subsidized land parcels that would cost one-tenth the cost (per square meter) of the parcels in the original industrial park. The land area for the new industrial park has been identified by the city's territorial master plan, and the city is negotiating its purchase.

Territorial approaches to productive development require governance networks that can mobilize resources and engage in coordinating activities at multiple institutional and governmental scales (Davoudi et al. 2008). Sindimol has undertaken this role and established fruitful relationships with state government agencies like Bandes and the governor's Economic Development Secretariat (SEDES), quasi-public entities like the Small Business Development Agency (SEBRAE), and federal financial institutions. These relationships allow the furniture entrepreneurs to articulate the needs of the sector while ensuring that public investments in the sector are used to promote productive improvements. This relationship is evident in a number of instances described previously, such as the efforts to attract (and eventually launch) an MDF producer to the region and incentives to help firms relocate their plants to the industrial district.

Sindimol's ability to undertake vertical coordination of policies at multiple scales can be seen in its work with Bandes. Currently, Sindimol and Bandes are developing a program to help the state's furniture firms upgrade their productive capacities. For small firms that serve as subcontractors for large firms, the program creates a line of credit with favorable interest rates for businesses to purchase new machinery and productive technologies. The firms are required to undergo a consulting assignment with experts from SEBRAE, after which they are given a set of recommendations of new procedures they can undertake to improve productivity. Bandes sees these investments as lower risk (therefore allowing for more favorable terms), since the consulting will help firms to improve in areas that will directly enhance their profitability. For medium and large enterprises, Sindimol and Bandes have focused their investments on modular furniture lines. Modular furniture allows for a high degree of customization to meet a client's (and their architect's or interior designer's) specifications using computer-aided design technologies. This process requires firms to establish a venue for direct interaction with their clients, such as their own franchised stores. The Bandes program will provide credit for furniture producers to establish direct retail locations in order to facilitate the shift towards modular production. In this case, the investment in a commercial enterprise is directly linked to productive improvements, as it will allow firms to enter into more profitable niches of the furniture market than the low-end products in which the region currently specializes.

Thickening the local supply chain in a peripheral region

One of the primary bottlenecks for firms in this peripheral region has been accessing important inputs for furniture production. Although the industry evolved around native hardwoods in the 1960s, loss of that resource through deforestation and a shift in the mass-produced furniture subsector towards less expensive and more flexible fiberboard materials forced a restructuring of production in the region. Linhares's distance from other urban areas also meant that other inputs were difficult to come by and required large orders and high transportation costs. The furniture entrepreneurs in Linhares have addressed this challenge by creating partnerships between themselves and business owners in other sectors to produce the needed inputs locally, thereby thickening the supply chain in the region.

One of the early examples of this approach was the need for cardboard boxes to package the furniture pieces of various sizes for shipping. Linhares firms had to import the boxes from major urban centers in the south, which required large upfront investments, storage capacity, and high transportation costs for a relatively cheap and light product. In 1999, seven investors, four of whom were from the furniture industry, raised the capital to build a cardboard box factory in Linhares that now produces a significant portion of the boxes local industry requires. Local firms can now make smaller, more frequent orders that match exactly what they need in terms of their workload, can increase or decrease orders at the last minute, and pay almost zero transportation costs. As plants from other industries have located in Linhares, the firm has diversified its client base and supplies sectors like food processing, metal/machinery, and soft drinks.

The success in establishing the box factory has also given local entrepreneurs confidence to venture into other needed inputs for the furniture sector. For example, the high costs and inaccessibility of the most important and costly input in the furniture production process, the medium density fiberboard, is illustrative. MDF makes up 30–40% of production costs of a typical furniture piece, 20% of which is related to the cost of transporting the slabs of the material as much as 1,200 kilometers from the factories in southern Brazil. For decades, firms have engaged in various collaborative strategies for mitigating these costs, such as engaging in *dobradinhas* to purchase bulk amounts at more favorable conditions, maintaining large stocks of the materials in house, and, in the case of subcontracting relationships, receiving the materials from the larger firms. In the mid 2000s, the trade association started to discuss the idea of establishing a partnership among themselves to build a local factory to produce MDF in the Linhares region. The consulting firm Ernst & Young conducted a feasibility study but found the project to be too ambitious, concluding that there would not be enough local demand to build such a factory.

The idea resurfaced in 2012, and the trade association approached paper pulp investors to gauge their interest. The group traveled to several other MDF factories in Brazil and commissioned another study, which this time showed the possibility of a profitable factory that would meet the monthly demand for MDF in the Linhares region. This small group of seven investors attracted more partners (currently at 42) by selling shares of the project until they could raise enough capital to purchase land for the plant and harvest the eucalyptus trees that would be transformed into MDF. The group financed the expensive machinery through favorable loans from Bandes and a German bank. They decided to locate the factory 100 kilometers to the north, in the small municipality of São Mateus, so they could be eligible for additional fiscal incentives for generating 150 new jobs in a region whose economy depends on sugar cane and cattle (Cordeiro 2014).

The project will cost BRL 275 million, from an initial estimate of BRL 90 million, yet trust among the actors has held the group together and they negotiated a longer repayment window in exchange for a larger, potentially more profitable, but likely riskier venture. One of the greatest benefits to the region's firms is that they will not have to keep large stocks of MDF on site, locking up their capital. Rather, they will be able to pick up the materials from the nearby factory as they need to fill particular orders. Several of the firm's investors also noted that the MDF firm is not expected to supply its shareholders exclusively or preferentially. Rather, they stressed the fact that the mix of investors from various different sectors will ensure that the firm will need to stand on its own two feet and therefore sell the MDF at market prices. The factory broke ground in June 2016 and is expected to begin production by early 2018.

Conclusion: territorial vs. sectorial development

The Linhares case highlights the challenges of catalyzing local economic development processes in peripheral regions, as well as the importance of building networked forms of governance across the public and private spheres. Linhares developed from a primarily resource extraction and commodities-producing region into a fledgling manufacturing hub with limited regional reach in the 1960s and 1970s, and finally into an industrial region with national importance since the 1990s. The early changes were driven by adaptations to economic shocks (the overexploitation of local hardwood forests and collapse of the coffee industry), and the region's firms entered into the mass-produced furniture sector led by Movelar. From the beginning, networked forms of production chain governance were evident, as Movelar outsourced much of its production to smaller subcontractors, many of whom were its former employees who had learned the business in their years working for the firm. As other firms grew, they formed the trade association Sindimol to articulate their needs with the public sector. The APL has developed since the 1990s through a variety of networked forms of governance operating at different scales.

The most basic form of governance is the production chain arrangement between firms to achieve production efficiencies while maintaining flexibility and adaptability to market conditions. In Linhares these arrangements are structured vertically, with a leading firm subcontracting production of intermediate inputs to smaller workshops, and the horizontal *dobradinhas*, a system that has allowed small firms to remain competitive. This mode of chain governance has also been successful in thickening the local supply chain by attracting investors inside and outside the furniture sector to produce key inputs in the Linhares region. Sindimol has played an important role in facilitating these networked arrangements, both by functioning as a conduit for social interaction and building trust among members, but also in making connections with outside investors, from both the public and private sectors. Finally, Sindimol has been able to articulate the needs of the APL to municipal and state government agencies, targeting infrastructure in industrial parks and investments in the region's productive capacity.

The findings from this case study have important policy implications. Industrial policies (at the national and subnational level) have made a strong comeback in recent years. Multilateral institutions like the World Bank (Rodrik 2008) and the Inter-American Development Bank (Crespi et al. 2014), and powerful domestic institutions in Brazil such as the National Economic and Social Development Bank (Cassiolato, Lastres, and Stallivieri 2008) have actively promoted such policies, with cluster-based approaches seen as an important driver in the development of regions outside major metropolitan areas.

In Peterson (2015), I categorize the Linhares model of APL development as *territorial*, because it seeks to improve the productive capacity of its firms through broad-based investments in infrastructure, thickening the local supply chain, and facilitating collaborative relationships among actors. I contrast this approach with sectoral interventions that are narrower and more targeted towards a given set of firms, with less of a chance of positive spillovers for the region. The territorial approach has been crucial for the development of Linhares, as firms have been able to upgrade their capacities as a result of equivalent improvements among their competitors as well as the region's productive infrastructure and institutions. As this chapter demonstrates, this territorial development model requires the development of strong, networked governance that is able to organize local firms and engage with actors in other economic sectors as well as with state actors, across multiple scales.

Notes

1 The following statistics are taken from an annual survey from the Ministry of Labor (RAIS/MTE) for all municipalities in the Linhares region (see Figure 6.1), which are Linhares, Aracruz, Ibiraçu, Rio Bananal, and Sooretama.
2 Labor productivity is calculated as industrial value added per worker.
3 Profit margin is calculated as revenues minus production costs divided by production costs.
4 This is a similar type of organization to the *fabbrica diffusa* (widespread factory) of the paradigmatic industrial districts of the Third Italy (Bagnasco 1977; Brusco 1982; Piore and Sabel 1984).
5 An expert on the furniture industry from Espírito Santo's development bank, Bandes, made this point during an interview in August 2014.

References

Bagnasco, A. 1977. *Tre Italie: La problematica territoriale dello sviluppo.* Bologna: Il Mulino.

Block, F. 2008. "Swimming against the Current: The Rise of a Hidden Developmental State in the United States." *Politics & Society* 36 (2): 169–206.

Brusco, S. 1982. "The Emilian Model: Productive Decentralisation and Social Integration." *Cambridge Journal of Economics* 6 (2): 167–84.

Cassiolato, J. E., H. M. M. Lastres, and F. Stallivieri. 2008. "Introdução: políticas estaduais e mobilização de atores políticos em arranjos produtivos e inovativos locais." In *Arranjos Produtivos Locais: Uma alternativa para o desenvolvimento*, edited by J. E. Cassiolato, M. Pessoa de Matos and H. M. M. Lastres, Vol. 2, 11–38. Rio de Janeiro: E-papers.

Cordeiro, L. S. 2014. "Project: Placas do Brasil S/A." *Powerpoint, Pinheiros, ES.*

Crespi, G., E. Fernández-Arias, and E. Stein, eds. 2014. *¿Cómo repensar el desarrollo productivo? Políticas y instituciones sólidas para la transformación económica.* Washington, DC: Inter-American Development Bank.

Davoudi, S., N. Evans, F. Governa, and M. Santangelo. 2008. "Territorial Governance in the Making: Approaches, Methodologies, Practices." *Boletín de La Asociación de Geografos Españoles* 46: 33–52.

Evans, P. B. 1996. "Government Action, Social Capital and Development: Reviewing the Evidence on Synergy." *World Development* 24 (6): 1119–32.

Giuliani, E., C. Pietrobelli, and R. Rabellotti. 2005. "Upgrading in Global Value Chains: Lessons from Latin American Clusters." *World Development* 33 (4): 549–73.

Granovetter, M. 1985. "Economic Action and Social Structure: The Problem of Embeddedness." *American Journal of Sociology* 91 (3): 481–510.

Jessop, B. 1998. "The Rise of Governance and the Risks of Failure: The Case of Economic Development." *International Social Science Journal* 50 (155): 29–45.

Negoita, M., and F. Block. 2012. "Networks and Public Policies in the Global South: The Chilean Case and the Future of the Developmental Network State." *Studies in Comparative International Development* 47 (1): 1–22.

Peterson, P. 2015. "Local Production, Territorial Governance: The Political Economy of Subnational Industrial Policies in Brazil." PhD diss., University of California, Berkeley.

Piore, M. J., and C. F. Sabel. 1984. *The Second Industrial Divide: Possibilities for Prosperity*. New York: Basic Books.

Polanyi, K. 1944. *The Great Transformation: The Political and Economic Origins of Our Time*. New York: Farrar & Rinehart.

Putnam, R. D. 1993. *Making Democracy Work: Civic Traditions in Modern Italy*. Princeton, NJ: Princeton University Press.

Rodrik, D. 2008. "Normalizing Industrial Policy." Working paper. Commission on Growth and Development. Washington, DC: World Bank.

Schmitz, H. 1999. "Collective Efficiency and Increasing Returns." *Cambridge Journal of Economics* 23 (4): 465–83.

Sepulveda, L., and A. Amin. 2006. "Decentralizing Industrial Policies: Threat or Opportunity in Developing Countries." In *International Handbook on Industrial Policy*, edited by P. Bianchi and S. Labory, 321–41. Cheltenham, UK: Edward Elgar.

Vieira, P. S., and G. L. Barcelos. 2014. "Uma análise do setor moveleiro no estado do Espírito Santo: Fragmentação e reorganização produtiva." In *Proceedings from the V Encontro de Economia Do Espírito Santo*. Vitória, ES.

Villaschi, A., and F. de Oliveira Bueno. 2000. *Elementos dinâmicos do Arranjo Produtivo Madeira/Móveis no Nordeste Capixaba – Linhares*. Rio de Janeiro: IE/UFRJ.

Villaschi, A., E. S. Felipe, and U. J. de Oliveira. 2011. "*O mercado funcionou! O aprofundamento da desautonomia do estado e a diversificação da economia capixaba nos anos* 1980–2000." In *Elementos da Economia Capixaba e Trajetórias de Seu Desenvolvimento*, edited by A. Villaschi, 105–35. Vitória, ES: Flor & Cultura.

Woolcock, M. 1998. "Social Capital and Economic Development: Toward a Theoretical Synthesis and Policy Framework." *Theory and Society* 27 (2): 151–208.

7 From individual to shared leadership in Arauco, Chile

Elements of an emergent process

Miren Estensoro and Susana Franco

Introduction

Since the middle of the 1990s the focus of local economic development (LED) has rested on the generation of favorable business environments through such activities as investment in soft infrastructure (development of human resources) and on the development of new governance modes (World Bank 2003). In this case, the tools needed are systemic vision – to generate an environment that facilitates economic activity – networks and collaboration among communities, collaborative relationships among firms, and clusters. Helmsing (2001) argues similarly when referring to the systemic approach of the new LED policy generation, as do Collinge and Gibney (2010) when describing the new approach to localized policy intervention. Horlings and Padt (2013) go further, underlining that the longevity of territorial development processes and policy making depend on the leadership modes developed for that.

As is argued by Sotarauta and Beer (2017), leadership studies share the challenge of understanding how territories answer to the core question of resilience, that is, their capacity to adapt to changing circumstances. These authors specifically refer to the place leadership approach or concept as an emerging body of research that has the potential to contribute to different current academic inquiries and add an "'agential' lens through which issues and relationships of structure and agency can be explored" (Sotarauta, Beer, and Gibney 2017, 189). They also argue that "distributed place leadership can become a shared development effort" (Sotarauta et al. 2017, 190), referring to the potential to foster inclusive territorial development and answer to "intractable 'wicked' problems" (Sotarauta and Beer 2017, 212), based on shared leadership processes as new solutions.

Even if the presence of catalytic actors who are highly motivated and can trigger collaboration to respond to complex situations is crucial in any governance structure, it is not sufficient. Catalytic actors can be considered network leaders who can guide the activities of the network in the desired direction. They are necessary to spark a process of dialogue and start to generate a common vision for local development. However, for the process to endure it is also necessary to overcome the reliance on such catalytic leaders and build a process of shared leadership, where the members involved in the new governance develop a common vision for the territory that is not dependent on any particular individuals but is owned collectively. The construction of shared leadership requires, first, owning the change from previous governance modes and second, repeatedly acknowledging explicit and implicit conflicts in order to reach the consensus that will allow the process to advance. The longevity of the structure and the process will depend on various factors, including the characteristics of those in charge of creating the conditions so that the process advances.

In this chapter, the concept of complexity (Karlsen 2010) is used to show that shared leadership is necessary if the aim is to tackle territorial challenges that obstruct LED. But what are the challenges to developing shared leadership in governance structures for LED in peripheral territories, where decentralized institutions are new and governance may be fragile? How can local actors overcome these challenges? This chapter analyzes the case of a Public Private Board created in Arauco, one of the four provinces in the Chilean Bío Bío region, to articulate the implementation of a project of territorial economic development. At the time this case was analyzed, it showed signs indicating that a process of shared leadership was emerging.

The chapter seeks to enrich academic literature on the topic of shared leadership and place leadership as important elements in LED, something that has been undertheorized so far (Harmaakorpi and Niukkanen 2007; Sotarauta et al. 2017), particularly in the context of peripheral territories (see Chapter 1). In addition, the chapter also aims to help local development practitioners in comparable territories (small peripheral territories) to reflect on how they can apply these concepts to their own circumstances. In order to better achieve both aims, the chapter is structured in a way that intertwines theoretical concepts and frameworks with lessons extracted from the analysis of the case. It has been done in such a way to clarify how the construction of shared leadership takes place. Therefore, the case is introduced from the beginning together with the research methodology.

The chapter is structured as follows. After we explain the case and methodology in the next section, the following section introduces the concepts of shared leadership and territorial complexity in order to justify why the former is necessary to tackle the latter. Complexity will emerge in governance structures to foster LED, so leadership modes will have to adapt in order to manage such complexity. The following section elaborates on the argument that the different actors should feel the need to collectively act and change the way they interact to respond to complex situations, and the argument is illustrated with lessons extracted from the case. Experiences from Arauco exemplify how this feeling should be constructed with the help of catalytic actors that can activate the process. In the next section, we discuss the importance of capacity building and conflict management to improving the construction of shared leadership. The crucial role that facilitators, together with other factors, have on the durability of the process is detailed in the following section. Finally, we offer some concluding remarks.

Introducing the case and methodology

Arauco is one of the poorest provinces in Chile (26% poverty rate compared to 21% in the region and 15.1% nationally[1]). With a population of around 170,000 inhabitants, economic activity takes place mainly within the agricultural, fishing, tourism, forestry, and commerce sectors. The forestry sector exploits around 58% of the provincial area; three big firms in the sector are the owners of 80% of that land. Fishing activity is mainly carried out through artisanal fishing, which was seriously damaged by the earthquake and seaquake in 2010. According to the 2002 census, 21,000 inhabitants (13.5% of the population in the province at the time) are Mapuche, mainly located in the south of Arauco, contributing to a very strong multiethnic identity.

The governance structure analyzed in this chapter is linked to a program supported by the Multinational Investment Fund (MIF) of the Inter-American Development Bank. The program included the creation of a local institutional arrangement, a Public Private Board (PPB), which was responsible for the design and implementation of LED strategies and action plans.

Following Yin (1998), we undertook the analysis of the case primarily in a *descriptive* way within an analytical approach. As the focus is on understanding the particular *process* by which a new governance mode and the resulting structure have emerged, qualitative methods are particularly relevant, because they help to understand processes that later generate actions or other outcomes (Patton 1990; Merriam 1998; Maxwell 2004). Moreover, qualitative methods also facilitate the understanding of how actions are shaped by the unique circumstances in which they occur (Maxwell 2004).

Specifically, for this report we conducted 40 in-depth semi-structured interviews in August 2012. The majority of the interviewees were members of the PPB or beneficiaries of projects supported by the PPB with resources from the MIF program. Other relevant actors we interviewed were members of the beneficiary unions of main employment programs, NGOs, and the University of Bío Bío, the institution that carries out some of the projects promoted by the PPB in Arauco. We complemented these interviews with nonparticipant direct observation of a plenary session of the PPB and secondary document review. Finally, we held a group session with the Executive Committee of the PPB. The aim of this workshop was to gather multiple reflections in order to understand the governance approach developing through the PPB in the provincial context.

Arauco has a fragile governance structure characterized by limited collaborative culture. This was mentioned by several interviewees, such as two representatives of the private sector in the PPB, who stated

> there is a lack of associations . . . there is a tendency to individualism, mistrust of working together . . . they each want to make their own decisions. . . . Breaking with that has been difficult, we have been trying for many years.

Arauco also has centralized decision-making procedures at the regional and national levels (something characteristic of Chile), and both the governance structure and the procedures are obstacles for the generation of spaces where a common vision for the territory could emerge. However, the MIF program has been committed to implementing a LED project involving public and private actors in the decision-making process, and there were some actors who have been crucial for such a process to evolve. The PPB responsible for the implementation of the project is composed of 22 members, half from the private and half from the public sector.

Catalytic actors who have helped the process to emerge and evolve come from both private and public sectors, taking the form of individual persons or institutions. On the public side is the Regional Development Undersecretary (SUBDERE), part of the Chilean Ministry of the Interior, which had established an office in the province as a pilot experience to promote economic development through public–private collaboration and clearly backed the creation of the PPB. On the private side, the first president of the PPB, a local businessman, showed strong motivation and was very actively involved in the project. This was acknowledged in several interviews. For instance, one of the members of the PPB said: "The president dedicated a lot of effort to this project and that helped to keep some people involved, because they saw that he was not only pursuing his own benefit." The other catalytic actors were CIDERE BIOBIO (the organization that managed the project, named for the Spanish words for industrial corporation for regional development) and MIF (who provided technical assistance and funds). This was also acknowledged in several interviews; as one of the mayors explained,

> I was aware that we had to create alliances. . . . in 2004 we already started working on public–private partnerships for productive development, but they were very weak. . . . Then, in 2008, [the representatives of] CIDERE came to tell me that they were coming to work on a project and they had a different perspective and I realized that they could help us and then the MIF program that was going to strengthen the (existing) public–private partnerships appeared, and this was key.

Without the impulse of these catalytic actors, the project would never have occurred. Their role was particularly crucial at the beginning, but, as will be discussed, the process would have stagnated if it had remained dependent on them.

The PPB members took on the very complex issue that spurred creation of the Board: the low education levels in the province, which hinder employability and entrepreneurial activities (Dini 2012), triggering the need to improve their capacities so they could take advantage of new or existing opportunities. As the members of the Executive Committee of the PPB explained during the group session, the PPB members realized that they had different views on how to tackle the problem but recognized this forum as a legitimate space to address it.

Rather than something imposed by the catalytic actors, through dialogue they all decided this was the main problem they had to overcome, agreeing upon several actions to address it. Through dialogue, the shared leadership process started to emerge.

Shared leadership to manage complexity

Power plays and a dependence on unilateral decision-making can monopolize the development of networking processes, thus becoming potential obstacles for developing collaborative processes. *Shared leadership* is thus a critical element, essential for the consolidation of governance structures and networking processes to foster LED. As defined by Sotarauta (2005) and Karlsen and Larrea (2012), shared leadership is a *collective process* with no place for absolute power or one leader. It is about a joint process where many different interdependent actors participate and influence each other.

When shared leadership is constructed, participants feel that they are part of the results of these networking processes. As they learn of the importance of the network, they are motivated to work for the achievement of common goals. This sense of belonging makes them aware of their responsibility in critical situations or conflicts. Shared leadership is, therefore, the sum of all actors that join forces in LED processes. As Sotarauta (2005) states, it is this sharedness and dispersedness among the actors that causes the mission to be accomplished.

This sense of belonging and engagement comes from mutually influencing mental frameworks and cannot be imposed top down: it must originate in relationships. "It is not about a super hero that can solve a crisis and create a common ground for action" (Karlsen and Larrea 2012, 212). Accordingly, the development of these collective capabilities reduces dependency on individual participants and favors the continuance of networking processes beyond the rotation of individuals. The particular participants in these networking processes are going to change. This is inevitable. Therefore, the generation of stable participation mechanisms is necessary to construct shared values and mechanisms for collaboration (Haga 2007); shared leadership is, in the end, the result of collective learning processes.

Shared leadership is critical to tackle territorial complexity; that is, situations that encompass conflicts of interest among territorial actors (Karlsen 2010). These actors will have different interpretations and opinions about a concrete situation, problem, or challenge in the territory; accordingly, their views about solutions to overcome it will differ too. At the same time, none of the actors have the necessary resources or authority to compel the others to a consensus. Karlsen (2010) advocates activating collaboration processes and innovative governance modes that alter previous leadership modes in order to address these situations and favor shared leadership modes. Shared leadership makes it possible to manage the complexity that will emerge in any governance structure where different actors are involved or in any territorial challenge that involves more than one actor. This can also be related to what Sotarauta and

Beer (2017, 212) define as the relational and processual nature of place leadership and its capacity to develop "new and creative solutions to apparently intractable 'wicked' problems."

Participants must be conscious of the existing complexity in the governance structure and in territorial challenges; they have to be able to make the complexity explicit and share their motivation to address it. This implies that the other actors' interests and intentions have to be respected. Participants also need to assess their willingness to participate in this dialogue and their skills for reaching decisions to achieve the common aim. As a result, engagement of an emotional nature ensues. This emotional engagement is a critical element for enabling change processes and developing responsibility in actors to follow up decisions in order to implement them. Whereas the collective conversation among involved actors is a powerful tool to connect the different opinions and perspectives about the same problem, consensus is not necessarily the result. With this in mind, Karlsen (2010, 49) states that it is

> necessary to create rules for the governance network, such as for learning and reflection, for handling negative effects of conflict and consensus and for creating decision making rules. The rules created and agreed by the participating actors make it easier to use them in practice.

While creating such rules, the path to developing shared leadership continues.

First step: feel the need

As Karlsen and Larrea (2012, 217) argue, constructing shared leadership is a critical way to consolidate and provide the networks with a new platform for revitalized development:

> Shared leadership is a process that can be constructed; it is not an asset that is available from the beginning. . . . It is about generating a sense of belonging and engagement in the territorial processes that will make the responsibility of the territorial actors emerge in critical moments. . . . This engagement is expressed through the desire of individuals to make a difference and it is related to the culture and social structure of the region.

A collective approach is essential to progresssing in shared leadership processes. This collective sense, however, is constructed over time too. In the case of Arauco, local networking processes required individual and strong leadership modes at the beginning, often making these processes dependent on the capabilities of individual promoters or catalytic actors. These strong individual leaders (such as the first president of the PPB), who act as initial levers in order to start new action for territorial development, are critical to facilitate the conditions for new governance processes to emerge. This role is related to the "slack resources" referred to by Sotarauta and Beer (2017).

However, in terms of the durability of these processes and the path to develop a shared leadership process, we must keep two points in mind. The first one is that their capacities must spread to the rest of the territorial agents over time. This does not mean that the catalytic actors need to step out or be removed, but if other actors do not develop new capabilities, the process will always depend on a handful of institutions or individuals and, therefore, it will not be sustainable. The second point is that the *knowing*[2] these agents possess is going to influence the development path of the process. As their influence decreases, the dependence on their role will soften and so will the dependence on their particular knowing.

To develop shared leadership, participants need to be aware of the limits of acting in an individualistic way. According to Estensoro (2015), among the critical factors that facilitate the development of socially innovative governance modes, shared leadership will emerge if catalytic actors and the rest of the territorial actors are conscious of the need to change governance modes to foster LED in the territory. Catalytic actors must recognize the interconnectedness and interdependence among territorial actors and be aware of the need for generating new mechanisms for acting together to manage complexity and face territorial challenges. This is because none of the actors will be able to generate change on their own; at least not with the same transformative capacity. That is, they have to be aware of the need to act in a collective way and feel the need for new governance modes. This was the case in Arauco: local actors recognized that they were not able to solve the challenge of improving the province's educational level on their own. Thus, we must recognize not only the need to act in a collective way but also the need to change how we interact.

The awareness of the need for change can be sparked in different ways. It will depend on who has the catalytic role to initiate a dialogue and raise questions among local actors, as well as who can understand their perceptions and motivate them to change previous modes of interaction. This will involve delegating and sharing power, while creating conditions for others to believe in the process and feel that they are part of it. This feeling of belonging and ownership contributes to the establishment of honest communication channels, allowing participants to share their main motivation (their common challenge or problem) and making it worth the time they are going to invest trying to solve it.

Catalytic agents become powerful actors in the process and influence others, but they also assume responsibility to achieve shared objectives. They recognize themselves as "change agents," because they facilitate and encourage change. This often leads to a change in their language, with the use of the first person plural becoming the common way of talking, which reflects the emergence of a *covenantal culture*, defined by Dovey and Muller (2011, 621) as an intuitive sense of "all being in it together." This was clearly apparent in the case of Arauco, as illustrated by this literal quote by one of the members of the PPB, interviewed during the fieldwork: "we know that if we work separately it will be more difficult to seek an audience anywhere or to access consultancy services . . . or even to get resources."

In Arauco, local actors took part in the initial group reflection to define the main challenge on which the PPB should focus. However, there were several factors that hindered the critical step of recognizing the need to act in a collective way through new interaction mechanisms. Although several factors can be highlighted, we underline the ones that are most crucial and common in other peripheral regions in Latin America. The first factor is the centralist policy-making mode that characterizes Chile and other countries in the area. Despite the fact that regional and national policies advocate the creation of new governance structures to promote productive activity and economic development, the top-down approach to policy making is still prevalent. These new governance modes at subnational level are considered instruments that give capillarity to the system, but their potential to create bottom-up policy-making modes is ignored. Moreover, the case of Arauco shows that one of the main challenges related to the emergence and continuance of shared leadership processes in these partnerships is the creation of a multilevel governance mode to address the multilevel character of economic development and its articulation among different policies.

Another factor is also related to a challenge common to poor peripheral territories in Latin America: the image of a poor, antagonistic, far, and undeveloped territory has a significant impact on the generation of new governance modes. This image may reinforce the motivation to be more proactive in order to build a better future for new generations, as when a board member stated:

> I was born in Lebu and although I didn't study here, I came back. . . . My sons don't live in this province, but it is my province, I want to live here and I would like to see it as a developed territory. . . . If I can do something for that, I will do it. . . . I thought that by being a member of the the PPB I could contribute to the development of Arauco.

But it may also hinder proactivity and motivation to start new initiatives for territorial development. In the case of Arauco welfare policies, rather than being catalytic, welfare became a mere subsidy on which people depend; they prefer to continue receiving such subsidies rather than start any new ventures. That was the opinion of most interviewees about ProEmpleo, a program established by the National Training and Employment Service in Chile that was designed as an answer to the high unemployment rates in Arauco. Even if the idea was to promote employment in both the public and private sectors, the beneficiaries were mainly employed by the municipalities in menial jobs at minimum wage, offered few possibilities to develop new and competitive skills. While the interviewees acknowledged that the program was providing subsistence income to many otherwise unemployed people, they felt it also constrained them from applying for other jobs and acting on their entrepreneurial attitudes:

> Employment policies are the worst policies that we have ever had . . . these policies are the curse of our times. . . . They are generating division and selfishness among the population.
>
> (Beneficiary of a project supported by the PPB)

> These programs have provoked the loss of our main values, such as education or proactive attitude for working.
>
> (Woman in the Female Entrepreneurship School of Curanilahue)

The third factor refers to the culture of collaboration in the territory, which conditions the governance mode that may emerge, mainly because it facilitates or limits the development of new interaction modes and the interest of local actors in collective action. In this sense, one of the main challenges in the case of Arauco was the lack of networks, associations, or partnerships among local firms and producers, something that hindered starting bottom-up modes to foster LED in the province.

> The efficient articulation of private producers is one of the challenges and difficulties in this province . . . but we have to work on that and it is about changing behaviors.
>
> (Private actor, Member of the PPB)

> The collaboration requires a medium long-term perspective . . . local producers are not willing to wait.
>
> (Private actor, Member of the PPB)

Conditions for shared leadership to advance: capacity building and conflict management

Karlsen and Larrea (2012), borrowing from Sotarauta (2005), argue that different capabilities help shared leadership to emerge. We focus on the three capabilities that must go into the capacity-building process that we outline in this section and that, as Karlsen and Larrea (2012) state, the three that are relevant in understanding how a policy network evolves to make shared leadership emerge or stagnate. The first is institutional capability. *Institutional capability* is the ability to connect the different sets of actors in the territory, to develop the network and create a common ground for action. Without this basic capability, the following two cannot be developed. In the case of Arauco, the PPB managed to integrate several private actors (although it is not clear how representative they were, due to the private sector's lack of voice in the territory and the difficulties in incorporating members of the Mapuche communities) with the main public institutions. In fact, as one of the members of the PPB stated

> one of main results (of the PPB) in positive terms has been the generation of new connections that did not previously exist and sharing a common vision about the territory's development and about the challenges. More than any concrete actions, the process of articulation has been the most interesting part.

However, they still had to resolve issues of overlap with other public decision-making institutions in the territory (further discussed at the end of this section).

Second, the *networking capability* refers to the capability to generate trust, mutual dependency, loyalty, and solidarity among the participants. According to Karlsen and Larrea, the institutional and networking capabilities create the arena for shared leadership to emerge, because they allow agents to connect and create a trusting atmosphere. The third critical capability in their argument is the *socialization capability*; that is, the ability to socialize the members of a network so they feel that the network is important for them and that they will be working to achieve common goals. This opinion was expressed by several members of the Board. For instance, one of them declared: "We think that we can go away from that backwardness and the PPB is an example of a space where we can work together to change things."

These three capabilities are not necessarily innate, but can be developed and learned during the process, constituting an example of what was termed in Chapter 1 "communities of practice" that socially construct knowledge to help the process to advance. In this case, the knowledge they are generating is not meant to initiate new economic activities; rather, it focuses on capabilities related to the functioning of governance structures. This learning may be sparked by experts who share what has been codified about these topics or tell stories that disseminate best practices (Sørensen and Torfing 2009), but it is only through experiencing it themselves that these capabilities will jell.

The three capabilities are necessary for shared leadership to emerge in the process of making either conflict or consensus explicit. Unless the common goals are important enough for participants, they will not make conflict explicit, and unless they make conflict explicit, shared leadership will not emerge. As Karlsen and Larrea (2012, 222) point out,

> the process of collectively setting the rules of the game, the procedures involved in decision-making, and the roles of the participants constitute an excellent process for the development of socialization capability in the network and for rendering conflict explicit so as to reach consensus. Such processes must be managed so that conflict is made explicit in a controlled way, without paralyzing the process by breaking relationships, and without letting it stagnate due to the lack of capacity to go beyond the initial apparent consensus.

Types of conflict

Governance structures are, by nature, spaces of conflict, as different agents with different interests participate in them. The inability to manage conflict hinders the feeling of being part of the process and the durability of the process. Consensus, however, is not always positive. While it is necessary to set objectives or shared actions, if participants do not see the need to change, or if the most powerful actors do not want to change, the obstacle can block innovation (Karlsen and Larrea 2012). Conflict, on the other hand, can reveal the diversity of values, problems, and solutions and demonstrate that the process is democratic, with different voices expressing different points of view. Hence, conflict is not a negative situation per se. The key is how to manage it to facilitate change.

Different types of conflict may arise (Larrea, Aranguren, and Arrona 2013; Estensoro and Franco, 2015), such as *conflicts between hierarchy and networks*. If governments promote new governance structures to design participatory policies while simultaneously maintaining hierarchical governance structures, these structures might become consultative bodies without real decision-making power. Hierarchical structures are not exclusive to the public sector. Firms and private members might also replicate hierarchical ways, because generating a network does not necessarily imply that power asymmetries will disappear. There are usually nodes in the networks that concentrate more influence or information, which might cause conflict.

Another type of conflict is *linked to the definition of roles*. The creation of new governance structures is not a result per se but an ongoing process that will keep transforming to achieve initial goals or even to define new ones. In these processes the roles of the participants will need to be redefined, and these changes can generate conflict. But if participants manage to reach consensus that results in these changes, they will see the consequences of their work and the feeling of belonging will increase.

A third potential conflict might occur *between particular governance structures and analogous institutions* in the territory if they do not coordinate their activities. Institutions that articulate their activities and detect synergies decrease uncertainty and create the institutional context to promote LED (Ferraro and Costamagna 2000). This coordination supports governance modes that are simple enough to reduce territorial complexity while being consistent with real processes (Jessop 1998).

The argument here is that the phase when actors assume responsibility to work together and act as change agents will be critical to develop socialization capabilities. Acting together facilitates feelings of belonging, and socialization capabilities motivate collaboration. Meanwhile, the feeling of belonging will help participants face the conflicts that will naturally emerge in the networking process. Once conflicts are made explicit, a dialogue about differences becomes necessary to build consensus. This dialogue is conditioned by the mechanisms defined in the governance structure: communication channels, ways of interacting, etc. Such mechanisms are themselves redefined by these dialogues, through a continuous decision-making cycle based on conflict and consensus. Governance modes that emerge from conflict management are then the result of negotiation that prevents power plays or contradictory interests. These resulting structures might be more complex than what could be considered ideal, but they are probably the only way to get consensus for action.

In Arauco the process went through a critical phase when the board president of the PPB resigned from the presidency to continue as a mere member of the PPB. He had been such a charismatic, trust-inspiring leader and neutral participant that the continuation of the PPB was called into question, as several interviewees mentioned. This is an example of one of the conflicts they had to overcome. However, some of the other members offered a compromise, actively searching for a new president. There were several meetings and discussions where the board members demonstrated their ability to compromise, a sign that indicates that socialization capability had already emerged among the members of the PPB, giving them the fortitude to take the process forward.

Another sign of emerging shared leadership in the PPB was the restructuring of the initial governance structure, in which all 22 members participated in all the meetings. This was inefficient, because the number was too large to permit sharing information and prioritizing actions. The members went through a process to select their main areas of intervention (economic development, tourism, etc.) and decided to create one commission comprising several members for each area. Therefore, the reorganization of the decision-making mechanism they had previously designed was the outcome of a collective decision process. Through this process, a common vision was generated. This is an example that reflects their advances in the three institutional, networking, and socialization capabilities and a means to solve a conflict linked to role definition.

A critical factor for those capabilities to arise was a strong element of identity, the feeling of belonging that exists in the territory and characterizes some of the board members. This feeling impelled them to act both individually and as a group for the development of the area.

Unresolved conflicts

The case also shows other examples of conflicts that remained unresolved during the fieldwork. One of them is the lack of involvement of the Mapuche community in the PPB. A historical land dispute has resulted in violent confrontations, and several efforts have tried to resolve the situation. However, while some interviewees felt that this conflict still exists and is evident in daily life, others thought that the conflict had been overcome and a balanced situation for living together had been reached. Yet at the time the authors visited, one of the participants in the PPB who belonged to a Mapuche association had stopped attending meetings. She represented a group of Mapuche female entrepreneurs and could not understand the logic of participating in the PPB. This is an example of an implicit conflict that, at the time when the fieldwork took place, had not been managed.

Another example of unresolved conflict can be found in the lack of coordination and the overlap between the various organizations that shared the goal of promoting territorial development in Arauco. This is the case of the PPB and the Technical Advisory Committee (TAC), a space for the coordination and supervision of public services supported by the provincial government. All the initiatives depending on the provincial government had to be accepted by the TAC; this shows that any attempt at bottom-up decision making proposed by the PPB was blocked by the hierarchical logic of the TAC.

Ongoing process: clues for longevity

The case of Arauco shows that once the stage has been set with shared rules, procedures, and roles, the process of addressing territorial challenges and solving conflicts requires continuing capacity building and collective learning processes. As Karlsen and Larrea (2012) argue, this is an ongoing process in which continuous reinvention is necessary to face the unpredictable challenges that appear. This shows that shared leadership is not about ticking boxes. It is about an ongoing capacity-building process provoked by unpredictable challenges and responded to via changing actions and actors. Thus, shared leadership processes will be forced to adapt to this ongoing development process.

The continuity of the capacity-building process will depend, however, on a key factor: the role of the network managers in charge of facilitating these collaboration processes. Several authors underline the critical role of these intermediary actors for supporting and developing learning processes through networking. For instance, Lane (2001) argues that network managers must systematically develop knowledge of and experience with networks in order to create and exploit learning opportunities. This means identifying different mental maps and learning styles among participants, helping them detect conflicts and understand how to manage situations. The concept of metagovernors as described by Jessop (1998) or Sørensen and Torfing (2009) (see Chapter 2) also emphasizes the strategic and collaborative competences that network managers must develop in order to "metagovern" governance networks.

Beyond being network managers, development facilitators are people or groups who provoke continuous reflection–action–reflection processes in actors (ConectaDEL 2013). They facilitate collective learning processes and are in charge of knowledge management in participation processes (Estensoro 2015). Developing shared leadership is going to require specific forms of knowledge, knowledge that will facilitate the transformation of traditional, deep-seated assumptions regarding the modes by which actors in a territory interact with one another. Accordingly, the central argument here is that knowledge facilitators will condition shared leadership to emerge, and consequently facilitators can foster or impede shared leadership. If facilitators have specific capabilities to carry on these processes, the potential for change and overcoming shared territorial problems and challenges is consequently maximized. The capacity to manage conflict will depend on that.

The role of the facilitators was critical to keep the process going in Arauco too. In this case the president of the PPB and the staff of CIDERE BIOBIO managed the project and kept it going. However, the lack of stable resources to maintain the PPB threatened the capacity of these facilitators, and during the fieldwork this was one of the primary concerns of the members of the PPB.

Building a common vision and leadership requires time. In this case the emerging process was highly dependent on the resources linked to the MIF project. Even if the members had built trust, were committed to the process and had developed the necessary capabilities, leveraging the necessary funds to keep the process going was not easy.

Political rotation and the lack of stable resources, typical in peripheral territories, hinder the capacity to develop long-term projects and strategies, because these outlast the time individual members stay in the process. Also, in connection with the centralist way of policy making, in this case there was an apparent limitation on the extent to which the PPB could evolve to become a space where actors could discuss and influence policies that were really place-based.

Other critical elements in shared leadership include political compromise and common language in the policy-making process. As Estensoro (2015, 542) states:

> The involvement of policy makers in collaboration processes for territorial development can be counterproductive because hierarchical policy-making processes can be replicated. . . . Beyond knowing the need for a change in governance modes to encourage sustainable LED, policy makers must feel that their political objectives would be achieved and that the new governance mode would provide ways to advance these goals. The direct dialogue and knowledge cogeneration between the facilitators and policy makers are crucial. The specific approach that would be followed in the collaboration process must be clarified and shared, and the dialogue between facilitators and policy makers can facilitate this clarification.

The development of a common language, however, must also include other actors beyond policy makers in order to take advantage of the transformative potential of these collective learning processes. The capacity to share learning with involved actors and respond to shared challenges requires social and cognitive proximity. Social proximity refers to a mechanism to share objectives between agents. Although the generation of local linkages is critical, it does not necessarily follow that knowledge will be exchanged through these linkages. According to Lorentzen (2009), cognitive proximity ensures knowledge exchange will occur between different agents. Cognitive proximity refers to mental, cultural, and technological structures that facilitate common understanding between agents. The success of some actions derived from the PPB in Arauco shows that the involvement of local actors (who are considered beneficiaries of actions) in the design phase is critical in order to reach these two types of proximity and advance shared leadership. Likewise, the implementation phase of some actions based on shared leadership very often results in self-management procedures that contribute to the durability of governance structures.

Likewise, the continuation of such projects then depends on securing funds for a longer period than what international organizations usually provide. The risk is that stakeholders who have started to develop the capacities required to move to a shared leadership mode of governance might see the process interrupted if resources to support it dry up. Agents might be reluctant to reignite the process for future projects.

Conclusion

Local economic development depends on the capacity to address territorial complexity, which in turn demands adapting leadership modes and moving from individual to shared leadership. Hence, while catalytic actors are essential to spark the process, shared leadership is necessary not only for the durability of new governance structures for LED (which cannot depend on single individuals or institutions), but also for their transformative capacity in the territory. However, developing shared leadership is a lengthy process.

This chapter has shown how the development of shared leadership processes in governance structures to foster LED requires time and various enabling conditions to manage complexity and tackle complex territorial challenges. We used the analytical framework presented throughout the chapter to analyze the case of Arauco, concluding with several lessons.

Table 7.1 summarizes the different phases for developing shared leadership and the contextual elements that must be managed in each. These contextual elements, derived from the analysis of the Arauco case, are features common

Table 7.1 Phases of shared leadership and features of peripheral territories

Phases	*Contextual elements*
Activation: the role of catalytic actors	Lack of economic resources
Recognition of the need to change governance	Centralist policy-making culture Rooted negative image Lack of collaborative culture
Capacity building and conflict management	Lack of stable and capable facilitators Difficulties developing political compromises and constructing a common language Lack of long-term funding

to many peripheral territories dealing with decentralization processes. What is more, these elements are not restricted to such territories and might apply to advanced territories that face situations of territorial complexity.

In peripheral regions that lack economic resources, the role of catalytic actors who can encourage and motivate other participants is particularly critical. Stakeholders must feel an imperative to change the governance mode present in the territory, which might be hampered by centralist policy-making modes (with major decisions being made by national authorities outside the region), a rooted negative image (which might affect the attitude of the people and their interest in changing their situation), and a lack of collaborative culture.

In situations of territorial complexity, conflict is inherent. Trying to avoid it would either postpone its emergence (probably in a more virulent way) or cause the process to stagnate. Making the conflict explicit also has its perils if the capacities to manage it do not exist. Therefore, it is important to stress the role of facilitators as conflict managers with capacities to build consensus and provoke processes of reflection–action–reflection. Hence, while investing in hard infrastructure might still be necessary to promote LED in some peripheral territories, this chapter has stressed the importance of these soft capacities to the development of shared leadership. The capacities themselves will vary from place to place according to the particular circumstances.

Managing conflict, building consensus, and developing shared leadership does not mean that all stakeholders will agree on everything. It means that they agree on the essential elements that will allow the process to advance. Advancement will require, though, that all relevant stakeholders are integrated into the process. Otherwise, some latent conflicts will remain unaddressed: if all are not part of the process, their different views will not be taken into consideration and they might undermine the process from outside. What is more, they will not be able to contribute to territorial development. In Arauco, this was evident with the Mapuche communities, but in other regions it might refer to different collectives, such as women, immigrants, or others.

Finally, because these are long-term processes, the lack of resources, particularly in peripheral regions that might have lower capacity to attract funds, can hamper the process. In any case, it should be stressed that processes of shared leadership will need to be developed in place, taking into account the particular reality of each territory.

Notes

1 Results from Casen (Social Situation Survey) in 2009 in Plan Arauco Avanza (Ministerio Secretaría General de Gobierno – Gobierno de Chile 2012)

2 Knowing is defined here as the knowledge that is applied for action or which is put into practice (Karlsen 2007), what Lundvall and Johnson (1994) refer to as "know-how" (see Chapter 2). The knowledge of an individual could be greater than his or her knowing, but if the individual does not act upon such knowledge, it is not considered knowing.

References

Collinge, C., and J. Gibney. 2010. "Connecting Place, Policy, and Leadership." *Policy Studies* 31 (4): 379–91.

ConectaDEL. 2013. *Taller regional de investigación acción para el desarrollo territorial: Sistematización de la experiencia.* Workshop on Action Research for Territorial Development, Bueno Aires, Argentina, February, 25 – March 1, 2013. Workshop report. www.conectadel.org/wp-content/uploads/downloads/2013/06/Sistematizacion_TallerIA_web.pdf.

Dini, M. 2012. "Informe final de evaluación intermedia del proyecto BID-FOMIN en Arauco." Unpublished.

Dovey, K., and L. Muller. 2011. "Dangerous Learning in Edgy Contexts: Creativity and Innovation in the South African Arts Domain." *International Journal of Lifelong Education* 30 (5): 613–29.

Estensoro, M. 2015. "How Can Social Innovation Be Facilitated? Experiences from an Action Research Process in a Local Network." *Systemic Practice and Action Research* 28 (6): 527–45.

Estensoro, M., and S. Franco. 2015. "*Gestión del conflicto.*" In *Mecanismos de gestión público-privada para el desarrollo económico territorial: Una guía para la práctica*, edited by N. Laguyas and M. Romis, 83–89. Washington, DC: Fondo Multilateral de Inversiones (FOMIN)-Banco Interamericano de Desarrollo (BID).

Ferraro, C., and P. Costamagna. 2000. "*Entorno institucional y desarrollo productivo local. La importancia del ambiente y las instituciones para el desarrollo empresarial. El caso de Rafaela.*" Working paper for the Economic Commission for Latin America and the Caribbean (CEPAL), Buenos Aires.

Haga, T. 2007. "Orchestration of Networking Processes." PhD diss., Norwegian University of Science and Technology, Trondheim, Norway.

Harmaakorpi, V., and H. Niukkanen. 2007. "Leadership in Different Kinds of Regional Development Networks." *Baltic Journal of Management* 2 (1): 80–96.

Helmsing, B. 2001. "Externalities, Learning and Governance: New Perspectives on Local Economic Development." *Development and Change* 32 (2): 277–308.

Horlings, I., and F. Padt. 2013. "Leadership for Sustainable Regional Development in Rural Areas: Bridging Personal and Institutional Aspects." *Sustainable Development* 21 (6): 413–24.

Jessop, B. 1998. "The Rise of Governance and the Risks of Failure: The Case of Economic Development." *International Social Science Journal* 155: 29–45.

Karlsen, J. 2007. "The Regional Role of the University. A Study of Knowledge Creation in the Agora between Agder University College and Regional Actors in Agder, Norway." PhD diss., Norwegian University of Science and Technology, Trondheim, Norway.

Karlsen, J. 2010. "Regional Complexity and the Need for Engaged Governance." *Ekonomiaz* 74 (2): 36–55.

Karlsen, J., and M. Larrea. 2012. "Emergence of Shared Leadership in Situations of Conflict – Mission Impossible? Long Term Experiences from a Local Network in the Basque Country." In *Leadership and Change in Sustainable Regional Development*, edited by M. Sotarauta, I. Horlings, and J. Liddle, 212–33. Abingdon, UK: Routledge.

Lane, C. 2001. "Organizational Learning in Supplier Networks." In *Handbook of Organizational Learning & Knowledge*, edited by M. Dierkes, A. B. Antal, J. Child, and I. Nonaka, 699–715. New York: Oxford University Press.

Larrea, M., M. J. Aranguren, and A. Arrona. 2013. "The Role of Governance in the Sustainability of Public Private Partnerships: Reflections on a Long Term Case in the Basque Country." Unpublished.

Lorentzen, A. 2009. "*Las redes de conocimiento en el espacio. Reflexiones de una geógrafa sobre la literatura de los sistemas regionales de innovación.*" *Ekonomiaz* 70 (1): 170–83.

Lundvall, B. A., and B. Johnson. 1994. "The Learning Economy." *Journal of Industry Studies* 1 (2): 23–43.

Maxwell, J. A. 2004. "Causal Explanation, Qualitative Research, and Scientific Inquiry in Education." *Educational Researcher* 33 (2): 3–11.

Merriam, S. 1998. *Case Study Research in Education: A Qualitative Approach*. San Francisco, CA: Jossey-Bass.

Ministerio Secretaría General de Gobierno – Gobierno de Chile. 2012. "Arauco Avanza: Programa de Desarrollo Integral. *Año 2012–2014*" www.intendenciabio bio.gov.cl/filesapp/PlanAraucoAvanza.pdf.

Patton, M. Q. 1990. *Qualitative Evaluation and Research Methods*. 2nd ed. Newbury Park, CA: Sage.

Sørensen, E., and J. Torfing. 2009. "Making Governance Networks Effective and Democratic through Metagovernance." *Public Administration* 87: 234–58.

Sotarauta, M. 2005. "Shared Leadership and Dynamic Capabilities in Regional Development." In *Regionalism Contested: Institutions, Society and Governance*, edited by S. Halkier, 53–72. Urban and Regional Planning and Development Series. Farnham, UK: Ashgate Publishing.

Sotarauta, M., and A. Beer. 2017. "Governance, Agency and Place Leadership: Lessons from a Cross-National Analysis." *Regional Studies* 51 (2): 210–23.

Sotarauta, M., A. Beer, and J. Gibney. 2017. "Making Sense of Leadership in Urban and Regional Development."*Regional Studies* 51 (2): 187–93.

World Bank 2003. *Local Economic Development, a Primer. Developing and Implementing Local Development Strategies and Action Plans*. Washington: The World Bank.

Yin, R. K. 1998. "The Abridged Version of Case Study Research." In *Handbook of Applied Social Research Methods*, edited by L. Bickman and D. J. Rog, 229–59. Thousand Oaks, CA: Sage Publications.

8 Intergenerational leadership and local economic development

Towards a new kind of artisan association in Mompox, Colombia

Sergio Montero and Nathalia Calderón

Introduction

Given the growing importance for institutions to understand local and regional development (Pike, Rodríguez-Pose, and Tomaney 2017; Rodríguez-Pose 2013), economic development strategies and policies in cities and regions of Latin America have increasingly placed emphasis on factors such as building governance and collaborative networks between public and private actors (Chapple, Montero, and Sosa 2012). Despite the optimism in the local economic development literature about the possibility that governance and networks can provide new mechanisms for better understanding and addressing territorial imbalances, networks and associations are not new in most small and medium-sized cities and peripheral regions of Latin America, where solidarity relations and cooperatives have existed for decades. Furthermore, several authors have shown that governance mechanisms can fail and become an obstacle to local economic development (Jessop 1998). Governance processes involve collaboration among actors with different agendas that can easily become bottlenecks to local economic development if mechanisms for inclusion, leadership, and conflict management are not in place. In this context, it is critical to understand how certain forms of networks and association can be translated into local economic development results. Using Mompox as a case study, this chapter analyzes the relationship between association structure, leadership, and local economic development, to identify some theoretical and empirical elements that improve our understanding of this relationship in the context of smaller cities in Latin America.

Mompox, a Colombian municipality located in the northwestern part of the country and declared as World Heritage Site by UNESCO, is a small and economically disadvantaged city that has, nevertheless, great economic potential given its rich cultural heritage. With a population of less than fifty thousand inhabitants, Mompox's local economy is distinguished by a long artisan tradition, specifically, the art of filigree. This technique is a complex process using fine gold and silver threads that mixes European, Arab, and indigenous knowledge and draws from more than 230 years of tradition. In addition to gold and silver filigree, other important Mompox artisanal activities include woodworking, hand embroidery, pottery, and food products such as *queso de capa* and lemon desserts. Artisanal work represents more than half of the municipality's income (De La Hoz 2011). As of 2011, there were 82 associated micro-enterprises: 38 filigree workshops, 28 carpenter's workshops, and 18 women's associations. There are even more artisan workshops: 96 carpenter's workshops, employing on average six to ten workers, and 80 filigree workshops, with six to 22 employees depending on their size (De La Hoz 2011). Artisanal activity in Mompox is not only important for its income generation potential, but is also a crucial cultural element of *Momposino* local identity. The fact that this knowledge has been transmitted from generation to generation is often a source of local pride.

According to calculations by the mayor's office, in 2012 there were 120 filigree artisans in the municipality, most of which are part of the local filigree artisan association ASOMOM (Alcaldía de Mompox, 2012). As in other Colombian municipalities dependent on artisanal work to sustain the local economy, in Mompox different governmental entities, foreign development agencies, and NGOs have tried to increase artisan productivity and income, often through the creation of cooperatives or associations of artisans. This has led to the proliferation in recent decades of association initiatives in response to the arrival of a particular agency or project. Often, however, the same local leaders are repeatedly selected to head these initiatives and similar schemes are replicated while funds last. The consequence of these initiatives has been low levels of satisfaction and trust about the creation of new associations and their potential contribution to the development of the municipality, because these leadership choices reinforce existing hierarchies among artisans and do not allow younger generations to participate. This, in turn, results in low levels of product innovation, significant youth migration to larger cities, and fragile association structures that often disappear after some years.

This chapter analyzes the case of a recently created group of young artisans in Mompox that has broken with the traditional type of association. The case also shows how NGOs and development agencies can support and fund local associations of artisans and producers in ways that are more inclusive, endogenous, and sustainable than previous efforts at creating associations.

Twenty interviews were conducted between July and September 2016 with community leaders, artisans, and local public servants in Mompox, and five interviews were conducted in Bogotá with officials from the Ministry of Culture, the National Planning Department (DNP) of Colombia, and experts in local economic development from Artesanías de Colombia and the Japan International Cooperation Agency (JICA). Through these interviews, primary information was collected to conduct an analysis of governance and economic development dynamics within associations of filigree artisans in Mompox.

This chapter is structured in three sections following this introduction. The first section provides a review of some of the main debates concerning local economic development, with special emphasis on the role of associations and leadership. The second section analyzes the dynamics of association and leadership in the case of artisanal filigree work in Mompox. It examines the case of the Grupo de Artesanos Independientes (GAI) as a new kind of association in Mompox that has the potential to create more inclusive local economic development processes. Specifically, this chapter analyzes three key elements that characterize this new form of association: (1) the gradual growth of the association supported by promoting entities through progressive trust-building tactics, (2) collective decision making on production processes, and (3) the involvement of young people in leadership positions. In the third and final section we reflect on how the experience of the GAI and Mompox can provide lessons and policy recommendations for other Latin American regions. We show the importance of developing intergenerational leadership so that associations can translate into inclusive local development.

Associations, leadership, and local economic development in Latin America

Although the first regional development planning initiatives in Latin America emerged in the 1930s (Boisier 2012), it was not until the second half of the twentieth century that local and regional development studies, as well as government interventions to boost the economic development of peripheral regions, expanded significantly (Moncayo Jiménez 2004; Alburquerque 2014). From more mainstream economic visions that gave special emphasis

Figure 8.1 Young leaders of Grupo de Artesanos Independientes (GAI) in Mompox

Source: Ana María Leaño (Universidad de los Andes)

to the central government as a promoter of the development of peripheral regions through strategies such as growth poles, there has been a gradual transition to a vision that emphasizes the importance of decentralization and local and regional institutions as a key force behind the development of territories (Chapple et al. 2012). From this perspective, the idea that local development strategies have to go beyond the economic realm to incorporate sociocultural and institutional dimensions (Méndez, Michelini, and Romeiro 2006) has become consolidated in the region, and terms such as *networks, governance*, and *institutions* have become common denominators in Latin American territorial development policies (Gallichio 2004; Aguilar 2010; Montero 2015). For instance, Cabrero, Orihuela, and Ziccardi (2003) assert that in order to achieve cities capable of attracting investment, generating employment, and improving the quality of life of citizens, the interaction of governmental, social, and economic actors at the local level is essential. Similarly, Méndez et al. (2006) have defined innovative cities as those that use strategies to acquire or generate network knowledge. The importance of networks has become so significant that their absence is seen as a possible obstacle to the innovation and development path (Méndez 2002). Therefore, given the perceived ineffectiveness of centralist and top-down approaches and policies to boost territorial development in the past, there is a growing interest in Latin America to better conceptualize and understand what kind of institutions, networks, and practices produce and reproduce economic development (Caravaca, González, and Silva 2005).

However, several authors in the governance literature have shown how governance and networks can also fail as an approach to promote local economic development (Jessop 1998; Montero 2015). These failures can reside in the impossibility of solving conflicts among multiple participants or the lack of representation of some actors in participatory mechanisms (Jessop 1998). The greater number of actors involved in governance processes has become a double-edged sword. Networks have the advantage of allowing the design and implementation of a strategy that may include different actors, yet who is – and who is not – represented in the process or in the network is the biggest disadvantage of this way of making decisions. The lack of representation of certain actors, either directly (not invited to participate) or indirectly (invited to participate but unfamiliar with the language and dynamics of participatory planning or unable to counter existing power dynamics), can lead to the reproduction of existing social hierarchies or the design of agendas that harm vulnerable or underrepresented populations (Montero 2015). We cannot therefore assume that the fact that decisions about local economic development are made through networks or associations means that they are automatically horizontal or more inclusive.

The success of associations and networks in fostering local economic development is usually determined by territorial variables such as trust or social capital (Rodríguez-Pose 2013). In particular, trust, defined as a socially constructed phenomenon that allows the emergence and stability of networks over time, is an element that contributes to the local economic development of territories

(Murphy 2006). Trust is decisive not only in the quality or intensity of associations and networks, it also influences the degree of openness of networks to new participants and ideas. But the effective functioning of governance mechanisms of a territory also requires catalytic actors with the capacity to influence others to achieve common development goals and objectives (Uyarra et al. 2017; Sotarauta, Horlings, and Liddle 2012; Stimson, Stough, and Salazar 2009). In early stages, these actors can appear as individual leaders. However, to guarantee the sustainability of local economic development processes, they need to move towards shared leadership arrangements that allow leaders and participants to make collective decisions with a common view of territorial development (Beer 2014). In this context, the capacity of these leaders to act as agents of change is key. Karlsen and Larrea (2012) distinguish among three types of capabilities that facilitate the emergence of shared leadership processes: institutional, networking, and socialization capabilities. Institutional capability refers to the ability to connect actors in a network and provide spaces for action. Networking capability consists in the ability to build trust, solidarity, and loyalty between actors. Socialization capability refers to the ability of members of a network or association to value the network and work towards the achievement of common goals.

Yet the literature on leadership and local economic development has said very little about the importance of intergenerational leadership to promote inclusive processes of local economic development. Indeed, one key finding of this chapter is the widespread disenchantment in Mompox with traditional forms of association in which a small number of individual leaders – often male and older *maestros* – become representatives of all local artisans. The empirical evidence in the following sections will show that this kind of leadership structure reinforces pre-existing hierarchies among artisans, not allowing younger generations to be included and represented in these associations. In this context, a group of young artisans that emerged in 2015 offers an interesting example of a new kind of association in Mompox that breaks with the old model of associations built around traditional leaders and provides a renewed force for collective action among younger generations. While still new and quite fragile, the analysis of this new association shows the importance of including factors such as intergenerational leadership to better address the relationships among association structure, leadership, and local economic development.

Mompox: disappointment with traditional forms of association in the filigree business

Our interviews in Mompox show a general perception of disenchantment with traditional forms of associations, especially in the filigree business. These findings confirm the results of a 2013 study of Artesanías de Colombia, a public entity committed to the development of the handicraft sector in Colombia. This study identified a weakness in the promotion of associative processes among artisans in Mompox due to an individualistic attitude among artisans and a lack of trust in collective initiatives. The study also emphasized the weakening of leaders of organizations due to the low generational change and the large number of responsibilities that rest on them, the lack of communication among members of associations, and the naïveté of external organizations that come to support processes of economic development in the region (Artesanías de Colombia 2013). As in other poor and peripheral Colombian municipalities, in Mompox public agencies, development agencies, philanthropic organizations, and NGOs often condition their investments in local economic development on the creation of a new association. This has led to a proliferation of associations in Mompox, often created to respond to the arrival of a particular project. This is the case of Comercializadora Filigriclin, which was related to a project of Proexport, or the network of filigree artisans Mompox Filigrana, which was the result of a project of Fundació Corona with the purpose of internationalizing the filigree of Mompox. Often, the funds for these initiatives disappear over time along with the association, undermining local expectations about the creation of new associations and their sustainability.

Currently, there are two major filigree associations in Mompox: Asociacion de Orfebres Momposinos (ADOM) and Asociación de Orfebres del Municipio de Mompox (ASOMON). The first one, created in 1996, has 36 members, and the second one was created in 2012 as a result of a call launched by the One Village One Product (OVOP) Program, an initiative of JICA to promote local development, with approximately 52 members. Due to particular interests and disagreements between its members, both associations refused to create a single union of filigree artisans (Artesanías de Colombia 2013).

One of the main reasons given by our interviewees to justify their skepticism about associations is the corruption in the administration of associations, along with the co-optation of benefits by certain leaders. This has led to the filigree community being less confident in the potential of associations. One artisan dedicated to filigree jewelry, who has lost his faith in associations after his experience in several association initiatives in Mompox, reported:

> When the board members of an association pursue personal interests, then the other members get disappointed and they all lose confidence in the association. . . . There is a loss of credibility, a whole process gets lost, a whole story, because two or three leaders took advantage. Recovering from this is much more difficult than creating a new association.
>
> (Artisan 1, 2016)

The presence of individual leaders who remain in power for long periods of time has been a constant complaint about associations in the filigree business in the municipality. For example, one of the territorial coordinators of the OVOP project emphasizes the existence of "negative long-term leaders" as one of the major challenges faced by artisan associations: "The problem is that when a negative leader is empowered, it starts to become exclusionary because he is going to choose his friends, his beneficiaries" (JICA Officer 1, 2016).

This is the case with associations such as ADOM and ASOMON, whose boards have tended to be chaired by the same representatives year after year. In addition to not allowing the rotation of leadership, this type of leadership has been characterized by personal gain at the expense of the association and the work of the rest of the members:

> The initial experience in the association we started was quite difficult. We saw how the leader pursued his personal goals and not those of the community. . . . There was that identity and enthusiasm from all members, but we saw that all the management was directed only to his own benefit, we saw the discrepancy that in a short period of time he remodeled his house, bought his own car, set up his own business and we felt that we did not own anything.
>
> (Artisan 2, GAI member, 2016)

This kind of leader behavior means that the resources they receive as an association do not affect all members equally. This thus illustrates the lack of a collective vision of territorial development in the association. Some of the members took advantage of networking contacts for their personal benefit, leaving the impression among other members that they had been used to meet particular interests. From their experience with associations in Mompox, including ADOM and ASOMON, several interviewees claimed that when machinery or resources are provided to the association, it is quite common that they stay in the house of one of the members, preventing others from enjoying the resource. This feeling is common among many artisans of the community:

> They [filigree artisans] said that when they were in those associations [ADOM and ASOMON] they felt that they had no voice, that they were simply the workforce for fairs or for workshops, that they had no leadership, participation, or good representation.
>
> (JICA Officer 1, 2016)

Towards more inclusive associations in Mompox: Grupo de Artesanos Independientes

Against this landscape of disenchantment and fatigue with traditional forms of association in the filigree business, a new kind of association, the Grupo de Artesanos Independientes (GAI), emerged in Mompox in 2015. GAI was born as a result of a call made by Artesanías de Colombia and JICA. The purpose was to bring together a group of artisans who worked independently and had not had the opportunity to show their work in commercial places. The group is currently made up of 20 artisans organized for a common cause: the making of a new group of filigree business leaders that includes young people and women, to break with the traditional figure of the older man (or *maestro*) who usually leads artisan associations. Although most of the current members are young artisans, they are also all masters and benefit from the experience and trajectory of older people in the group, who are considered *maestros de maestros*. The intergenerational collaboration and more horizontal structure encourage the sense among the youngest of belonging to the filigree business. A young artisan member of GAI says:

> We were in another association before, but we have obtained more profit and benefits in this group; in a short time we have obtained more. Here we receive, there we could only contribute. Here we make the group together and we all benefit. In associations where not all members benefit equally, we feel discouraged.
>
> (Artisan 3, GAI member, 2016)

In contrast to self-serving individual leadership, shared leadership is a process in which different interdependent actors influence each other with a common shared vision or a "common dream," as some of our interviewees put it. It is a collective process in which actors must collaborate to achieve goals that otherwise would not be achieved (Karlsen and Larrea 2012). Unlike other traditional associations, which emphasize forms of cooperative organization and a limited and small number of leaders, in the case of the GAI, leaders and other members of the group make decisions together and obtain benefits equally. Likewise, the work of leaders is voluntary and not-for-profit, allowing all members to be at the same level. A young member of the GAI says:

> The results are all the same, we are all on the same level, that makes us believe in a dream and we all believe in this same dream because there is no one who can legally say: I am going to receive these resources and I will decide how to use them.
>
> (Artisan 2, GAI member, 2016)

The ability to make decisions collectively and profit equitably without asymmetries of power strengthens trust and the sense of belonging – and makes it possible for leadership to be shared within the group. Building and maintaining trust in leaders is essential to ensure the success of projects and the sustainability of the group. Based on her own experience in another association, a GAI artisan member is aware of the negative impact of a leader who does not guide collective processes for everyone's benefit: "You get hurt when you delegate trust and responsibility to one artisan partner and he fails the community. Then that disappointment is the impact we all receive" (Artisan 2, GAI member, 2016).

The following sections analyze three key elements that characterize this new form of association in Mompox with the potential to create more inclusive local development: (1) the gradual growth of the association supported by promoting entities through progressive confidence-building tactics, (2) collective decision making about production, and (3) the involvement of young people in leadership positions.

Gradual growth and trust-building tactics

Usually, the creation of artisan associations in small and intermediate cities and peripheral regions of Latin America is totally or partially funded by governmental entities, NGOs, or international development agencies. It is also common that the role of these entities is limited to granting resources at a specific initial moment during the creation of an association, without generating the necessary tools for its proper administration and development. This phenomenon can generate patterns of dependence by the community on the promoting entities and the funds they offer (Chapple and Montero 2016). In the creation and consolidation of Mompox's GAI, the financial support and guidance of two promoting entities – JICA and Artesanías de Colombia – were decisive. Given the past experiences of both entities with associations of artisans and small producers that disappear within a few years or months, together with the frustration concerning the process of associating in Mompox, the GAI was explicitly designed from the beginning to create gradual trust- and confidence-building processes among the group, even before the main transfer of resources occurred. Both promoters and group members consider this characteristic key to the success of the GAI:

> We have been receiving responsibilities gradually, and that makes us feel that we have a father and mother that are these two entities. . . . We have been growing with them; we feel that each time the group is assuming more responsibilities until finally it can take off by itself.
>
> (Artisan 2, GAI member, 2016)

Together with this gradual support, our interviews also revealed another successful characteristic of the GAI, the importance of creating processes and institutions to build trust among its members, or what we call in this section "trust-building tactics." In the case of the GAI, two of these tactics were particularly important: the creation of self-saving groups and a system of internal accountability.

Self-saving groups

One of the methodologies proposed by JICA to strengthen teamwork and trust among artisans is the "self-saving group." This methodology works as a cyclical fund so that artisans manage their own resources with a common objective, which translates into goals in cycles they define together. This methodology allows all grouped artisans to make collective decisions about the resources they get from a common objective that is defined by them. Lending circles and women's solidarity groups have been extensively discussed in the microfinance literature, since this has been a significant novelty of the now well-known Grameen Bank microfinance model (Christen 2006). One form of microfinance is self-help groups (SHGs), in which an NGO, government agency, or bank promotes the formation of groups and gives them support services. An SHG is an economically and socially homogenous group of 10 to 20 people who come together voluntarily to collect savings on a regular basis and use the resources of the group to lend to each other (Christen 2006; Jakimow and Kilby 2006). SHGs generally begin by collecting and lending their own savings, sometimes for a long period of time, before receiving a bank loan, which tends to generate more disciplined groups (Murray and Rosenberg 2006). SHGs in India are an important development tool that has encouraged the development of leadership roles among its members, particularly women (Jakimow and Kilby 2006; Harper 2002; Reddy and Manak 2005). In this context, numerous studies have shown both the potential of these circles to create social capital among poor peasants (Dowla 2006) and the limits of this generated social capital to produce significant development outcomes in the long term, given that it hardly questions existing financial hierarchies (Rankin 2002).

Artisans in Mompox often do not have access to institutional credit. They need to work with their own resources or borrow in the informal market at high interest rates, limiting their capacity for expansion. According to De La Hoz (2011), despite being part of an association, many artisans operate on their own, which limits their ability to improve competitiveness, as well as achieve economies of scale. According to one of JICA's officers involved in the GAI project in Mompox, the first cycle of self-savings groups was very useful not only to provide alternative funding to artisans but also to create trust among them:

> It helped them learn how to save, to have a saving culture and a common goal, to generate trust, teamwork, and collaboration among them, but above all to have a common goal. They did a first cycle and they did it quite well, they were very happy and they started the second cycle and they are doing it by themselves now, they define their board, the accountants, the prosecutor, the one with the keys, the one with the box, etc.
>
> (JICA Officer 1, 2016)

In addition to promoting a saving culture in the group, this strategy is designed to generate trust. Although the initial guidelines were proposed by JICA, artisans have control and autonomy over the group and are in charge of managing resources and defining the rules. As one GAI member expressed:

> There was something that has also led us to be more united and this was that we had an auto-saving group, which was created within the GAI. There, we have some initial rules that were led by people from JICA, but right now we have control of the saving group. When we started this second cycle, we already had a goal: it was the purchase of raw materials for the production of the end of the year. We already have rules that we will be changing and adding to this new cycle.
>
> (Artisan 2, GAI member, 2016)

Internal accountability

In addition to the self-saving group, another trust-building tactic developed for the GAI from the beginning was the creation of a system of accountability that works as a way both to train artisans in basic accountability and to give them feedback tools:

> By being together there are responsibilities. If an association representative goes [to trade fairs or events], they have to report to the whole group. . . . This is to avoid what always happens in other associations and previous trade fairs . . . usually the members that do not go to Bogotá [to a trade fair] do not receive that information. . . . The representative, on the other hand, he gets to know everything, but the one who stays, the one who sends his or her product, they do not know that feedback [unless someone tells them].
>
> (JICA Officer 2, 2016)

In addition to allowing more transparent processes, a proper accountability system allows artisans to know how customers perceive their products and lets them build the trust needed to create shared leadership that ensures the continuity of collaboration established through the association. Despite the recency of its formation, the experience of GAI shows the great potential of local economic development initiatives based on shared and intergenerational leadership. Although the GAI is not yet legally constituted and its members are still in the process of consolidation (which is part of the gradual growth strategy), the GAI represents a new type of association that demonstrates that it is not necessary to adopt a formal structure from the beginning to build trust and successful collaborative networks. Rather, one path to achieve this is through gradual growth strategies and various trust-building tactics.

Collective decision making

Within the dynamics of the group, it is also important to highlight the group's collective decision making regarding production. These decisions allow artisans to get involved and feel linked to the group, and yet maintain certain personal independence:

> We cannot say that we are all going to have machine-made jewelry that will weigh exactly the same. But there is a balance to avoid disproportion between artisans. We seek that everyone's sales are somehow balanced and that everyone is satisfied with their work. We always gather before producing, we are always integrated.
>
> (Artisan 2, GAI member, 2016)

The absence of this kind of decision making in other associations of artisans in Mompox created a lack of credibility and skepticism about the benefits of associating. For example, reflecting on the lack of collective decision making regarding production in other associations, a member of the GAI says that this was, in fact, one of the main causes of mistrust in previous associations: "That is the distrust where one says: I do not believe in association" (Artisan 3, GAI member, 2016).

Interviews conducted in the field show that equitable allocation of roles in the production process contributes to the formation of social capital as well as the creation of networks of intergenerational collaboration among artisans. In the case of the GAI, everything begins with Mr. Luis Jiménez, who is the oldest in the group and because of his great experience is responsible for La Casa del Artesano. Mr. Jiménez is in charge of the first production steps, which involves tasks on a large scale. From there, each artisan in the workshop produces his product, but all are involved in the work of the group throughout the process:

> Mr. Luis Jiménez is the oldest in the group. He is very old and he is the person who takes care of La Casa del Artesano. That is where the process begins. He is the one who helps us in the first part of the measurement process, lamination, etc. That which is done on a large scale, that part is supported by him. From there, everyone in the workshops begins to elaborate their product and we are all involved, because the partner in the first production made a design, that design might be made by other partner in the second production, then the one who did it first transmits the knowledge to another partner and supports and advises him so he can make the jewelry similar to the one made by the previous partner.
>
> (Artisan 2, GAI member, 2016)

There are important networks of collaboration and trust generation in the process of designing filigree jewelry. The artisan who makes a design in the first part of the production transmits the knowledge to another partner, supporting his work throughout the process so he can make a similar piece of jewelry. This ability to work in a network throughout the production process reinforces the trust and feelings of cooperation among artisans. The existence of shared leadership also becomes an important mechanism for conflict resolution based on dialogue and collective decisions. For example, when on one occasion GAI artisans found a quality defect in the filigree production of one of their members, the production was divided among three artisans to make sure it met minimum quality standards. As one GAI member puts it, the partner learned the lesson and understood that he must deliver on time and in optimal conditions: "We have failures, but we all talk about it and try to solve it" (Artisan 2, GAI member, 2016).

Youth involvement and intergenerational leadership

The absence of young people in leadership positions in traditional associations of artisans in Mompox has resulted in a lack of interest among the younger generation to continue the tradition and ancestral knowledge that filigree jewelry represents. Many of them prefer to migrate to bigger cities and engage in other activities. Particularly in relation to associations of filigree artisans, the general perception is that the dynamics within them do not favor fair economic retribution for the great majority of artisans and only a few manage to obtain any benefits at all. In addition to the risk involved for the continuity of artisan knowledge, the lack of young leaders also leads to stagnation and lack of innovation in the activity, since new generations are more familiar with new technology tools and have the greatest potential for contributing with creative and innovative ideas. The GAI, contrary to traditional associations, offers an opportunity for young people to get involved and find economic opportunity in artisan handicrafts:

> This is not like the other two associations [ADOM and ASOMON], where it is always the old artisans who get to go to Expoartesanías.[1] Instead here we have a new wave of "we are young, we will start well from the beginning, we are going to establish our own rules".
>
> (JICA Officer 2, 2016)

One of the members of the GAI emphasizes the importance of the group in preserving the artisan activity that has tended to disappear due to the lack of interest in filigree among younger people:

> To own and retake our tradition, our culture, all that ancestral and traditional work . . . there are moments in which the new generations end up being put aside and this group has older people who are the parents, the teachers, but it has many young people too who are also welcome to own this legacy, and at this moment our work is to promote this tradition, to show it to many people, to start valuing what we do and translate these achievements in the personal life of each member.
>
> (Artisan 2, GAI member, 2016)

In addition to significant participation of people in their thirties and forties in the group, some have younger assistants who have the opportunity to learn the work:

> There is a base of young people between the ages of thirty and forty who are doing the work, but some of them have also involved assistants. . . . I was in the workshops and they are really younger than them, I saw young people of eighteen, twenty, twenty-two years. That is good because they are transferring knowledge to the younger ones.
>
> (JICA Officer 1, 2016)

According to the JICA interviewees, although the GAI is not exempt from the vices of self-serving individual leadership, the participation of young people saves the group from being vitiated by these traditional forms of leadership. The contribution of the younger generation is reflected in new impetus and renewed energy transmitted to the rest of the members, without ignoring the great experience and trajectory of older artisans and the importance they have within the group. As one GAI member says: "there is a balance between youth and *maestros*' knowledge." The joint presence of intergenerational collaboration translates into positive effects for the group:

> With the strength of youth we are going to take advantage of the energies, we have to keep moving forward. But those old teachers that we have within the group are also the force to be able to support them and move forward, all of us at the same time.
>
> (Artisan 2, GAI member, 2016)

Table 8.1 sums up the characteristics of traditional artisan associations and the new Grupo de Artesanos Independientes.

Table 8.1 Comparison of the traditional and the new forms of artisan association in Mompox

	Traditional associations (ADOM / ASOMON)	*New forms of association (GAI)*
Type of leadership	Self-serving individual leadership repeated over time; legal representative figures	Shared leadership; nonprofit, volunteer leadership figures
Mechanisms of participation	Only a few have a voice in decision making, most of them older men (*maestros*, or master artisans).	Greater diversity of leaders; an effort is made to include young people and women in leadership positions.
Conflict management	Absence of effective conflict resolution mechanisms	Mechanisms of conflict resolution through dialogue in place
Dependence on promoting entities	High dependence on funds and external resources in initial stages	Gradual independence and acquisition of responsibilities by members over time
Decision making	Decisions made by the directive board	Collective decision making
Trust level	Low levels of trust; trust is assumed to exist from beginning	Increasing levels of trust; trust-building tactics in place
Accountability	No effective accountability and feedback mechanisms in place	Accountability and feedback mechanisms as an important part of the association
Generational involvement	Little presence of young people in leadership positions	Greater presence of young people working together with senior *maestros*

Conclusion

In our fieldwork in Mompox we found a widespread disenchantment with the continual creation of artisan associations that frequently benefited only a limited number of individual leaders, usually *maestro* artisans who are often older men. However, the emerging group of artisans known as GAI provides an inspiring example to foster a new, if fragile, kind of association that contributes to the creation of intergenerational shared leadership, and therefore, more inclusive local development. In this chapter, three distinctive features of this new model of association and leadership were analyzed in depth: (1) a gradual growth of the association supported by promoting entities through progressive trust-building tactics; (2) collective decision making on production processes; and (3) the involvement of young people in leadership positions.

This emerging model of artisan association can offer important lessons for local leaders and economic development planners in other small and peripheral regions, particularly those dependent on the production of artisan goods and handicrafts. First, the process of creating an association must be understood as collective, progressive work that is successful only when members see decisions made in a collaborative manner. Both privileging horizontal mechanisms of participation that allow all members to be at the same level and obtaining benefits in an equitable way encourage members to own the association. In the case of the GAI, the presence of volunteer leaders capable of channeling processes for the benefit of all has been a key factor in the effective functioning of the group. In this sense, collective decision making regarding production processes has been an important issue for creating networks, not only regarding attendance at fairs and commercial activities but also in different steps of production.

Second, it is important to take into account the role of the youth and intergenerational collaboration in building associations, enabling these partnerships to have a long-term impact on local development and benefit a large and diverse number of people. The traditional dynamics of Mompox's local artisan associations reinforced pre-existing hierarchies among artisans and did not allow younger people to be represented and own the profession. This has translated into low levels of product innovation, high out-migration of young people, and fragile structures of association that often disappear after a few years. In the case of the GAI, including older and younger leaders contributed to the empowerment of young people and opened up new possibilities for creating a more inclusive strategy of local economic development.

Finally, while promotional organizations such as NGOs and government and development agencies are important in fostering initiatives and convening participants, the success and sustainability of producer associations depends on the ability of these agencies to facilitate gradual mechanisms that lead to the building of trust among association members. This is a slow and tricky task, and therefore activities and tactics must also be designed to create trust in the group to improve collective self-management and acquisition of new responsibilities, in order to avoid patterns of dependence on the initial source of funding. In the case of the GAI, Artesanías de Colombia and JICA used mechanisms such as the creation of self-saving groups and a system of collective accountability. Although it is a newly formed group, Mompox's GAI makes it clear that not all associations need to be formalized to build networks of trust and collaboration, nor is legal formalization necessarily the first step in strengthening an emerging process of association. On the contrary, the progressive appropriation of specific roles and collective decisions allows the valuing of the work of each member within the group and encourages the achievement of common results. Likewise, favoring horizontal mechanisms of participation and shared leadership models that allow all members to participate in collective decisions encourages trust building. In this sense, Mompox's evidence suggests that public policy efforts for associations and local economic development should focus on fostering such evolutionary processes gradually, with an emphasis on activities and tactics that generate trust building and intergenerational leadership and collaboration before formalization.

Note

1 Artisans participate annually in Expoartesanías, the main specialized handicraft fair in Latin America, held in Bogotá. It is an initiative of Artesanías de Colombia and Corferias that seeks to promote traditional artisan products with high-quality standards and to boost artisan activity. See https://expoartesanias.com/index.cfm.

References

Aguilar, L. F. 2010. *Gobernanza. El nuevo proceso de gobernar.* México DF: Fundación Friedrich Naumann.

Alburquerque, F. 2014. "*Política regional y desarrollo territorial en América Latina y el Caribe.*" *Informe GEPEC* 18 (2): 177–204.

Alcaldía de Mompox. 2012. *Línea de Base Plan Municipal de Desarrollo "Alianza por el rescate de Mompox" 2012–2015.* Mompox: Alcaldía de Mompox.

Artesanías de Colombia. 2013. *Fortalecimiento e Implementación del Componente Asociativo como Estrategia de Sostenibilidad de la Estrategia OVOP. Diagnóstico Empresarial de las Doce Iniciativas OVOP Resultado de la gestión adelantada por Gestando a través del Voluntariado.* https://goo.gl/iJQJGm (accessed August 2, 2016).

Beer, A. 2014. "Leadership and the Governance of Rural Communities." *Journal of Rural Studies* 34: 254–62.

Boisier, S. 2012. "A Theory is Search of a Practice or a Practice in Search of a Theory? A Brief Review of Territorial Policies in Latin America during the 20th and 21st Centuries." *Regional Development Dialogue* 33 (1): 1–19.

Cabrero, E., I. Orihuela, and A. Ziccardi. 2003. "Ciudades competitivas – ciudades cooperativas: Conceptos claves y construcción de un índice para ciudades mexicanas." *CIDE Documento de trabajo* 139, *División de Administración Pública, Centro de Investigación y Docencia Económicas.*

Caravaca, I., G. González, and R. Silva. 2005. "*Innovación, redes, recursos patrimoniales y desarrollo territorial.*" *EURE* 31 (94): 5–24.

Chapple, K., and S. Montero. 2016. "From Learning to Fragile Governance: Regional Economic Development in Rural Peru." *Journal of Rural Studies* 44: 143–52.
Chapple, K., S. Montero, and O. Sosa. 2012. "Evolving *Regionalismos*: Latin American Regions in the 21st Century." *Regional Development Dialogue* 33 (1): iii–xv.
Christen, R. P. 2006. "Microfinance and Sustainability: International Experiences and Lessons for India." In *Towards a Sustainable Microfinance Outreach in India*, 43–67. Mumbai, India: National Bank for Agriculture and Rural Development.
De La Hoz, J. V. 2011. *La economía anfibia de la isla de Mompox*. Bogotá: Banco de La República–Economía Regional.
Dowla, A. 2006. "In Credit We Trust: Building Social Capital by Grameen Bank in Bangladesh." *The Journal of Socio-Economics* 35 (1): 102–22.
Gallichio, E. 2004. "*El desarrollo local: ¿Cómo combinar gobernabilidad, desarrollo económico y capital social en el territorio?*" *Cuadernos del CLAEH* 27 (89): 55–68.
Harper, M. 2002. "Promotion of Self Help Groups under the SHG Bank Linkage Programme in India." Paper presented at the Seminar on SHG-bank Linkage programme at New Delhi on November 25–6, 2002. www.ruralfinanceandinvestment.org/node/508.
Jakimow, T., and P. Kilby. 2006. "Empowering Women: A Critique of the Blueprint for Self-Help Groups in India." *Indian Journal of Gender Studies* 13 (3): 375–400.
Jessop, B. 1998. "The Rise of Governance and the Risks of Failure: The Case of Economic Development." *International Social Science Journal* 50 (155): 29–45.
Karlsen, J., and M. Larrea. 2012. "Emergence of Shared Leadership in Situations of Conflict – Mission Impossible? Long Term Experiences from a Local Network in the Basque Country." In *Leadership and Change in Sustainable Regional Development*, edited by M. Sotarauta, I. Horlings, and J. Liddle, 212–33. London: Routledge.
Méndez, R. 2002. "*Innovación y desarrollo territorial: Algunos debates teóricos recientes.*" *EURE* 28 (84): 63–83.
Méndez, R., J. Michelini, and P. Romeiro. 2006. "*Redes socio-institucionales e innovación para el desarrollo de las ciudades intermedias.*" *Ciudad y Territorio Estudios Territoriales* 38 (148): 377–95.
Moncayo Jiménez, E. 2004. *Nuevos enfoques del desarrollo territorial: Colombia en una perspectiva latinoamericana*. Bogotá: Universidad Nacional de Colombia.
Montero, S. 2015. "*Planeación y gobernanza regional en América Latina.*" *Estudios Jaliscienses* 101: 6–19.
Murphy, J. T. 2006. "Building Trust in Economic Space." *Progress in Human Geography* 30 (4): 427–50.
Murray, J., and R. Rosenberg. 2006. "Fondos de préstamos gestionados por la comunidad: ¿ Cuál de ellos funciona?" *Enfoques* 36.
Pike, A., A. Rodríguez-Pose, and J. Tomaney. 2017. "Shifting Horizons in Local and Regional Development." *Regional Studies* 51 (1): 1–12.
Rankin, K. N. 2002. "Social Capital, Microfinance, and the Politics of Development." *Feminist Economics* 8 (1): 1–24.
Reddy, C. S., and S. Manak. 2005. "Self-Help Groups: A Keystone of Microfinance in India – Women Empowerment and Social Security." Andhra Pradesh Mahila Abhivruddhi Society (APMAS). India: Hyderabad.

Rodríguez-Pose, A. 2013. "Do Institutions Matter for Regional Development?" *Regional Studies* 47 (7): 1034–47.

Sotarauta, M., I. Horlings, and J. Liddle, eds. 2012. *Leadership and Change in Sustainable Regional Development*. London: Routledge.

Stimson, R., R. Stough, and M. Salazar. 2009. *Leadership and Institutions in Regional Endogenous Development*. Cheltenham, UK: Edward Elgar Publishing.

Uyarra, E., K. Flanagan, E. Magro, J. R. Wilson, and M. Sotarauta. 2017. "Understanding Regional Innovation Policy Dynamics: Actors, Agency and Learning." *Environment and Planning C* 35 (4): 559–68.

9 Fragile governance and local economic development policy

Concluding thoughts

Karen Chapple and Sergio Montero

In peripheral regions around Latin America, actors are actively reorganizing how they promote and govern local economic development (LED). In the face of ongoing outmigration of youth, low levels of trust, and a weak private sector, regions are mobilizing networks, enhancing learning processes, and sharing leadership to unleash local economic development processes. They thus engage in an endogenous development approach that contrasts with dominant economic development strategies that center on exports, high-tech parks or creative talent attraction. Building on local knowledge and relationships, they develop innovative – yet fragile – governance processes to manage LED in the context of decentralization and the inability of the market to intervene.

In this book, we have suggested that Latin American peripheral regions are often characterized by what we called *fragile governance* or emergent – and often informal – processes of planning, coordination, and collaboration that take place in weak institutional environments. In using the term *fragile* as opposed to weak, we sought to emphasize the temporal and evolutionary possibilities of governance transformation. Something *fragile* can be easily broken. But if tended properly, it could be transformed into something strong. We might characterize fragile governance along a continuum, from the experimentation in countries with a long history of decentralization, to that in those experiencing incipient decentralization. In some cases, the new governance structures have deep historic roots, suggesting that at a minimum, elements will continue into the future. Others are more tenuous and informal, in part because they lack regular funding and even specific projects. Yet, even without this kind of institutionality, they are engaged in ongoing planning and have developed new capacities for governance.

This book analyzes six cases where this new capacity to learn, collaborate, and manage change is emerging. It is too early to characterize these as successes, and indeed we cannot claim to have identified the causes behind these new governance capabilities. Even though governance is emerging, it is fragile and can easily disappear. Still, the story of how these spaces of experimentation developed over time has important lessons for other smaller cities and peripheral regions, in Latin America and beyond.

Both Córdoba and Linhares have developed associational approaches to LED to counter the dominance of other regions (in this case, Buenos Aires, Rio Grande do Sul and São Paulo) in the competition for (mostly) national markets. In these cases, associations govern competitive, established sectors (IT and furniture) in an environment with supportive infrastructure. In the Argentinian context, associativity develops in part because of the political differences between the regional and national government, exhibiting an approach to LED in explicit opposition to the narrative of multinational-driven development subsidized by Argentinian taxpayers. These associations grow out of particular local social networks that may not survive. Yet, the presence of the triple helix of business–university–government, as well as ongoing tensions with the national government, suggests that others will appear in its stead.

The Brazilian case, Linhares, differs in its roots: rather than growing out of opposition to the central government, local associations benefit from the long history of decentralization and thick LED institutions in that country. Shaping the emergence of the furniture cluster is the national APL policy, the Sindimol trade association is one of many such legal entities, and financing from the state development bank, Bandes, plays a critical role. As Peterson notes, the success of this case is rooted in a networked governance model that originates in the organization of production of the furniture industry in Linhares. As Sindimol works to thicken the local supply chain and facilitate collaborative relationships, territorial economic development results. Again, even if this is a fleeting moment in the development of one industry, the presence of this collaborative capacity seems far from fragile.

In contrast, the stories of Lurín and Quetzaltenango are about drawing from a rich history of local institutions and networks to build a new infrastructure for LED in the context of decentralization. Like Córdoba and Linhares, these cities are constructing an identity in reaction to their country's capital cities. Yet decentralization processes are quite recent, giving these areas an opportunity to define their future trajectory. Both are trying to navigate the complexities of the tourism sector in a context of poor infrastructural development. Both benefit from local strong tie networks in building associativity, but the Lurín case is further along in building commons governance because of its ability to incorporate different forms of learning and activate both horizontal and vertical ties with public sector actors. Here, even if the new governance capacities are emergent, their rootedness in local culture suggests the potential durability of governance. But perhaps because Guatemala presents a less stable national context, the new associations planning for economic development seem fragile indeed, failing to connect effectively with the state in order to push forward projects.

The most fragile cases are Arauco and Mompox, where decentralization is very recent and local networks are continually adapting. Here are the most recent efforts at collective action around economic development issues, shaped by a dominant central government (in the case of Chile) and an array of NGOs (in Colombia). Both cases illustrate innovative new capacities – for shared leadership in Arauco and intergenerational associativity in Mompox. But these remain governance experiments, illustrating new engagements that may or may not lead to sustained local economic development.

In the following sections, we explore lessons from each of the cases on the three key variables we chose in this book to analyze fragile governance processes: learning, networks, and leadership. We conclude with some thoughts on the implications of our analysis to rethink LED policy, as well as some of the limitations of our approach and avenues for future research on these issues.

Learning

The field of regional development has long championed the idea of tacit knowledge, which is localized in so-called learning regions (or regional innovation systems). Although this conception undoubtedly characterizes global city-regions well, it falls short for rural regions and even secondary cities. As our cases illustrate, the economies of peripheral regions struggle primarily with access to markets, rather than innovation. They are embedded in particular cultural contexts that tend to produce communities of practice that construct meaning together and learn via social relations. Practices such as storytelling help to create new aspirations and motivate actors to acquire new capabilities.

As in the literature, these cases illustrate the role of networks in transmitting tacit knowledge and facilitating learning. But tacit knowledge here is not just a shared understanding of how to do business, or non-codifiable technical expertise. Instead, it is more about know-how by doing: actors gain experiential knowledge which then gives them the confidence to act, and in some cases overcome the lock-in brought by strong tie, familial social networks. Technical expertise, particularly about access to markets, is of course not tacit, because it does not exist. But when storytelling and experiential knowledge build trust in local actors, they are well positioned to benefit from technical expertise as well.

Thus, in Lurín, when experts try to impart knowledge, it is not well received. Only when multiple forms of learning combine do locals gain enough trust to construct new meaning, in the form of infrastructure investment as well as an incipient vision for regional economic development. Trust is also key in Mompox, where a new accountability system builds trust and helps to show artisans in Mompox a different way to collaborate in filigree production. In Arauco, it is the crisis of a leadership change that helps actors develop new networking and socialization capabilities that gives locals the trust to manage the change. Quetzaltenango illustrates how a national network can spur local groups to learn through similar processes. Thus, in each case, learning is about the interaction of human capital, broadly construed, with social capital.

Networks

In this book, we view governance as the "process of co-ordinating actors, social groups and institutions in order to reach objectives which have been collectively discussed and defined in fragmented, even nebulous environments" (Bagnasco and Le Galès 2000, 26). While governance as an analytical term has flourished in the last two decades, it remains unclear how to link governance networks and economic development at the local and regional levels in practice. Self-coordinating networks might exist in an economic sector, spatial territory, or any other system, and they will consist of both firms, associations and related institutions. To be effective, they should be reflexively self-organized, meaning that they develop a common language and vision around an issue, but also they need to learn from failure and continuously adapt their behavior. This can create collective efficiency, or effective joint action, either horizontally – between stakeholders in equivalent positions (such as associations) – or vertically, in hierarchies (as between levels of government). Yet, just as networks can facilitate the transfer of knowledge and provide trust, they can result in lock-in and limit collaboration, or reinforce entrenched power structures. Networks also shape the durability – and the fragility – of governance. Where networks are rooted in local institutions, such as a university, they offer an opportunity to become part of local economic development culture. Such a networking capability is readily replicated.

Though these cases clearly illustrate both sides of networks, they also show that networks provide critical capacity for governance, particularly in the instable context of decentralization. Networks enable learning and form the basis of shared leadership. As networks extend into different regions and higher levels of government, they help locals develop new capacities to manage change.

The Quetzaltenango and Mompox cases illustrate the potential for lock-in. The insular Grupos Gestores struggle to interact meaningfully with the public sector, and a few associations monopolize NGO attention in Mompox. Yet from Linhares to Mompox, the cases illustrate different ways of constructing connections that will leverage local developmental assets. In Linhares and Córdoba, associations emerge out of the local context, in particular the structure of the furniture and IT industries and their relationship to national and global production. Associations develop in both cases despite their distinct relationships to their respective national governments (supportive in Brazil and oppositional in Argentina). In Lurín, it is local leadership, as well as presence of the *mancomunidad*, that act as connective tissue between local communities and national NGOs and government. And despite issues of lock-in and power in Quetzaltenango and Mompox, each case still illustrates the potential of networks: the RNGG expands throughout Guatemala due to the ability to leverage local ties, and locals innovate new forms of association in Mompox, learning from the failure of older systems.

Leadership

Effective territorial governance mechanisms require catalytic actors with capacity to influence others towards the achievement of common development goals and objectives (Sotarauta et al. 2012; Stimson et al. 2009). In early stages, these actors are essential for the implementation of processes and can appear as individual leaders. However, to guarantee the sustainability of processes, the ideal is to move towards a shared leadership that allows participants to make collective decisions with a common view of territorial development.

Several leadership scholars (Beer 2014; Davies 2009; Peters 2012; Purdue 2001) distinguish between transactional and transformational leaders. Transactional leaders are those who take the initiative to make contacts to exchange something of value (Peters 2012). But more applicable for rural development is the transformational leadership model, which includes "leaders and followers working together to develop common goals" (Rada 1999, 18). The main purpose of this kind of leadership is to guide followers to levels where they can achieve tasks associated with a project or take charge of it without the direct involvement of the leader (Davies 2009). Consequently, transformational leaders in rural development aim to build capabilities so that rural actors are able to respond to new challenges (Davies 2009).

These cases each illustrate the importance of shared leadership, as well as its deep connection to learning and networks, in the context of peripheral regions. For example, learning processes in Lurín did not take hold until the transformational leadership brought together first the comunidad of Tupicocha and then the entire river basin. Networks in Mompox are insufficient to revive associations until elders shared leadership with younger generation and female members. Shared leadership in the Xela case makes possible learning through communities of practice, but also falls short, due perhaps to the heavy hand of the RNGG.

Implications for local economic development (LED) policy

Many recent explanations of differentiated development outcomes among nations and regions highlight the importance of institutions (Acemoglu and Robinson 2012; Storper 2011; Rodríguez-Pose 2013). In this context, international development organizations and governments around the world have embraced institutional approaches. The World Bank, for instance, introduced the "good governance" approach in the 1990s after the recognition of the failure of the Washington Consensus' emphasis on market mechanisms and the privatization of the delivery of public goods and services (World Bank 1992). While this emphasis on institutions is welcome, three aspects of local and regional development still need careful consideration in order to design and implement development policies that have an impact.

First, the institutional turn in development has often meant increasing attention to the role of formal institutions such as building government capacity, rule of law, decentralization, accountability and democracy – at the expense of informal institutions (Pomerantz 2011). When informal institutions have been explored, these have been mostly conceptualized in terms of social capital or trust levels (Amin 1999; Rodríguez-Pose 2013). And yet, as we have argued in this book, peripheral regions in Latin America need particular attention to the "soft" or informal institutional aspects on which fragile governance processes are often based.

Second, national governments and international development organizations, particularly the World Bank, still rely on "one-size-fits-all" quick fixes that adopt space-neutral policy solutions for regional development despite the vast empirical evidence, both in the EU and in developing countries, that have called for place-based approaches to regional development policy (Pike, Rodríguez-Pose, and Tomaney 2006; Barca, McCann, and Rodríguez-Pose 2012). This space-neutral strategy has materialized in regional development policies that often rely on two policy instruments: 1) investments in infrastructure (particularly roads); and 2) tax subsidies to attract industries to territories with a weak industrial base. This spatially blinded approach, however, is doomed to fail because it does not recognize the institutional diversity and particular institutional bottlenecks that each city and region experience.

Third, this insistence on space-neutral policies based on market and institutional reform at the national or macroeconomic levels has led to a view of mega-cities as a solution to development – in other words, the idea that migration to large cities is almost a necessary step for development. Yet, urbanization does not equal development (Henderson 2010): several studies have shown that rapid urbanization in countries of the global South have often brought a new set of development problems such as the lack of proper housing, mobility and employment (CAF 2010).

Thus, this book concludes that we need to rethink local economic development policy. A different kind of local and regional development policy is needed, one that imagine a multiplicity of development paths beyond the reliance on global city-regions. We also need development policies that take into account the role of informal institutions in local economic development processes, particularly in smaller cities and rural regions. Even so, this does not mean that what worked in a small city or peripheral region will work in another one.

The case studies presented in this book gave us some hints about how different cities and regions in Latin America are transforming their fragile governance to unleash local and regional economic development processes. We see the particular policies or institutional arrangements adopted not as "solutions" but examples that suggest some basic policy principles for other regions to follow.

- **Support multiple forms of learning** both within and across territories (Lurín);
- While fostering bottom-up networks in civil society and the private sector, **ensure connection to and collaboration with the public sector** (Xela);
- **Build collaboration based on existing networks**, and use intermediaries to help strengthen networks (Córdoba);

- **Organize action across scales and sectors** (economic as well as public/private/nonprofit) (Linhares);
- **Stay engaged – and provide resources –** over the long term (Arauco);
- **Build trust** by ensuring that benefits and responsibilities of associations are widespread and divided equitably (Mompox).

Limitations and future research

Several factors limited the scope of this research and suggest the need for future research on the relationship between governance, institutions, and local economic development. Here we explore the issue of time, the limitations of case selection, the potential for omitted variable bias, and more generally, challenges in understanding local embedded knowledge.

The extent to which governance is fragile of course depends on when we view it. With the perspective of time, the most fragile of arrangements may stabilize, and permanent, strong institutions may emerge. Likewise, what appears to be fragile may actually be deeply rooted in a region's history and culture. On the one hand, our cases do identify a relationship between the extent to which localities can act as authors of their own development, and the state of decentralization (both fiscal and administrative). On the other, it is hard to know the extent to which these regions have adapted a lasting capacity to learn, collaborate, and manage change. The innovation may be fleeting and weak, or actors may continue to adapt, with new kinds of fragile governance emerging. Future research should revisit these cases and actors to identify patterns of adaptation (or collapse).

In a related vein, we know little about the success of the cases. We selected cases because they had emergent fragile governance – but in some cases they illustrate governance failure as much as success. Thus, our research seeks to explore and develop this concept rather than establish the causality behind its success. It is entirely possible that the processes of learning, networking, and leadership that we highlight are rooted in regional particularities that we do not explore herein. What appears to be success in organizing activity in a sector – from IT in Córdoba to furniture in Linhares to filigree in Mompox – may be just as much about the particular moment in that sector's trajectory. Again, this is an issue that future research might explore, by identifying cases that have succeeded – or even just continued to evolve new capacities.

In our effort to analyze and trace collaborations between public and private actors, we devote little effort to exploring government and fiscal factors that may have played a key role in our cases. For instance, local electoral politics, such as short terms for mayors, may have shaped the imperatives for action. Likewise, we know little about the extent to which higher levels of government have infused our case study regions with resources, which then may have influenced the formation of networks or the interest in learning. Not only did our research design not focus on political and fiscal issues, but also in many cases data (for instance on local budgets) is not readily available.

Finally, one of the primary concepts explored in this volume is tacit knowledge. These cases all explore governance in the context of socially and historically embedded knowledge. As outsiders, there are limits to what we can know about each region. We chose to tell our story using the umbrella concept of fragile governance but it is our hope that in writing this book, we help local voices to emerge and help rethink local economic development theories and policies from the perspective of small cities and peripheral regions, in Latin America and beyond.

References

Acemoglu, D., and J. Robinson. 2012. *Why Nations Fail: The Origins of Power, Prosperity, and Poverty*. New York: Crown Business.

Amin, A. 1999. "An Institutionalist Perspective on Regional Economic Development." *International Journal of Urban and Regional Research* 23(2): 365–78.

Bagnasco, A., and P. Le Galès (Eds.) 2000. *Cities in Contemporary Europe*. Cambridge, UK: Cambridge University Press.

Barca, F., P. McCann, and A. Rodríguez-Pose. 2012. "The Case for Regional Development Intervention: Place-Based versus Place-Neutral Approaches." *Journal of Regional Science* 52(1): 134–52.

Beer, A. 2014. "Leadership and the Governance of Rural Communities." *Journal of Rural Studies* 34: 254–62.

CAF. 2010. *Desarrollo Local: Hacia un Nuevo Protagonismo de las Ciudades y Regiones*. Caracas: Corporación Andina de Fomento (CAF).

Davies, A. 2009. "Understanding Local Leadership in Building the Capacity of Rural Communities in Australia." *Geographical Research* 47(4): 380–89.

Henderson, J. V. 2010. "Cities and Development." *Journal of Regional Science* 50(1): 515–40.

Peters, K. 2012. "Socially Embedded Leadership." In *Leadership and Change in Sustainable Regional Development*, edited by M. Sotarauta, L. Horlings, and M. Liddle, 145–63. London: Routledge.

Pike, A., A. Rodríguez-Pose, and J. Tomaney (Eds.) 2006. *Local and Regional Development*. London: Routledge.

Pomerantz, P. R. 2011. "Development Theory." In *The Sage Handbook of Governance*, edited by M. Bevir, 160–78. London: Sage Publications.

Purdue, D. 2001. "Neighbourhood Governance: Leadership, Trust and Social Capital." *Urban Studies* 38(12): 2211–24.

Rada, D. R. 1999. "Transformational Leadership and Urban Renewal." *Journal of Leadership & Organizational Studies* 6(3–4): 18–33.

Rodríguez-Pose, A. 2013. "Do Institutions Matter for Regional Development?" *Regional Studies* 47(7): 1034–47.

Sotarauta, M., L. Horlings, and M. Liddle (Eds.) 2012. *Leadership and Change in Sustainable Regional Development*. London: Routledge.

Stimson, R., R. Stough, and M. Salazar. 2009. *Leadership and Institutions in Regional Endogenous Development*. Cheltenham, UK: Edward Elgar Publishing.

Storper, M. 2011. "Why Do Regions Develop and Change? The Challenge for Geography and Economics." *Journal of Economic Geography* 11(2): 333–46.

World Bank. 1992. *Governance and Development*. Washington, DC: World Bank.

Index

Note: Page numbers in *italics* denote tables and in **bold** denote figures.

For Product Safety Concerns and Information please contact our EU representative GPSR@taylorandfrancis.com Taylor & Francis Verlag GmbH, Kaufingerstraße 24, 80331 München, Germany